TOURNAMENT

TOURNAMENT

David Crouch

Hambledon and London

London and New York

Hambledon and London

102 Gloucester Avenue
London, NW1 8HX

175 Fifth Avenue
New York, NY 10010
USA

First Published 2005

ISBN 1 85285 460 X

A description of this book is available from the
British Library and from the Library of Congress.

Typeset by Carnegie Publishing, Lancaster,
and printed in Great Britain by Cambridge University Press.

Distributed in the United States and Canada
exclusively by Palgrave Macmillan,
a division of St Martin's Press.

Contents

III: Documents on the Tournament

Illustrations

Illustration Acknowledgements

For permission to reproduce the illustrations, the author and publishers are grateful to the following: the Bibliothèque Nationale, Paris, plates 4 and 7; the Pierpoint Morgan Library, New York, plates 6 and 8; the Universitätsbibliothek, Heidelberg, plates 1, 2, 3 and 5.

Acknowledgements

It has recently been said that the tournament is a field that has been relatively well cultivated in recent years, after being ignored by academics since the beginning of academic history.[1] I would differ. Its latter years and decline have certainly been well treated. But there has been rather less about its early years and prime. What has been entirely lacking to date is any serious attempt to reconstruct how a tournament was experienced, and what it really meant to medieval society. Academic historians began to take a serious interest in the tournament only in the 1980s, since when our knowledge of its development and nature has certainly expanded enormously. Historical and literary texts have been searched for clues and perspectives and a mass of new evidence has emerged. But my purpose in this book is not just to provide a summary of what has been discovered. With the help of some neglected texts, I have also given what is the most detailed reconstruction to date of what the tournament was like in its heyday. But more than that, I will be putting the tournament in a new context, its place in the evolution of aristocracy itself.

I would like to thank for a variety of reasons Martin Aurell, Martha Carlin, John Gillingham, Maurice Keen, Graham and Lisa Scott, Guilhem Pépin, Xavier Storelli and Eve Turner. All assisted in the writing of this book, and at the very least they listened sympathetically and encouragingly. It would have been impossible to write it at all without the magnificent collection of French literature and periodicals offered by the Brynmor Jones library of the University of Hull. The Institut Universitaire de France offered a fellowship which materially assisted me in completing the book. I must also thank Martin Aurell and the CESCM at Poitiers for hosting the fellowship. Thanks also to Martin Sheppard and Tony Morris of Hambledon and London, for an opportunity to get the resulting book into print and for encouraging its appearance.

My family is to be thanked as usual for its forbearance. I dedicate the book to my two sons, Simon and Timothy, because they like sport and have taught me a good deal about the mentality of the sportsman, which I do not possess.

Scarborough   November 2004

Abbreviations

Ann. Dunstable	*Annales de Dunstaplia*, in, *Annales Monastici*, ed. H. R. Luard (5 vols, Rolls Series, 1864–69), iii.
Baldwin	J. W. Baldwin, *Aristocratic Life in Medieval France: The Romances of Jean Renart and Gerbert de Montreuil, 1190–1230* (Baltimore, 2000).
Barber and Barker	R. Barber and J. R. V. Barker, *Tournaments: Jousts, Chivalry and Pageants in the Middle Ages* (Woodbridge, 1989).
Barker	J. R. V. Barker, *The Tournament in England, 1100–1400* (Woodbridge, 1986).
Bertran	*Poésies complètes de Bertran de Born*, ed. A. Thomas (Bibliothèque méridionale, first series, no 1, 1888). Poems translated into modern French in R. de Boysson, *Études sur Bertrand de Born: sa vie, ses œuvres et son siècle* (repr. Geneva, 1973). Page references to the Thomas edition.
Bumke	J. Bumke, *Höfische Kultur: Literatur und Gesellschaft im hohen Mittelalter* (Munich, 1986), translated as *Courtly Culture: Literature and Society in the High Middle Ages*, trans. T. Dunlap (Woodstock, New York, 2000). Page references to translation.
Charrete	Chrétien de Troyes, *Le Chevalier de la Charrete*, ed. M. Roques (Classiques français du moyen âge, 1983).
Cligés	Chrétien de Troyes, *Cligés*, ed. A. Micha (Classiques français du moyen âge, 1957).
Chauvency	Jacques Bretel, *Le Tournoi de Chauvency*, ed. G. Hecq (Société des Bibliophiles Belges, no. 31, Mons, 1898).

Couci	Jakemes, *Le Roman du Castelain de Couci et de la Dame de Fayel*, ed. M. Delbouille (Société des anciens textes français, 1936).
Crouch, *Marshal*	D. Crouch, *William Marshal: Knighthood, War and Chivalry, 1147–1219* (2nd edn, London, 2002).
de Dornon	A. de Behault de Dornon, 'La noblesse hennuyère au tournoi de Compiègne de 1238', *Annales du Cercle archéologique de Mons*, xxii (1890), 61–114.
Denholm-Young	N. Denholm-Young, 'The Tournament in the Thirteenth Century', in, *Collected Papers of N. Denholm-Young* (Cardiff, 1969), 95–120.
d'Oisy	Huon d'Oisy, *Li Tournoi des Dames*, in, A. Jeanroy, 'Notes sur le tournoiement des dames', *Romania*, 28 (1899), 240–44.
Flori, *Chevaliers*	J. Flori, *Chevaliers et chevalerie au moyen âge* (Paris, 1998).
Gerbert	Gerbert de Montreuil, *Le Roman de la Violette ou de Gerart de Nevers*, ed. D. L. Buffum (Société des anciens textes français, 1928).
GM	*La chronique de Gislebert de Mons*, ed. L. Vanderkindere (Brussels, 1904).
Gui	*Gui de Warewic: roman du xiiie siècle*, ed. A. Ewert (2 vols, Classiques français du moyen âge, 1932).
Ham	*Le Roman de Ham*, in, *Histoire des ducs de Normandie et des rois d'Angleterre*, ed. F. Michel (Paris, 1840), 213–384.
HWM	*History of William Marshal*, ed. A. J. Holden and D. Crouch, trans. S. Gregory (3 vols, Anglo-Norman Text Society, Occasional Publications Series, 4–6, 2002–6).
Joinville	Jean de Joinville, *Vie de Saint Louis*, ed. J. Monfrin (Paris, 1996).
Keen	M. Keen, *Chivalry* (New Haven, 1984).
Lancelot	*Lancelot: roman en prose du xiiie siècle*, ed. A. Micha (9 vols, Geneva, 1978–83).

Lancelot do Lac	*Lancelot do Lac*, ed. E. Kennedy (2 vols, Oxford, 1980).
Laon	A. Långfors, '*Le dit des hérauts* par Henri de Laon', *Romania*, xliii (1914), 222–25.
Liechtenstein	Ulrich von Liechtenstein, *Service of Ladies*, trans. J. W. Thomas (University of North Carolina Studies in the Germanic Language and Literature, 63, 1969).
Manekine	Philip de Remy, *La Manekine*, ed. H. Suchier (Société des anciens textes français, 1884).
Méry	Huon de Méry, *Le Tournoi de l'Antéchrist*, ed. G. Wimmer and trans. S. Orgeur (2nd edn, Medievalia, no. 13, Orléans, 1995).
MP	Matthew Paris, *Chronica Majora*, ed. H. R. Luard (7 vols, Rolls Series, 1872–84).
Niger	Ralph Niger, *De re militari et triplici via peregrinationis Ierosolimitane*, ed. L. Schmugge (Beitrage zür Geschichte und Quellenkunde des Mittelalters, 6, Berlin, 1977).
Parisse	M. Parisse, 'Le tournoi en France, des origines à la fin du xiiie siècle', in, *Das ritterliche Turnier in Mittelalter: Beitrage zu einer vergleichenden Formen- und verhallengeschichte des Rittertum*, ed. J. Fleckenstein (Göttingen, 1985)
PL	*Patrologiae cursus completus: series Latina*, ed. J-P. Migne (221 vols, Paris, 1847–67).
Renart	Jean Renart, *Le Roman de la Rose ou de Guillaume de Dole*, ed. F. Lecoy (Classiques français du moyen âge, 1962).
RHF	*Recueil des historiens des Gaules et de la France*, ed. M. Bouquet and others (24 vols, Paris, 1869–1904).
Sone	*Sone von Nausay*, ed. M. Goldschmidt (Bibliothek des litterarischen Vereins in Stuttgart, ccxvi, Tübingen, 1899).

1

Beginnings and Sources

The tournament was a remarkable medieval obsession. It was a sport organised by and for aristocrats, but it was not just the obsession of wealthy medieval males. Aristocratic women were enthusiastic spectators and sponsors; even people of lower social groups shared the fun, and many of them found business opportunities in the tournament's not inconsiderable support industry. The history of the tournament has been studied haphazardly since the eighteenth century, and it has been an enduring fascination of reconstructionists from the beginning of the nineteenth century up till the present day. The tournament has always been recognised as an important historical phenomenon, but I think that its importance is still underestimated in social terms. One reason it was so important was that in its heyday the tournament touched on the lives of by far and away the majority of the members of the aristocracies of Latin Christendom. Participation in the tournament in the middle ages was more of a class characteristic than is any modern elite sport.

But what was the period of the tournament? An important distinction has first to be made. 'Tournaments' and 'jousts' were not the same thing in the middle ages, a point insisted on by the poet Jean de Condé in the early fourteenth century.[1] The tournament was a mass activity. At the heart of it was a mock battle involving hundreds and sometimes thousands of knights fighting across a very large area. Jousts, on the other hand, were single combats on horseback in a confined space. The 'mêlée tournament', to define it properly, appeared in north-eastern France late in the eleventh century, but went out of fashion and disappeared in the mid fourteenth century. Jousts grew up alongside tournaments, and indeed, as we will see, were initially an integral part of tournament festivities, but from the beginning of the thirteenth century jousts became increasingly preferred by knights, and became more dominant in aristocratic culture. 'Tournaments' after 1350 were almost invariably organised fields of jousts. There were other activities which were not tournaments, but which were involved with them, not least the intriguing activity called 'bohorts' or 'béhourds'. Both these and jousting will be dealt with in the book, but they are not principally what this book is about.

Origins

By 1150 the tournament had developed into its mature form. By then we know that the game had great and wealthy patrons, and that knights travelled all over the French-speaking world to compete in it. We cannot be absolutely sure that the rules of conduct, as they were known in the later twelfth century, were in operation in 1150, but the likelihood is that they were. The passion for the tournament, drawing hundreds and thousands of males to travel hundreds and thousands of miles to compete with each other, was certainly already in existence in the early 1120s. The first great tourneyer of whom we know much was Count Charles of Flanders (1119–27). Galbert of Bruges, who wrote the sad story of his murder, tells us that in happier days in the early 1120s the count – then late in his thirties – 'for the honour of his land and to train his knights' enjoyed travelling to encounter the counts and barons of Normandy, the Île de France and of other places with a company of 200 select knights 'and there he fought the tournaments (*tornationes*) ... and so raised his reputation and the power and glory of his county'.[2] There is an indication that he travelled into the western Empire to tourney in a reference in one of his written acts of 1122 to a successful knightly tour he made of neighbouring lands in the Empire.[3] Where had Charles found this compulsion to tourney? Although the younger son of a king of Denmark, he had spent his boyhood and youth in Flanders, and it was here, in his mother's native country in the first decade of the twelfth century, that he must have been bitten by the enthusiasm for the tournament. Indeed, it is likely that Charles was doing no more in the 1120s than his young and gallant predecessor, Count Baldwin VII (1111–19) had done in his day, for Baldwin died as a result of a blow he received while skirmishing with the household of Henry I of England in 'military games' held outside the besieged castle of Eu in Normandy.[4] Baldwin was well known in Normandy and a close friend of the Norman border counts; friendships formed perhaps on the tournament field.

Much of the earliest evidence of tourneying relates to the county of Hainault, which from 1058 shared a ruling dynasty with neighbouring

Flanders. In 1122 Count Charles journeyed into Hainault 'for a contest of arms (*de conflictu armorum*) held between myself and Godfrey de Valenciennes', presumably at Valenciennes itself. At any rate he returned to Arras, as he said in an act to the abbey of St-Vaast in the town, 'with knightly honours (*cum gloria militari*)'.[5] Since there was no war at the time between the counties of Hainault and Flanders, this trip to Valenciennes must have been a tournament in which he had distinguished himself. But there is an even earlier reference to tournaments which also comes from Hainault. It has been pointed out that the Peace legislation enacted by Count Baldwin III for the town and region of Valenciennes in 1114 referred to the possibility that the keepers of the peace in the town might leave it 'for the purpose of frequenting javelin sports, tournaments or suchlike'.[6]

This is probably the earliest reference to the tournament by name, and it is an evocative name. The word comes from the ancient French verb *torner*, meaning 'to revolve' or 'whirl about'. Knights whirling around in a mêlée is exactly what happened in tournaments, and the word itself seems to have been conjured up as a metaphor by the participants to describe what they did when they tourneyed, rushing round and round like leaves in a tornado. In 1114 the 'tournament' may have been a new word for a new thing. It has been argued that the tournament was then a recently-devised recreation with the new feature of a charge with lances followed by mounted skirmishing with swords. The word *torneamentum* was therefore newly coined to described the sharp turn made by the knights after the charge to swing round and engage their opponents with swords. *Torneamentum* was a word devised to distinguish the tournament from an older and different form of mounted exercise with javelin, what was called in Latin the *hastiludum* ('spear-game').[7]

But it is unlikely that the tournament was a new sort of knightly recreation in 1114. We are on reasonably firm ground in suggesting that it was in existence in the 1090s. Hermann of Tournai, writing in the early 1140s, recalled the death in 1095, in his grandfather's days, of Count Henry III of Brabant at Tournai in something that sounds very like a tournament. The count had travelled with his Brabazon retinue west across the River Scheldt to the Flemish city to indulge in a peacetime meeting with the castellan of Tournai's household, which had a high reputation for skill in arms. The count's death occurred at the beginning of the meeting, when he unwisely called out a knight from the opposing ranks for an individual joust in front of the teams and was accidentally killed in the encounter. The description of the circumstances of the count's death certainly bears a marked resemblance to the *commençailles* of the tournament as they were staged a century later (see pp. 83–5), that is, preliminary jousting between the lines of the opposing teams – although Hermann called the meeting not a joust or a tourney, but a 'military game' (*militaris ludus*).[8]

Despite the fewness of the references, we have good reason to assume that the itinerant world of the tourneyer was in existence in and before 1100. Can we go back further? Here direct evidence fails us, so we are driven back on the circumstantial. To begin with, what do we make of such Latin phrases associated with the tournament which contain the element *ludus* ('game') or of writers who treat it as a military exercise? In the 1120s Galbert of Bruges made much of the way Count Charles trained his knights by frequenting tournaments. We get a glimpse of this world of war games in the *Song of Roland*, a work produced in the environment of late eleventh-century aristocratic society. As the emperor sits in his camp in Spain the 'active young knights' (*bacheler leger*) of his army exercise in arms, as the older warriors sit around under the trees playing chess or backgammon.[9] Youngsters had to let off steam by intensive training and armies had to be drilled, especially mounted armies. We find these needs mentioned as far back as one and a half centuries earlier. There is information from the Carolingian writer Nithard that the armies of his day might divide into teams to rehearse battle tactics, as the Saxons, Gascons, Austrasians and Bretons did at Worms in 842. On that occasion we are told that the mounted royal households practised how to pursue a fleeing enemy.[10] Such mounted games give us at least a context out of which the tournament might have developed.

By the early twelfth century, knights were so imbued with the need to parade their skills that the line between war and game often became blurred. The Norman monk-historian, Orderic Vitalis, refers to early 'military' or 'knightly' exercises which took place at the siege of Falaise in 1106, in which the nobleman, Roger, sheriff of Gloucester, was killed, presumably in a personal encounter or joust. Orderic describes something similar again at the siege of Bellême in 1113, where knights of the garrison rode out hoping for 'single combat', only to be swamped by the besiegers, who had no time for such military niceties.[11] Another Norman chronicler refers to mounted 'military games' held between the bored besieged and besiegers of Eu in 1118 where Count Baldwin of

Flanders was fatally injured. The army besieging Ludlow in 1139 annoyed King Stephen by organising military games when they should have been concentrating on the castle. The biographer of William Marshal preserved a memory that the royalist garrison of Winchester Castle 'tourneyed' with the Angevin forces besieging them in the summer of 1141.[12]

These feats of arms were not of course recreational tournaments, but they speak of a world where an irrepressible competitive spirit sometimes showed itself even on the field of war, especially if there was little action happening at the time. Armies continued to nominate champions to fight the sort of single combat in front of the ranks which had been familiar since the ancient world. When some decades later Wace of Bayeux described a combat between individual knights of the the armies of King Henry I and Duke Robert, he imagined the archers and infantry sitting down like spectators as the rival champions rode each other down between the armies with levelled lances.[13] There is no doubting the power of the idea of heroic single combat over the warriors of the twelfth century. In 1119 King Louis VI of France exploited it by offering personally to fight his rival, Henry I of England. He suggested that they should fight between their armies (separated by a swift stream and a rickety plank bridge) to settle their differences once and for all. Henry's abrupt refusal made Louis look good and himself timorous. Since both kings were very stout men, the armies were amused at the thought of what would happen if they fought on the bridge.[14] Preliminary single combats were a feature of the tournament, and indeed, Count Henry of Brabant apparently died in one in 1095 at Tournai, a Goliath fallen to a David.

Although the long history of military games between armies in the field gives us some context for the tournament's appearance, it does not help us explain or date it. There is a clue at least to the date, however, in that the tournament was meant to be a peace time and not a war time activity. The early references to the tournament all cluster around the region of Flanders, Picardy, Brabant and Hainault. In the eleventh century this was a political cockpit on the marches of the Empire, where the king in Paris had long ceased to exert any influence and where petty conflicts and armed feuds were perpetual and pervasive.[15] Great princes in Flanders, Hainault and Vermandois were attempting to impose their authority on lesser, rebellious dynasties which had emerged at places like Namur, Boulogne, Guines, Hesdin, Ponthieu and St-Pol. Warfare was endemic in this region but there were also robust and persistent attempts by princes and bishops to contain it. These attempts are called by historians, the Peace Movement. They had the aim of restricting and containing wars, and during the 1020s and 1030s peace councils met in Flanders, Champagne and Normandy with the aim of binding all males by oath to keep public order. The counts of Flanders were particularly keen on pursuing it, and sponsored proclamations of the Peace three times in the early eleventh century, in 1024, 1030 and c. 1042.

It is not too fanciful to suggest that the tournament may have been an unintentional side-effect of the proclamations of the Peace within the regions of Flanders, Hainault and Picardy in the 1020s and 1030s. One later pointer to this is that in the twelfth century it was the custom to hold French tournaments on the borders of lordships and counties. This traditional choice of site may very well have been the result of eleventh-century knights and their masters attempting to live up to the letter of the Peace, but also to maintain their skills and continue their perpetual competition for status and physical excellence. By tourneying on borders where no prince ruled, they could pretend to themselves that they were not technically breaking the oaths they had sworn. As the proclamation of the count of Hainault's peace at Valenciennes in 1114 reveals, ban on violence or not, it was expected that the knights of the region would still meet to tourney, although at sites some distance from the town. Another and even stronger link between the early tournament and the Peace movement is the way that the early eleventh-century councils might ban all violence during the period of Lent – the forty days of penitiential observance which preceded the Easter celebrations – and until the end of Easter week. This was one of the terms of the Peace as it was proclaimed at Verdun-sur-le-Doubs in Burgundy in 1016, and at Beauvais in Picardy in 1023.[16] Much later, in the mid twelfth century, we discover that there was just such a closed season which applied universally to the tournament throughout France. It is tempting to deduce from this that the tournament appeared in the days when Peace legislation necessarily closed it down for the Lent season, and that the traditional closed season was perpetuated in tournament practice even after the Peace proclamations went out of fashion amongst rulers and bishops in the middle of the eleventh century.

A third and final explanation for the origins of the tournament might lie in the social world of the higher aristocracy. The French historian,

Georges Duby, identified a hedonistic cult of youth amongst the twelfth-century aristocracy.[17] On coming to adulthood the wealthy heir to a great estate would be equipped with a tutor, a retinue and ample funds, and take to a wandering life in which attendance at tournaments was one of the frequent amusements. Such aristocratic vagabonds are frequently to be found in the sources for the later twelfth century. Were they to be found in the previous century? When Robert Curthose quit his father's court in Normandy in 1083 and went into voluntary exile in northern France for four years, he lived an itinerant and luxurious lifestyle with a group of male companions. He must have occupied himself in doing something compatible with his exalted status, and pilgrimage, sexual adventures, hunting and feasting would only have filled some of the time. The existence of a tournament circuit as early as the 1080s would help explain how Duke Robert occupied his itinerant life. It would also help explain his close association with the dukes and counts of north-east France and Flanders that came to fruition when they all took the cross together in 1095.[18] Time and again over the next two centuries, crusading contingents arose out of tournament fellowships. A tournament at Écry in Champagne in 1199, for instance, provided a major stimulus for recruiting the army of the Fourth Crusade.[19]

So much for circumstantial evidence about the tournament's origins. It can justify a theory that the tournament arose on the marches of the Empire and France at some time in the first half of the eleventh century. But it will only ever be a theory. Still, we can at least say when the tournament was not. One terminal point might be easily overlooked: the appearance of armour which was sufficiently effective to minimise injury in violent horseback military games.[20] This sort of protection did not exist before 1000. And it is clear that we are on safe ground in asserting that the tournament was being enjoyed in north-east France by the aristocratic generation which lived immediately before 1100. To this deduction we might add the fact that the tournament could not have happened at a date before it became customary for knights to charge with lances couched under their arms, a tactic which only became customary with cavalry early in the eleventh century.[21] The tournament could not have existed much before 1020.

We can say no more than that about the tournament's ultimate origins, but it is worth noting how ancient is the curiosity to find them. People around the year 1200 were as curious as we are about the origins of the tournament, and were willing to speculate. A later chronicler of Tours on unknown authority (or none) declared that an Angevin baron, Geoffrey de Preuilly 'devised (*invenit*) the tournament', when (innaccurately) noting his death in the 1060s.[22] At much the same time, Lambert of Ardres, the historian of the counts of Guines, refers to his ancestor Count Ralph as travelling around the tourney fields of France in 1036, where he met his end.[23] Although Lambert did not say that Count Ralph devised the tournament, he seems to have visualised an early eleventh-century world where his ancestors dominated much the same sort of tournament circuit as the one with which he was familiar in his day, over a century later. In both cases local patriotism was at work.[24] Such was the centrality of the tournament to aristocratic life by the end of the twelfth century that historians assumed it had always been central to noble life, and routinely noted its antiquity in their own localities.

There are good grounds for believing that the tournament arose in a distinct region, and I have already given my reasons for saying that it was in the western marches of the Empire and north-east France. The tournament's earliest appearances can be located in Brabant, Hainault, Flanders, Picardy and the northern marches of Normandy. There is one significant fact that tends to confirm this belief. The study of the origins of heraldry has found its earliest manifestations in exactly the same area and at the same period when the tournament was well established.[25] In its earliest proto-heraldic days, heraldry was the system by which individual magnates and their retinues could be identified by symbols and colours exclusive to them. It was a clever way of getting round the problem of identification of groups of heavily armoured knights, and where was this more regularly needed than during the tournament? Once the two great lines of the tournament had rolled together and the mêlée had begun, it was vital to know which anonymous armoured figure around you was an opponent, and which was a friend. Coloured shields, harness and robes could tell you that almost instantly, and couldn't easily be counterfeited, as an identifying warcry could. The time and place at which heraldry first appeared can only therefore be significant for the tournament, and to find it surfacing in Picardy and Flanders around 1100 is to me conclusive evidence that the heartland and origin of the tournament lay there.

It is not easy to plot the way that the tournament spread beyond its place of origin. Its spread may have been resisted in certain places and at certain times. There were social conditions which favoured its growth in north-east France, but the tournament did not necessarily flourish where the structure of lordship was different, and particularly where a king and prince was keen to impose order on his realm. It is for that reason a little surprising to find that tournament meetings occurring in England in the reigns of King Henry I (1100–35) and King Stephen (1135–54), in view of the high ideals of public order and royal control that prevailed there. The fact that the tournament was established in England at all may be due to the Normans being implicated in its origins. Perhaps the sons of the Conqueror had shared their aristocracy's obsession with it. It is no surprise at all to find that, during the civil war, King Stephen suppressed at least two planned tournaments. After Stephen's reign meetings of tournaments were abruptly terminated in England by order of the new king Henry II (1154–89) and they were not allowed to be held again for forty years. Even after 1194, when they were once again permitted, English tournaments were tightly controlled and the object of official suspicion.

Elsewhere the spread of the tournament was patchy. The biography of William Marshal, an early tournament champion, tells us that meetings were being held on the borders of lordships in Anjou and Brittany in the 1160s, and knights from further south, from Poitou, were attending them.[26] Although the biography mentions no tourneys further south, the prolific poetry of Bertran de Born, lord of Hautefort in the Limousin, indicates that by the 1170s, and probably before, knights of Guyenne and Gascony were going to tournaments. Most intriguingly, he described a tournament held near Toulouse around 1181 at which Catalan and Aragonese knights met those of Count Raymond. The spread of the sport across the Pyrenees must then have been recent because Bertran commented on the ineptitude and poor equipment of the enthusiastic Spanish.[27] In central France, it is clear that the Capetian king opposed the spread of the sport. He was not allowing tournaments to meet within the heart of his domain around Paris, although they did meet on its borders. Louis VI of France (1108–37) invested a large amount of his prestige in successfully curbing the violent excesses of the aristocracy of the Capetian lands in the Île-de-France. It seems probable that he, like Henry II of England later in the century, regarded the tournament as an unwelcome threat to the hard-won public order of his domains and so preferred that its devotees go elsewhere. It is not impossible that the papal condemnations of the tournament proclaimed in 1130 at a council at Clermont, and in 1131 at Reims within France, may have been promulgated in response to Louis's request, as much as through agitation by the bishops.[28]

The spread of tournaments eastward into the Empire was as slow as its spread south. Tournaments may have flourished at an early date in the marcher counties of the west, but they were not necessarily so welcome in the great duchies of Swabia, Franconia and Bavaria further east. The earliest reference to something resembling a tournament in Germany comes from 1127 when the army of the Hohenstaufen rulers of Swabia camped outside Würzburg in Franconia. In the days that followed, the imperial troops defending the city sent out knights to contend in military exercises with the Swabians, in the same manner as we know that contemporary French armies did. When thirty years later Bishop Otto of Freising described what happened at Würzburg he called it by the Latin name of a *tyrocinium* 'which is nowadays called in the vernacular a *turnoimentum*'.[29] The word 'tirocinium' has a technical meaning, a combat between 'tirones' or young knights. At Würzburg it seems that the younger knights in the armies were being given a chance to show their paces; as such, it was not a tournament but what was called in French a 'bohord'. Bishop Otto, educated at Paris in the 1120s, was choosing his words with care. He was commenting that Germans had only recently adopted the French word *torneiement* into their language in the 1150s and maybe they did not use it as carefully as he would have done.

Bishop Otto certainly seemed to be saying that the tournament was spreading across the Empire in the 1150s, however, and there is some evidence to support that belief. The chronicle of the abbey of Lauterberg says that on 17 November 1175 Count Conrad, son of the Wettin margrave of Lausitz on the march of Poland, was killed 'by a lance thrust in the military game that people call the *tornamentum*'. The chronicler added that 'this nuisance of an amusement had by then so permeated our region (the Ostmark) that in one year sixteen knights are said to have died in it'. He made the telling point that Conrad's kinsman, Archbishop Wichmann of Magdeburg (1152–92), had gone so far in 1175 as to excommunicate the tourneyers in his province and he would not therefore allow Conrad an ecclesiastical burial.[30] The Marshal biography indicates that knights from the interior of the Empire (*Tiheus* or 'Teutons') were travelling into France in the 1170s to join in the great tournaments, noting that a company of them was at the Ressons-Gournay tournament of January 1183.[31] Another monastic

chronicle, that of the abbey of Villers-en-Brabant, adds further confirmation. Although itself in the tournament's western heartland, the
abbey of Villers acquired a young abbot in 1197 from further east in the
Empire, Charles, a former household knight of the Emperor Frederick
Barbarossa. Late in the 1170s and early in the 1180s, Charles had pursued a vigorous tournament career for several years in the Rhineland
before entering a monastery. The chronicle mentions tournaments he
attended at Worms and Neuss on the Rhine, and implies that they were
being held in many more places in Germany.[32] Tournaments had established themselves as an aristocratic enthusiasm clear across the Empire
by the 1170s, and a flourishing German circuit – which may have been
recognised as worth visiting, even amongst the French – was meeting
up and down the Rhine. It can be noted that in the 1160s the Marshal
was said to have been known as a tourneyer beyond Flanders in
Avauterre (the Low Countries). In 1183 he travelled as far as Cologne
looking for employers, after quitting the service of the Young King
Henry. It is also worth suggesting that when in around 1180 Chrétien
de Troyes selected the name *Noauz* for one of his imagined Arthurian
tournaments, he was alluding to the famous Rhineland tournament site
of Neuss, downriver from Cologne.[33]

By 1180 the tournament was in its developed state. It was a widespread
aristocratic sport and Bertran de Born gives us a contemporary mental
map of the tourneying world in one of his two laments for the Young
King Henry of England, who died in 1183. Bertran sang that Henry
would be missed for his gaiety and tourneying abilities by the English,
Normans, Bretons and Irish (meaning the Anglo-Norman colonists of
Ireland), by the people of Guyenne and Gascony, of Anjou, Maine and
Tours, by the subjects of the French king as far north as Compiègne, by
the Flemish from Ghent to the sea, by the Germans, Lorrainers and
Brabazons.[34] We can already recognise by 1183 most of the tournament's
defining features. Major French tournament sites were located on lordship boundaries and tournaments were held on them throughout the
year, except from Ash Wednesday to the close of Easter. We can already
see some of its characteristic organisation: it began with single combats,
and the main event was the grand charge between two teams, which dis-
solved into a lengthy mêlée across a wide area of country. The
tournament already had some great patrons, like Charles of Flanders,
who spent freely on retaining large squadrons of knights which they
would lead from tournament to tournament over a wide area.

I have asserted that the tournament was a sport – contemporaries called it in French a *deduit* ('amusement' or 'recreation') and in Latin a *ludus* ('game'). It is possible (and permissible) to go so far as to say that it was a professional sport, in the sense that twelfth-century knights could use the tournament to find personal celebrity and the best of them could make a handsome living by it. As the sociologists of sport would rightly say, the tournament was not a 'modern' sport, the sort of recreation that the Victorians developed, with ruling bodies, handbooks, rulebooks and leagues. But neither was it much like 'traditional' or 'folk' sport such as the mass football, handball or hurling contests mentioned as part of popular festivals as early as the twelfth century. It was rather the precursor of eighteenth-century upper-class amusements such as the tennis, pugilism, golf, rowing, racing and cricket which were sponsored by the gentry and aristocracy, the sort called 'pre-modern' sports.[35] The tournament may not have been formally organised with leagues, rule books and points, but like them it was not generally animated by any spirit of malign violence, it was instead dominated by a competitive team mentality and each leading team and sporting celebrity was informally rated by onlookers.[36] The following chapters will examine in detail what were the organisation and principal features of this grandfather of all western sports, and look also at its widespread social consequences.

Sources

As we have seen, sources for what the tournament was do not become relatively plentiful till the second half of the twelfth century, by which time the tournament had been in existence for a century. From indications of earlier practices, however, it seems likely enough that the tournament in 1160 was much the same as the tournament had been in 1120. In fact the organisation of the tournament remained constant in its essentials till around 1250. There was certainly change in equipment and detail, but the main changes were to do with emphasis. This was particularly the case with the growing importance in the thirteenth century of the tournament's preliminaries, the jousting or *commençailles*. There was also a distinct shift throughout the period towards greater elaboration and stage-management of the event itself.

The first major sources for the tournament are historical and unveil the careers of two great champions of the same generation, William Marshal, earl of Pembroke (d. 1219), and Baldwin V, count of Hainault and eventually also count of Flanders (d. 1194). Both men were active in the tournament field from the late 1160s to the 1180s. William Marshal's son and executors commissioned a professional poet to create a French verse biography of the old man in the mid 1220s. The poet did a scrupulous job and, although his chief source consisted of the anecdotes of tourneying from the 1160s to 1180s told by the old Marshal and remembered by his sons and knights, he also used several older, lost sources for tourneying. These included a list of ransoms the Marshal had acquired during a single year of his career in a partnership with another knight, and a rhymed roll of participants in a grand tournament at Lagny-sur-Marne in 1179. Count Baldwin's tourneying career was reconstructed around 1200 by his former chaplain and chancellor, Gilbert (or Gislebert) of Mons, as part of his history of the county of Hainault. Gilbert relied in part on his own memories and notes but also, it seems, on some sort of contemporary record of the count's tournaments which he might have written himself. The Marshal biography and the Hainault chronicle are reliable and informative insights into the tourneying society of the 1170s and 1180s. A similar sort of source is represented by the reminiscences of the aristocratic clerk, Lambert of Ardres, on the history of the allied families of the counts of Guines and lords of Ardres. Lambert's family history was compiled around 1206 and contains numerous incidental references to the tourneying done by various former counts and lords.

From the 1170s onwards a major shift in literary genre suddenly introduced a new source for the reconstruction of the tournament. The great French poet Chrétien de Troyes began writing Arthurian fantasies set in a recognisably contemporary French world. Chrétien imagined a number of fictional tournaments and drew on contemporary tournament practices to give them colour and verisimilitude. Chrétien also developed (along with other contemporary writers, notably Walter of Arras) a new sort of romance, the fictional biography of the life and loves of imagined Arthurian or historical characters, a sort of romance called the *roman d'aventure*. The characters in such romances, people like the Greek knight Cligés, the Breton Ille, the Englishman Guy of Warwick, or the Welshman, Perceval, all helped make their names by their early prowess on the tournament field. For a century and more thereafter many French and German writers gave pen portraits of tournament life, which increased in detail and colour, and contemporaneity.

Another boundary was crossed soon after 1200. The writings of the

early thirteenth-century northern French poets Jean Renart and Gerbert
de Montreuil go a step further than Chrétien and Walter. Both set their
imagined tournaments in real places used for tourneying, and both significantly increased the detail and colour of their descriptions of what
happened in such places.[37] This approach was taken to its logical conclusion in the romances of the mid thirteenth-century Capetian civil
servant and poet, Philip de Remy. In his famous work *La Manekine*
(*c.* 1241) Philip described a tournament tour of northern France
embarked upon by an imagined king of Scotland, which culminated in
the most detailed description yet given of a tournament, set in the real-
life venue between Ressons and Gournay. It was plainly constructed out
of his memories of actual tournaments fought on that genuine tournament field. Philip wrote almost journalistically, and this is no surprise,
for he actually lived in a house on the edge of that very tournament
field.

The sort of approach taken by Philip is also evident in the anonymous
later thirteenth-century romances, *Sone de Nansay* and *Le Roman du
Castelain de Coucy*.[38] The hero of *Sone* (his unusual name is explained
to be from his mother's German relatives) pursues his career and for-
tune across France, Scotland, Scandinavia and the western Empire. In
the course of his travels he distinguishes himself in notable tournaments
and the new sort of jousting events called 'Round Tables'. The venues
chosen in *Sone* are real places and the characters are modelled on real
members of the thirteenth-century aristocratic world, although it is set
in an unspecified past. The romance of Reginald, the 'castellan of
Coucy', by a Picard poet called Jakemes, is a love story and a historical
novel. Like *Sone*, it is set in a historical past, the time of Richard the
Lionheart. In pursuit of his love, Reginald distinguishes himself in a
series of tournaments. In fact the tournament circuit becomes the place
where he can freely pursue his adulterous passion. The descriptions of
the fighting and the venues in both are relentlessly detailed and realistic,
and the places, characters, and even the heraldry, are all real-life.

The second half of the thirteenth century produced the culmination
of the poetic treatment of tournaments, in extended historical verse
descriptions of real events reported by eyewitnesses. We have the supposed chivalric autobiography of a Styrian magnate, Ulrich von
Liechtenstein, written around 1255. It includes Ulrich's reminiscenses of
his love life, jousting and tourneying from 1220 onwards. It is a fascinating study, packed with contemporary colour and bizarre anecdotes,

some of which may even be true. The main problems with it seem to be
that Ulrich's memory let him down on several occasions, and his exu-
berant ego and cavalier way with numbers mean that he cannot always
be trusted as to details. A more reliable source is the detailed story of
what was in fact a joust, not a tournament, held at Hem-sur-Somme in
Picardy over three days, 9–11 October 1278. It was recorded in verse
within months of the event by a northern French herald called Sarrazin,
who had been at the event and constructed much of his account from
the score sheets he had kept. Not long afterwards, in January 1280, a
three-day tournament met under the patronage of the count of Looz
and Chiny at Chauvency-le-Château in the duchy of Lorraine. The
reporter this time was a prominent Flemish poet by the name of Jacques
Bretel, who, being a busy man, apparently did not get round to writing
up his notes till September 1285. Between *Sone*, Ulrich, Jakemes, Sarrazin
and Bretel we are not short of detail as to how tourneys and jousts were
conducted in the second half of the thirteenth century. Nor are we short
of criticism of the tournament from other poets. A major source for
thirteenth-century practice is the *Dit des Hérauts* of Henry de Laon.
This poem is in fact little to do with heralds, but is rather a satire on the
corruption and decline the author observed in the tournaments. We
know nothing of Henry other than his name, but his vivid and intimate
portrayal of the experience of the tournament is one of the best sources
we have for what it felt like to ride on the field.

In England meanwhile the historical sources available for studying the
tournament steadily increased. From the 1190s onwards a major and
unique source is represented by the Chancery and Exchequer records of
the English monarchy. These include records of fines, trials and prohibitions relating to the English tournament circuit. No other European
nation preserves such records for this period. Also in England, the history of the England in the reign of Henry III (1216–72) by a monk of
St Albans, Matthew Paris, preserves a number of highly detailed
accounts of insular tournaments. Although a monk, Paris was clearly
fascinated by stories of the tournament field, nor was he alone, for a
later monk of his abbey, William Rishanger, did the same. The accounts
of the royal household in the reigns of Edward I (1272–1307) and
Edward II (1307–27) offer a complementary, if technical, perspective on
tournament arms and trappings.

All of these sources have their difficulties, even the avowedly historical ones. The *History of William Marshal* hardly ever describes his

defeats, for its purpose was to demonstrate that William was the best and most loyal knight in his world. The same is true of Ulrich von Liechtenstein's *Frauendienst*, for it was written to demonstrate his great military prowess and (mostly unrequited) passion for the female sex. We can assume therefore that there is a lot we are not hearing about William Marshal and Ulrich, and that we will never now know. The literary sources are the most difficult, and there are several reasons why this should be. Like the *History*, the *romans d'aventure* were devised principally to exalt their fictional heroes: their accomplishments are often inflated beyond the capacities of flesh and blood. For instance, Cligés is depicted as tourneying on four consecutive days in the tournament between Oxford and Wallingford, when we know for a fact that a twelfth- and thirteenth-century knight was physically able to tourney only for a day. The size and splendour of tournaments in this genre is undeniably much exaggerated. The thirteenth-century Arthurian tournament scenes also present problems. The romance authors seem to have imagined that in that remote sub-Roman past tournament and battle were much the same, and Lancelot and his friends sometimes go on killing sprees on their tournament circuit. But there *was* something beyond the texts, and the texts responded in several ways to contemporary reality. Authors liked to seduce the readers by an appearance of verisimilitude and allusions to familiar practices and increasingly, to familiar places. We can be sceptical about their stories, but soak up the literary details they feed us with a lot more confidence.

PART ONE

Staging the Tournament

2

Sponsorship

The tournament was a sport, of a sort. It is difficult to think of exact parallels in modern times for what the tournament was in the high middle ages. It had the social cachet of polo and showjumping, and also the popular appeal of professional rugby. But tournaments were also as dangerous and thrilling as extreme sports are a thousand years later. For a long while tourneyers formed a suspect subculture. Men died in the tournament for no good reason, and its violent and aggressive devotees made the roads dangerous to peaceful travellers. Something of that suspicion of the tournament can be seen in the traditional sites of twelfth-cenury tournament fields in France. They were mostly on the borders of principalities. This marginalisation tells of a time when early groups of tourneying knights might have to gather where public authority was weak and was less likely to interfere with their meetings. It might especially indicate a time when, as we have seen, moves to impose an enforced Peace on society was a major concern of counts and bishops. The fact that, when they fought, twelfth-century knights banded together into national teams – Normans, Bretons, English and Flemish – hints at a time when testosterone-charged warriors got together and issued challenges to their counterparts in neighbouring regions, as if they were at war rather than just training for it. But by the time chroniclers got interested in the tournament in the 1130s those days were nearly gone, and they were gone because tournaments had found patrons.

The twentieth century discovered that serious money radically changes the nature of a sport, but the twelfth century already knew that. Grand and noble patrons brought a whole new range of imperatives into play on the field: aristocratic status, social display and political scheming. Rich sponsors would hire the best knights available to safeguard their honour and reputation, and also to keep them safe from capture in the field. They would form what were, in effect, teams. The game was no longer about showing off skills of arms and horsemanship, and no longer about tempering warriors for war, or riding the rush of adrenalin. The first major patron of whom we know anything was, of course, Count Charles of Flanders (1119–27). It took just one such man to trigger a competition for prestige on the field amongst other rich young princes, and it may be that this was the way the tournament became the playground of the great and wealthy noblemen of the Anglo-French world.[1]

By the early 1140s we know of many more great tournament patrons. In the Anglo-Norman realm there are three counts who are known to have been involved. In 1142 we hear of Count William of Aumale and York and Count Alan of Brittany and Richmond, both great cross-Channel magnates, who promoted a meeting (called a 'military festivity') after Easter near York.[2] We hear of it because King Stephen chose to cancel the meeting as he intended to mount a campaign that summer and wanted no distractions. Another great Anglo-Norman tourneyer was David of Scotland (died 1153), earl of Huntingdon from 1113 and king of Scotland after 1124. We know this because one of his household knights was Osbert of Arden, who was accustomed to tourney in England and across the Channel in the 1120s. We may presume that when he did so he was following his lord. One of the places at which Osbert attended tournaments was Northampton, which was a royal town but one in and around which Earl David had large estates.[3] It may well be that David's patronage was the reason Northampton became an established tournament venue. David's early patronage helps explain the prominence in the sport of later members of the Scottish royal family, including his grandsons William the Lion (whom we find on the tournament fields of Brittany in 1166) and Earl David II of Huntingdon (who was on the field of Lagny in 1179). These early twelfth-century patrons were the amongst the highest of the Anglo-Norman or Anglo-Scottish nobility. William of Aumale and Alan of Brittany were cousins of the Norman royal house, while David was brother-in-law to King Henry I and a descendant of the house of Wessex. Together they indicate that the Anglo-Norman aristocracy of the 1120s and 1130s was already passionate about tourneying.

High tournament patronage can also be glimpsed in France in the 1140s. Between 1147 and 1149 much of the French aristocracy accompanied King Louis VII (1137–80) on a crusade to Syria. They began to filter back in the winter of 1148–49, and to pick up their old pastimes, rivalries and amusements. During the preparation of the crusade from 1146 onwards the tournament had been suspended across the kingdom. We know this because Abbot Bernard of Clairvaux reported to the regent of France with distaste that in 1149 returning crusaders proposed to revive the tournament season with the close of the Easter festivities that year (on 11 April). The abbot named as the two leaders of the revival Henry of Blois and Count Robert of Dreux.[4] Henry was the son of Count Theobald IV of Blois and Champagne, and a nephew of King Stephen of England. Count Robert was King Louis's younger brother, ruler of the small realm of Dreux on the borders of Normandy and the lordship of Yved-le-Braine in the tournament's heartland of Picardy. They were men of just the same sort of class that we find as patrons of the tournament in England: the most distinguished nobles of their day, close kin of the English and French royal families. Henry and Robert were probably in their late twenties or thirties at the time, much the same generation as their English counterparts.

Celebrity in the Tournament World

Tournament patronage was no passing fad in the early twelfth century. Generation after generation of the high nobility took the field as their fathers had done before them, escorted by companies of retained knights. We know a lot more about the next generation's patrons, and what we learn of them is intriguing. The tournament was not just for them an expensive amusement. Everyone who was anyone in the western aristocracies took to the fields of northern France, and this fact opened up international political possibilities which had not been previously there. The career of Henry, the eldest son of King Henry II of England, cannot be understood unless you fully appreciate how he made the international tournament circuit his very own. Henry, or the Young Henry as he was generally known, was born in February 1155. He was declared of age in 1170 when his father girded him with the arms of knighthood, settled a large income on him and had him crowned as associate king of England.

Henry was born to a world of unparalleled wealth, to a mother of legendary beauty and sophistication, and to a father of unsurpassed political power. A Latin poem by a court official written to commemorate his coronation hints at the charisma that already then hung around this charming and handsome young prince. It describes him in 1170 at the age of fifteen as an epicene youth of striking beauty, tall but well proportioned, broad-shouldered with a long and elegant neck, pale and freckled skin, bright and wide blue eyes, with a thick mop of the reddish-gold hair characteristic of his dynasty.[5] On that very day his quick and heedless wit was brought to public attention. When the archbishop of York congratulated him on gaining equality in rank with his royal father, Henry politely differed with him. He was the son of a king, he said, whereas his father was merely the son of a count.

The elder king entrusted his son to a household he had selected to give him a training in all the skills proper to his rank, including the military ones. Amongst the boy's new tutors was a young and charismatic knight in his early twenties who had been transferred from the queen's household to be Henry's master in arms. His name was William Marshal, and he was the younger son of a royal court official. He had been born in England around 1146 but brought up in Normandy in the household of William, lord of Tancarville. William had entered on the French tournament circuit with the Tancarville household in 1166 and found it a place in which he could be happy. He was a powerful and skilled young knight, active, physically coordinated and fearless. By 1170, at around the age of twenty-three, he had already secured quite a reputation as an international sportsman, and Queen Eleanor had retained him as a handsome and talented ornament to her court, happy that his continuing success in tournaments reflected well on her judgement of men. William's transfer to the Young Henry's household brought the impressionable young prince under the influence of one of the most accomplished and devoted of the tournament champions of his day.[6]

Henry was put into intensive training by his young mentor and proved an enthusiastic pupil. He was eager to accompany William 'his dearest friend' around the tournament fields of northern and central France in the early 1170s, and there he spent freely from his liberal allowance, so freely that before long he was sending for more money from his father.[7] Since his allowance amounted to several thousands of pounds a year, the money must have been poured out in retaining knights and financing tournaments. The teenage prince had found an exciting and lavish way to establish a reputation in his world, and there were many men other than William Marshal who were happy to help him spend his money. Young Henry's charters tell us that in the period after 1174 when he took to the tournament circuit he supported a permanent retinue of about twelve knights, mostly Normans, which was a farily modest size for that time.[8] But the expenses accumulated when he took on several score more knights for the season, equipping them and offering large cash fees for their service. Free-spending, charming, handsome, whimsical and funny, Henry became fiercely popular amongst a younger set of the Anglo-Norman aristocracy. He had a remarkable talent for attracting men, with his openness and charm, quite unlike the brusque and purposeful aggression of his father. Naturally he became a focus of discontent for those barons who did not get on with the elder Henry. He precipitated a serious rebellion in his father's realm in 1173. But he survived it, and even got an increased supply of money from his father, amounting to 15,000 *livres angevin*.[9] He spent it freely on a return to the tournament circuit, on which he lived more or less continuously from 1175 to 1182.

The Young Henry and his fellow spirits loved the road; when they were confined to England for a year they chafed for the wandering life. This was what nineteenth-century writers called 'errantry'. It was not really a life of hardship on the road, more a life of itinerant luxury: the best food, the best lodgings and very little responsibility. But feckless and rootless a life as it may seem Henry was not just being the eternal playboy. There was a greater game to be played. Henry's own reported view in 1175 was that:

> it could be a source of much harm to me to stay idle for so long, and I am extremely vexed by it. I am no bird to be mewed up; a young man who does not travel around could never aspire to any worthwhile thing, and he should be regarded as of no account.[10]

Here was the difference between the father the king and his son. Henry II thought what his son was doing was wasteful and trivial. He might well have agreed with the criticism of the Young Henry by Bertran de Born in 1182 that Henry was off fecklessly tourneying with his French friends and family when he should have been restoring public order in Aquitaine.[11]

But Young Henry found that on the contrary the tournaments made him a 'man of account'. It gave him an international eminence unsurpassed by any European prince other than his cousin, Philip of Flanders. It was an eminence raised upon the regard of other princes and the adoration of the leaders of knightly opinion: those who travelled the tournament fields of Picardy and Flanders. Bertran himself acknowledged this when he lamented Henry as a lost 'sovereign of the courtly knights', 'emperor of champions', and a king who had been 'captain and patron of the young'.[12] It is worth asking how much of his father's reported contempt for the Young Henry was based on an unease at precisely how prominent the young man became before his premature death in 1183; maybe it was even envy. The Young King Henry lacked the political calculation and vision of his father, but his former chaplain, Gervase, recalled him as a man not without sense. In the 1170s Young Henry was playing as much a cultural as a political game. The end of his game was to exceed all other knights, barons and princes in fame. On that capital he could command great influence within the European aristocracies. His former courtier, Ralph Niger, recognised this. In 1187 he lamented the tournament for the waste of money and talent there that could have been better employed than on the avid pursuit of what he considered empty prizes: public acclaim and popular celebrity.[13] His late master was of another mind.

The cost of living as Young Henry lived was high. When his team lost, as it did consistently in 1175 and 1176, he was still bound to repay the ransoms of his household knights, as well as pay them for their services, buy them the best equipment and give them the best horses. Knights became more expensive too, as other princes and magnates, such as Philip of Flanders, began to bid against Henry for the best to be had. For instance, early in 1183, after many offers, Count Philip was able to buy the services of William Marshal, who had fallen out temporarily with Henry. The price of the transfer is known to have been the rents of a quarter of the Flemish city of St-Omer: a stupendous fee, fully comparable with the international soccer transfer market of the present day.[14] We have some insight into the scale of Young Henry's generosity in what he paid to his grand retinue at the tournament of Lagny in November 1179. On that day he rode with more than two hundred knights, fifteen of whom were senior knights, or bannerets, with their own retinues. Not only did he pay his own knights, he also paid twenty shillings a day to the knights in his bannerets' retinues, thus relieving them of the expense. Each day this enormous tourneying company rode together it cost Henry over two hundred pounds, and he undertook to pay each knight the same sum from the moment they left their homes to join him. To give an idea of what was being offered daily, two hundred pounds was the annual income of a moderately wealthy baron, or the amount the county of Worcester owed the king every year. William Marshal's biographer commented: 'It was a source of wonder where this wealth was to be found', as well he might, and he speculated whether some of it was raised from the captures and ransoms the Young King's men had made. But he also was aware that much of it was raised on credit at the towns at which Henry was staying, and that he left a trail of debt bonds behind him wherever he went.[15]

The Young Henry's golden career was as brief as such careers tend to be. He died in the Linousin of dysentery in June 1183 at the age of twenty-eight, during the course of a second pointless rebellion against his father. There were remarkable scenes of grief at his deathbed, and in the countryside and towns his corpse was mobbed by hysterical crowds as it was carried north to Normandy for burial. Some believed that miracles were performed by his body and that a pillar of light stood over his bier at night. His popularity embraced all levels of society, and his death left a lasting legacy of disappointment.[16] Forty years later a French poet attached to the Marshal family called John, a man with historical interests and the biographer of William Marshal, assessed 1183 as a turning point in the history of the tournament circuit. He said that no later patron of the tournament was as generous as Henry, and 'Largesse' was left a widow at his death. He believed that knightly skills and display reached a high point in Henry's lifetime that it never attained again. John the poet was not alone in his assessment. 'His death,' said Young Henry's former chaplain, Gervase of Tilbury, 'was the end of everything knightly'; after the loss of his generosity 'the world went begging'. The southern poet, Bertran de Born, lamented at the time on the part of the 'household knights' the death of Henry, whose generosity was on a scale to make the most lavish man in the world seem like a miser. Bertran considered that the Young King would be missed most on the tournament grounds of Flanders and Picardy, where he was 'the bravest and most daring of all tourneyers'. It was the conclusion of the Young King's circle, and outsiders too, that his death removed the key patron from the late twelfth-century tournament circuit, the man who had brought the sport to yet higher levels of popularity and social consequence.[17]

The brief period of the Young King Henry's ascendancy amongst the Anglo-French aristocracy has its significance. It tells us a lot about the nature of that small international community. Henry was not only a king, he was a celebrity. What do we mean by that in a medieval context? It means that he stood at the centre of his little aristocratic world, and people were drawn to him and wanted to be known by him. Just to be close to him produced a frisson, sexual in nature for many. It was not merely that he was a king: other contemporary kings, like his father and his father-in-law, Louis VII, did not excite crowds and people by their very proximity. To begin with, all writers who knew him commented on his outstanding good looks.[18] He was an exceptionally handsome young man, and his beauty was a part of his personal charisma. People felt instantly moved by close contact with him, in ways that they did not by his plain and sarcastic father, who tended to intimidate and overawe. This instant sympathy towards Young Henry was cemented into real affection if contact turned into conversation. He was approachable, charming and without much need to impose his social eminence on those around him. Medieval royalty knew how to work a crowd. David of Scotland (died 1153), Henry's great-great uncle, is a case in point. His friend Ailred of Rievaulx said of him that:

> It would so happen that whenever he talked to priest, knight, monk, rich or poor man, townsman or pilgrim, merchant or peasant, he would openly and humbly discuss with each of them his own affairs and duties, so that each of them would think that he was taking note of their ideas, and so he would send all of them on their way happy and better informed.[19]

Stories of Young Henry's wit and playful humour circulated widely in the twelfth century. On one occasion, in an uncomfortably packed banquet, he sent everybody out of the hall whose name was not William; people thought this very amusing in a Brideshead sort of way. Clerics were as vulnerable to his charm as knights and barons. Once under his spell, men and women did not easily shake it off, surprisingly in the case of some. Seven years after Young Henry's death, William Marshal founded an Augustinian priory and instituted there prayers for the souls of all the three kings of England he had served; of the three kings, the Young Henry was the one whom he called *dominus meus*, 'my lord'.[20] Henry had a similar effect on women. Eleven years after his death, his second cousin, Countess Eleanor of Beaumont-sur-Oise, lady of Valois in Picardy and sister-in-law of Philip of Flanders, who must have seen much of Henry in his tourneying days, made a grant to the abbey of Ourscamp. She did so, she said, for the souls of her sister, her present and past husbands, 'and of the Young King Henry, my cousin.'[21] The international tourney field allowed him to extend the sphere of his influence across western Europe. Wherever he went, counts, dukes and barons clamoured to approach him, to be of use to him, to entertain him and hope for an invitation to his table. Just as the common recognition of celebrity within western media-dominated societies assists in

socially consolidating them, so it was also in the Young Henry's small
and aristocratic world, the world of the tournament.

The Tournament as Foreign Policy

Great devotee though he was, the Young King Henry was not unique in
his day. There were realms where the tournament attracted more popular enthusiasm than religion, and one of these was Hainault. Hainault
was a small French-speaking principality just outside the medieval
kingdom of France and within the Holy Roman Empire, wedged
between the county of Flanders, the duchy of Brabant and the bishopric
of Liège. The twelfth-century counts of Hainault lived in a dangerous
and war-torn region, surrounded by aggressive neighbours. Their
neighbours, the Brabazons, were notorious in the twelfth century as
hard-bitten and ruthless mercenaries. Circumstances put a premium on
warlike skills amongst the counts of Hainault and their vassals, and it is
no surprise to find that Hainault played a prominent and violent part
in the history of the tournament and that Hennuyers had a formidable
military reputation.[22] As we have seen, the earliest historical reference to
the tournament by that name comes from the county in 1114, in the
records of the town of Valenciennes. One of the great international
tournament sites was on the border of the counties of Hainault and
Namur, at Trazegnies, four kilometres north of Charleroi in modern
Belgium.

   Baldwin V, count of Hainault and Namur and (after 1191) count of
Flanders, was knighted at the age of sixteen in April 1168; he was three
years older than the Young King Henry. Like Henry he came into wealth
and position as a very young man. He succeeded his father in November 1171, before he was twenty years of age. As the writings of his devoted
chancellor, Gilbert of Mons, tell us, Baldwin was already by then a devotee of the tournament, and he led his retinue on to his first tourney field
at Maastricht ten days after he was knighted.[23] Over the next twenty or
so years, Baldwin was to be found on the great tournament sites of
northern France and Lotharingia whenever war and politics did not get
in the way. Between his knighting and his succession as count, Baldwin
took to the road in search of every tournament he could find, and like
the Young Henry he recruited to his retinue the most accomplished and
famous knights who could be hired. Young Henry's own circle learned
to regret meeting the Hennuyers (that is, the men of Hainault). Before

he took service with Young Henry, at some time in 1168 or 1169, William Marshal came off worst in an encounter with Baldwin's retinue on a field somewhere in northern France and lost his horse as ransom to a Hennuyer knight, Matthew de Walincourt. Marshal nursed his resentment at the incident for over a decade afterwards; he did not like losing.[24]

The Hennuyers under Baldwin were a tough crew. Late in 1168 they arrived on the broad ridge of Ressons-Gournay. It was already then a traditional site for tourneying between the knights of Picardy, Flanders and Hainault, on one side, and the knights of the French lands further south, on the other. Young Baldwin had conceived a dislike for his cousin, Philip of Alsace, count of Flanders (1163–91). When it turned out that too few French had turned up to make it a fair contest, Baldwin took the opportunity to cross over sides and appear in front of the French lists against the Flemings and Picards. Baldwin's team attacked the Flemings with such enthusiasm that Count Philip was alarmed enough to order up companies of infantry in battle order so as to intimidate the Hennuyers. But Philip left it too late and a Hennuyer knight, Geoffrey Tuelasne, rode him down and left him reeling in the saddle from a blow on his chest. The Hennuyers later claimed that they captured and held Philip, but that he was allowed to escape by a sympathetic knight.[25] Even so, Baldwin led his men to a victory that was long remembered.

The toughness of the Hennuyers was partly because local animosities made tournaments in Brabant or Hainault likely to be more violent than those held further south within France, or in England. At a tournament announced at Trazegnies in the summer of 1170, Baldwin marched three thousand infantry to the field with him, as a precaution against possible treachery by Duke Godfrey of Brabant, with whom he had a number of disputes. As the Roman road from Mons approached the field at Trazegnies, his scouts reported that a powerful Brabazon army was marching towards the thick wood where Baldwin had halted at Carnières. A full-scale battle, not a tournament, followed and Baldwin used the defensive advantage of being in woodland to rout a force of Brabazons much larger than his own, killing many of them.[26]

Baldwin celebrated his accession to the county of Hainault by embarking in 1172 on a grand tour of the tournament fields of northern France and Burgundy. Early in the new year he was tourneying in the fields between Bussy-le-Château and Chalons-en-Champagne, south east of Reims, with a household of eighty knights. After Easter, when the season resumed, he travelled further south, to Burgundy, where he attended a tournament between Montbard and Rougemont with a household of a hundred knights, all at his own expense. Despite the fact that a local magnate, the count of Nevers, had forbidden the tournament from taking place on his land, Baldwin occupied the count's town of Rougemont and fought anyway. The Hennuyers thought that it was very funny. Baldwin returned home and spent the next five weeks touring the region of Rethel in the Ardennes taking in all the local meetings. The rest of the year he spent in diplomacy and continuing the war against Brabant.[27] When campaigns and local rivalries gave him the chance, Count Baldwin spent the next twelve years attending tournaments in north-east France and Belgium, from the Channel south to Burgundy. In 1184 he even ventured to the imperial court at Mainz and Ingelheim to enjoy one of the first known meetings in the Rhineland.[28] Baldwin's tournament career is confirmation that, enthusiast though he was, the Young King Henry of England was not all that exceptional a devotee and patron of the tournament field. There were a number of other princes who came close to matching his expenditure and enthusiasm.

The case of Baldwin of Hainault demonstrates a different aspect of the princely use of the tournament. The Young Henry used the tournament both for his own personal enjoyment and as a way of gaining ascendancy in a political world where he was allowed no realm to rule. Baldwin came young to power over his ancestral lands, yet he was equally assiduous in his pursuit of tournaments. For him the purpose was to establish himself as a great warrior in his warlike region, without actually going to the danger and expense of a war. The tournament field allowed him to engage politically and even physically with his more powerful neighbours, who would have overwhelmed his armies in war. Hence the delight in worsting his most dangerous dynastic rival, Philip of Flanders. The victory over Philip in 1168 was all the more satisfying as Philip fancied himself to be the leader of the tourneying society of the time.

Patronage and Publicity

Apart from hiring expensive retinues, there was further expense for the would-be patron involved in staging tournaments. The patron had to take responsibility for publicising the event, if it was to be in any way an exceptional meeting which would earn him credit. In the case of a tournament held at Valennes in Anjou in 1166, we are told that someone unknown had footed the expense of sending out criers to announce the date and place, and these men had penetrated into the Breton March in one direction, eastern Normandy and Paris in another, and (presumably also) south and west into Poitou and Anjou. In the case of Valennes, we have no idea who this anonymous patron was, but in the case of the first recorded Ressons-Gournay meeting of 1168 there is no doubt that the patron was Count Philip of Flanders. We are told that 'Count Philip of Flanders and Vermandois invited a party of French to fight at a tournament between Gournay and Ressons'.[29]

James de Vitry, writing between 1190 and 1215, said that it was the promoter of the event who ought to despatch what he called in Latin *praecones* and *hystriones* to publicise the event.[30] These men, who you could call 'criers' or 'heralds' were the people that were called at the time *hirauts* (from which the word 'herald' comes). These *hirauts* were at that time for the most part lowly military attendants. The word 'hiraut' comes from the old Germanic word 'heer' which means 'army'. Many of them doubled as singers and poets in order to pad out their very uncertain incomes, which is why James de Vitry uses the word *hystriones* for them – meaning 'entertainers'.[31] From one stray piece of evidence it seems that the heralds publicising a tournament might well have needed to sing their announcement, a sort of 'joust-a-gram'. At some time early in the 1180s the great and noble Occitan poet Bertran de Born was approached by an emissary of the count of Toulouse, with an urgent request that he provide a suitable song to publicise a tournament the count was going to stage at his city for the magnates and knights of Aquitaine, the Midi and the Spanish March. Bertran obliged with a brilliant *sirventès* which gave the location, teams and length of time of the tournament (the dates would be added later by the criers once they had been fixed, one supposes). It artfully painted the grandeur of the proposed meeting and the magnates who had already consented to be present, and did its best to rouse regional feeling. The clear intention was that copies should be given to heralds who were to ride around the valleys of the Pyrenees singing it for the weeks before the event. It ended: 'Let each man look to his arms, for he is awaited at Toulouse. I wish that the magnates would always be so eager against each other'.[32]

Joint patronage of a tournament was not unknown. The Marshal biography says that a tournament at Joigny in 1178 or 1179 was organised

by a group of Champenois magnates, not any one individual.[33] A
century later, it was the Champenois and Berruyer knights present at
the final dinner of the meeting at Le Fère-Vendeuil who got together
and 'swore a tournament' to meet within a fortnight at Mezières-en-
Gâtinais, on the border between their lands, some 275 kilometres to
the south.[34] Perhaps individual patronage was more common, as there
would have been more honour in it for the sponsor. As we have seen,
tournaments in England also attracted noble and generous patrons. The
1142 York tournament was organised by the earls of Richmond and
York. When tournaments were revived after 1194, earls likewise came
forward to offer patronage. In the early thirteenth century, King
Henry III's uncle, Earl William Longespée of Salisbury, and William de
Forz, count of Aumale, are identified as patrons of meetings at
Northampton in 1218 and at Brackley in 1219.[35] The English patrons of
the tournament were doing no more than their French colleagues in
seeking distinction and status.

The problem for would-be patrons in England was that the royal
council began to stigmatise the holding of tournaments as a challenge
to royal authority and so tournaments became politicised, in ways they
did not in France. It is a testimony to the drawing power and fashion-
ability of the tournament that, nevertheless, sponsors still came forward
in England, and tried to find ways around the royal ban. A tournament
held near Chepstow in September 1227 was a stubborn response by the
younger Earl William Marshal (son of the Marshal who was tutor to
Young Henry) to Hubert de Burgh's ban on tournaments earlier in the
year at Northampton and Blyth. Despite a writ to forbid it, the tournament still met on or soon before 10 November on the probable grounds
that Chepstow was in the March and beyond the king's writ.[36]

The thirteenth-century French poet and civil servant, Philip de Remy,
writing around 1240, gives us some insight as to how a patron would
set a tournament in motion. The king of Scotland in Philip's romance,
Manekine, enjoyed himself so much at a tournament at Ressons-
Gournay that he sent criers out into the town to proclaim a tournament
at Épernay (another site in use in the 1170s and 1180s) in a fortnight's
time. Before this, he had consulted with his fellow participants at
Ressons to make sure that it would be acceptable, and, presumably,
that they would attend if he made the effort. He did not apparently
bother about asking whether the arrangement suited the citizens of
Épernay.[37] All our sources assume that the settlements which defined

the well-established tournament sites were happy to welcome meetings at any time. Since there was a lot of money to be made from the tourneyers, the assumption may well be correct.

Notice of anything from a fortnight to six weeks was given when an event was announced. Chrétien de Troyes preserves the good advice that the more notice of an event that was given, the further news would spread and the more people would present themselves. The biographer of William Marshal imagined that a fortnight's notice was given for the tournament of Valennes in 1166 – the same notice as Philip de Remy gives. A fortnight's notice seems to have been the accepted normal period of notice in literature, but this was not invariable because he also reports three weeks' notice given for a historical tournament at Pleurs in 1178.[38] The best evidence for the circulation and reception of tournament publicity that we have is the series of prohibitions issued by the English chancery between 1216 and 1250. The bulk of them note the day and date on which the coming tournament had been 'fixed' (*captum*) by its organisers. The writ to prohibit the tournament was also dated by the chancery clerks, so from them we can roughly work out the period of notice the king had before the event. Generally it seems that he knew of an impending tournament between five and eight days before it happened, although on one occasion in 1235 he knew of a tournament at Bury St Edmunds three weeks before it was due. It is probable that he was no worse informed than his subjects on the approach of tournament days, and therefore news circulated a week or two in advance of the event. This gave time for travel quite a considerable distance across England, both for participants and the couriers sent to prohibit the event. There are examples when the king apparently had only a day or two's notice before issuing the prohibition. In such cases it can never have reached the participants in time. This warns us that in some cases the prohibition was only a legal form issued so that the transgressors were technically in mercy for breach of the peace, and the king may well have known of the event for rather longer than the documents imply. The tournament organisers of course planned further in advance. When the king himself sponsored a tournament, which he arranged to meet at Stamford on Saturday 9 September 1228, he gave himself many weeks in hand. When in July he decided to change the date, he was able to do it with over six weeks' notice.[39]

We are less well-informed about the notice given for continental tournaments. When Philip de Remy's king of Scotland came to

Flanders, he came believing that tournaments would be happening somewhere in northern France, but not knowing where. He clearly had no expectation of finding a regular circuit of fixed dates and places. There is no evidence that medieval tournaments held at the same location were held on a regular date, like a fair. The three tournaments mentioned in the *History of William Marshal* as held in different years at Ressons-Gournay were held in early summer in 1176, in November in 1182, and on Saturday 15 January in 1183. The one we know of that was held there in 1168 was held in autumn. There was a tournament 'closed season', but otherwise no restrictions other than the avoidance of tourneying on Sundays and probably also on major holy days that fell on week days, such as the feast of the Ascension. Analysis of the English tournament dates in the Chancery rolls between 1216 and 1250 finds that tournaments happened in every month of the year. If there were favourite tourneying months they were, according to the English evidence, January and September, but the early summer months and November were also busy. In the Low Countries in the fourteenth century, winter tournaments were also popular, with February the busiest month. This may not have been true elsewhere. Ulrich von Liechtenstein in thirteenth-century Austria and Slovenia, did not tourney after the onset of winter. But winters in the Alps were more arduous than winters on the Atlantic coast, and that may well account for the tournament being seasonal there.

The Closed Season

Tournaments were rare in certain months. Few happened in August, and this was probably for the pragmatic reason that it was the harvest season, and even noble landholders did not want hundreds of knights trampling down their hay and crops and bothering their workers. They were rare in March because there was a strict embargo in tourneying in the penitential season of Lent, which almost invariably included most of March, at whatever date Easter fell (Easter could be as early as 22 March and as late as 23 April). This was also convenient for landholders, as the new grass began to appear in early spring and it needed to grow for stock to be driven out on it after the winter famine for the lambing season. It was not just the tournament that stopped in Lent. In England in the thirteenth century, the riotous mass football and handball matches fought between entire villages were customarily held on Shrove Tuesday, the last day before Lent began, and a day of feast before the season of penance began.[40]

Lent was a religious season which spanned the forty days from Ash Wednesday to Good Friday. It was kept with great solemnity and involved numerous spiritual exercises, notably almsgiving, fasting and changes in diet. When French bishops drew up public oaths to keep the peace in the troubled days of the early eleventh century, as the bishop of Beauvais did in 1023, they might use the solemnity of the season to require adult males to renounce violence to the unarmed poor and to travellers from the beginning of Lent to the end of the Easter festivities (which was reckoned as the Sunday after Easter Day). The tournament closed season in the twelfth century was exactly that period and this is probably not a coincidence. The twelfth-century Lent tournament ban may well be a relic of part of the peace legislation of the previous century. The Lent ban on tournaments was universally maintained by the knights themselves, despite the counter-attractions of the sport, which says something for the general level of piety in the twelfth century.

For the ban in Lent we have the further evidence of Bernard of Clairvaux, who reports with distaste that in 1149 the returning crusaders, Henry of Blois and Count Robert of Dreux, proposed to revive the tournament season with the close of Easter that year, after the ban imposed during the Second Crusade. Marie de France in her *Milun* says something similar in the 1180s: it was after Easter that tournaments, war and raids began.[41] Gilbert of Mons offers further historical confirmation of the antiquity of the Lent embargo when he describes the first Christmas court of Baldwin V of Hainault in 1171. It was followed by attendance at several tournaments until Lent began (on 1 March 1172) when he went off to Laon to do homage to the bishop. He resumed his tournament attendance after the close of Easter (23 April) and he travelled around Burgundy, tourneying with an entourage of a hundred knights for five weeks. The datable tournaments of William Marshal in the late 1170s and 1180s include meetings in May, June, November and January, which likewise indicate that they might be held at any time in the year other than Lent, and the account roll of the captures he had made with Roger de Jouy ran from Pentecost (forty days after Easter) to the beginning of the next Lent, which is excellent evidence of how knights themselves regarded their tournament year in the late 1170s.[42]

In the thirteenth century, Philip de Remy says, around 1240, that it was still then the accepted custom that no one should tourney after the beginning of Lent.[43] But the prohibition was beginning to be challenged at that time. In 1249 Matthew Paris reports that the pious King Henry III of England tried to forbid his arrogant and wastrel half-brother, William de Valence, from holding a general tournament at Northampton on Ash Wednesday (the first day of Lent). As it turned out, a two-day snow-storm forced its cancellation, which Matthew Paris seems to have put down to divine intervention.[44] By the early fourteenth century, however, tourneying and jousting was occuring regularly in Lent in the Low Countries. Indeed jousting was a regular occurrence even on a Sunday, all of which would have seemed incredible a century earlier.[45]

As well as Lent, there were other times when the Church and princes combined to close down the tournament for long periods. Perhaps under the impulse of eleventh-century peace legislation there was an idea that knights should not fritter away their energy and lives on the tournament field when Christendom was in danger. The French aristocracy refrained from tourneying from 1146 to 1149, when the Second Crusade was being prepared and was under way. The prohibition was all the easier to enforce as many of the French princes and knights who were keenest on the sport left France for Syria in 1147. The prohibition during the Second Crusade may well have copied a similar prohibition while the First Crusade was preached and assembled in the late 1090s, but there is no evidence that this was so. It would seem that the idea of a tournament prohibition was revived for the Third Crusade, as in 1187 the writer Ralph Niger urges knights contemplating taking the cross not to engage in them.[46] The prohibition was revived fitfully in the thirteenth century. When Christendom was trembling at the news of the approach of the Tartar hordes, Franciscan and Dominican friars harangued the knights who had gathered for a great tournament at Neuss on the Rhine on Monday 21 May 1241 that they should think of the Tartar danger rather than their own amusement. The knights ignored them and chroniclers report with satisfaction that between forty-two and sixty knights and squires were killed or wounded in the disastrous meeting that followed.[47]

Prizes and Souvenirs

The patron had to shoulder other expenses apart from the responsibility of publicising his event. Philip de Remy tells us, and the biographer

of William Marshal confirms, that the patron was expected to demonstrate his generosity in providing dinners and entertainment for the
distinguished participants in the tournament he was hosting. Often he
would have to provide the prize awarded to the man judged to be the
best tourneyer on the day. These seem to have been symbolic, but
nonetheless expensive, items, and became more expensive during the
course of the thirteenth century. They were generally either live animals,
or expensively made and gilded representations of animals. So at the
tournament of Chastel de Molin in the early thirteenth-century *Prose
Lancelot* just a sparrowhawk and a falcon were offered to the winner. In
the tournament of Chalons in the late thirteenth-century romance *Sone
de Nansay* a real sheep – hung with golden ornaments and chained with
gold – was a prize, while in another meeting a representation of a golden
stag was offered, its great tines hung with little golden bells.[48]

On occasion, however, the patron was relieved of the expense of providing the prize, if one was to be offered. Although women could not
participate physically in the tournament, they could help in its promo-
tion and in this way share the honour to be had. The more distinctive
the prize, the more honour was involved. In the *History of William
Marshal*, the prize of a record-sized pike was offered to the best knight
at the tournament of Pleurs by a whimsical aristocratic lady, 'who was
powerful and influential and keen to do good deeds'. In the tournament
of 1215 planned by Robert fitz Walter between Staines and Hounslow in
England a prize of a bear was donated by a certain unnamed noblewoman. The romance *Gui de Warewic*, composed in the 1190s, also
expected that animals should be prizes, and that a noblewoman should
supply them. It describes a tournament patronised by the emperor of
Germany's daughter: she offered prizes of expensive horses, falcons and
dogs, all distinctively white in colour.[49]

Patrons might finance or sponsor souvenirs of particular tournaments, or tournament seasons. Since poets clustered around the
tournament circuit looking for employment, a patron might commis-
sion one to immortalise his own event in some way and then circulate
the resulting composition. In November 1179 Philip II of France was
crowned at the traditional coronation church of Reims. At some time
soon after the young associate king hosted a great tournament between
Lagny and Torcy, on the boundary of the county of Champagne and the
royal domain, which was intended to be the largest and greatest of its
age, a reflection of the glory of the Capetian dynasty. To preserve

its memory a great poem was composed listing each of the noble participants present, with rhymed entries to commemorate each man, listed
by nation. The tournament roll of Lagny is lost, but a copy came into
the hands of William Marshal's biographer in the 1220s, and he quoted
from it liberally.[50] How did William Marshal have a copy? Perhaps he,
like the other principal participants, was presented with one as a sou-
venir of the great day and his presence there, or, if not, got hold of a
copy and had one created for himself. Young King Henry had a similar
idea, and he commissioned a clerk to record his own tournament suc-
cesses in a sort of 'tournament history' of the 1170s and early 1180s, some
or all of which came into the hands of the Marshal biographer, again
probably because the Marshal had picked up a copy, or had walked
off with the Young King's copy after his sudden death. The historian of
Hainault, Gilbert of Mons, might perhaps have used a similar sort
of document around 1200 when he went into quite a surprising amount
of detail about the tournament career of the young Count Baldwin V in
the 1160s and 1170s. It may be these sorts of documents that gave Ulrich
von Leichtenstein the idea of compiling an itinerary of his exploits as a
tourneyer in the 1220s.

It became a practice in the thirteenth century to commemorate the
greater tournaments by creating armorial rolls. The earliest extant
example survives from exactly a century after the tournament of Lagny,
recording those present at a tournament fought at Compiègne in 1279.
The tournament was again a notable one, a state occasion sponsored by
King Philip III of France in the vicinity of one of his great royal castles.
It was in part a celebration of the grand tour of his homeland by the
young Prince Charles of Salerno, heir to King Charles of Sicily, King
Philip's uncle. In part also it celebrated the simultaneous presence in
northern France of the young King Edward of England, there to nego-
tiate the return of the northern marchlands of his duchy of Aquitaine.
The Compiègne roll must have been compiled by a herald of arms as it
lists the princes and knights present by describing their coats of arms,
perhaps initially in words (the surviving later copy paints them individually).[51] We do not know whether or not it was done at the request of
a sponsor; it may have been simply too great an opportunity for recording large numbers of heraldic devices for any herald to miss. The first
surviving English roll, from a tournament at Dunstable in 1309, is a simple verbal description of the arms of each participant, organised by
retinues. These rolls, however, were not apparently made as souvenirs.

They seem to have been working documents compiled by heralds as a register of attendance and as an aide-mémoire for the arms that they had observed.[52]

3

The Site

The 'knight errant' (from the Old French 'errer', to travel) was an idea which charmed the Victorians. It was the idea of a noble young hero questing through dark forests and across trackless heaths in search of adventure, spiritual fulfilment or love. The knight errant was more than a Romantic illusion. The idea was drawn ultimately from the twelfth-century genre of the *roman d'aventure*, the story of the way a young knight would make his way in the world and find a prosperous marriage with a suitable noblewoman. The Victorians were drawn to the more spiritualised version of knight errantry which appeared with the monumental Arthurian cycles of the early thirteenth century. Childe Harold and Childe Roland and luminous pre-Raphaelite knights 'palely loitering' appealed to a Victorian public for many complicated reasons, becoming a stock literary image, to be exploited and sometimes satirised. But underneath this literary verdigris there is nonetheless some glitter of historical justification for knight errantry, and it lies in the culture of the tournament.

Twelfth-century knights and nobles did travel widely. The noble moved perpetually from one of his estates to another, and from his estates to the princely court. We know this from literary sources and royal records, but we can occasionally glimpse and track the movements of an individual nobleman. In the early summer of 1155 Waleran II, count of Meulan (1104–66), travelled with a great household between his chief castles and monasteries. He passed from the city of Rouen across the Seine to his castle of Vatteville for Easter; from there he moved to his castle of Brionne in the Risle valley, and thence downriver to his town of Pont Audemer and his abbey of Préaux for Whitsunday. After a solemn visit to the monks, he passed back upriver beyond Brionne to his southernmost castle of Beaumont-le-Roger. This for him was an itinerary of three months. We also know that, in the course of his political career, Waleran made the sea crossing between France and England at least fourteen times. His business took him at times as far north as

Scotland and as far south as Compostella in Spain. Crusade took him into Germany, down the Danube to Constantinople and thence to Syria. His luck ran out when he was shipwrecked in the Mediterranean in 1149 on the way home. He must have travelled hundreds of thousands of miles by boat and on horseback in his lifetime.[1]

Travel was a medieval compulsion for those with the resources, necessity and freedom. William fitz Stephen's pen portrait of London in the early 1170s pictures the stream of nobles, knights and foreigners that filled the streets of the capital night and day, crowding out the cookshops by the Thames. Knights might travel just for the sake of travelling, the true 'errants'. Gerald of Wales described a Breton knight who visited Britain in the 1140s at the end of a world tour, looking to see the strange customs and marvels of the island. It took a lot to keep some knights from the road. Around 1190 Prior Philip of St Frideswide in Oxford talked of a knight, Hamo de St-Ciry, taking to the road in pilgrimage to the tomb of Becket, falling ill there for a fortnight, and travelling on from Canterbury to visit some cousins in Berkshire on a social call. Hamo was at the time over ninety years of age, and had been blind and deaf for three and a half years. His pilgrimage had been to seek a cure for a paralysed left arm. Pilgrimage, business, curiosity, politics, social calls and crusade were all motives which drew men to the road. But the lure of the tournament was the most frequent reason for a nobleman and a knight to travel any distance.[2] Henry de Laon tells us that there was a name for the circuit of tournaments: the 'long tour' (*li long sejour*). As early as the 1170s, as the biography of William Marshal tells us, barely a fortnight passed without a meeting being arranged somewhere in northern France.[3]

One of the earliest mentions of tourneying reflects this roaming life. It is a document by which an English knight retained a servant as his attendant on the road to and from tournaments. In this document of the 1120s or 1130s, the Warwickshire knight Osbert of Arden reveals that he was planning to travel regularly from his home near Tamworth to tournaments at Northampton or London. He was also expecting to travel across the Channel to tournaments in (presumably) northern France.[4] For the enthusiastic English knight, it was already not enough to take the field in England; to increase his reputation and his prowess he had to visit the heartland of the tournament in Picardy, Flanders and Hainault. Osbert is not an unknown historical character; for such an early knight we know a good deal about him. He was the eldest son of

Siward of Arden (died 1139), a considerable English landowner in War-wickshire. Osbert was the grandson of Thurkill of Arden, one of the few surviving great English landowners recorded in Domesday Book, him-self the son of a royal thegn and pre-Conquest sheriff. It is very revealing of the changing nature of England in the reign of Henry I that noble-men of native lineage were competing in what English sources later called 'the French combats'. Intriguingly, we also know that Osbert was a senior member of the household of a great magnate of English descent, David I, earl of Huntingdon, son of King Malcolm III of Scotland, and himself to become king in 1124.[5] David was the brother-in-law and lead-ing courtier of King Henry I of England. He arrived at the English court as a young boy, and it is likely that it was there that he acquired the enthusiasm for the tournament. It seems logical to assume that when Osbert of Arden travelled in England and on the Continent to the tour-nament, he was travelling with his lord, King David, who was often in Normandy.

There is some evidence of travel into England from outside for the sake of sport. In 1194 King Richard refused to allow foreigners to apply for licence to tourney in England, which indicates that the king expected some French, or perhaps Scottish, knights to try to enter England to sample the new delights of an English tournament circuit. Perhaps the king did not want to give potential French agents an excuse to cross into his island realm. 'No few knights from overseas' were present at the Round Table at Walden Abbey in 1252.[6] Mostly, however, it was the Eng-lish aristocracy which continued to travel abroad to tourney, but it was not just the English. In 1166 the young King William of Scotland led his numerous retinue on to a tournament field on the borders of Brittany, where his sister was duchess. Four Scottish bannerets took the field at Compiègne in 1279 and the arms of King Alexander III (although not himself present) were displayed at the lists on that occasion along with those of France, England, the Empire, Navarre, Castille and Aragon.[7] Scotland was rated as a tourneying nation, as we see in Philip de Remy's romance of the *Manekine* (c. 1241), where the king of Scotland was depicted as one of the leading tourneyers of his age.

Travel to France for the tournament was apparently long regarded as an important part of the education of every young English nobleman. There was no better way of getting yourself seen and noticed than rais-ing your banner in some corner of a foreign field. This was such a fact of noble life that it was echoed in literature. The English romance *Gui de Warewic* (*c.* 1200–4) opens with its ambitious, young Oxfordshire hero falling in love, and then heading for France to make his name on the tournament circuit.[8] It did not occur to the author that this might have been done at home, although England was at least for him a good place for killing dragons. Entering the lists asserted a young knight's place in a noble society that remained international, even after the loss of most of the English king's continental lands. Earl Richard de Clare of Gloucester and Hertford (died 1262) is a well-documented historical case. Born in 1222, he was active in tournaments in England in the 1240s, and probably in France as early as 1250. There is reason to believe he was the patron of the round table tournament held in the fields next to Walden abbey in Essex in 1252. The annals of the Clare abbey of Tewkesbury record all the great family events and include mention of their foreign tours. The earl's younger brother William, knighted at Christmas 1250, found the lure of the French circuit irresistible and undertook a tourneying tour of France in the summer of 1252, which turned into a nightmare when he lost everything and was publicly humiliated. Earl Richard made a special trip abroad later in the year to reassert the family honour. He distinguished himself by reclaiming everything that his brother had lost and, according to the chronicler, triumphed in every field he entered. Earl Richard enjoyed himself so much that he crossed the sea with an expensive retinue again after Christmas, in company with the king's half-brother William de Valence, to pursue his celebrity further. Unfortunately his luck did not last, and in a tournament in Poitou the French knights took his retinue apart, captured and ransomed him, and left the earl so bruised and battered as to need hydrotherapy.[9] Nothing daunted, his son, Earl Gilbert, crossed to France in his turn, and was to be found amongst the English tourneying at Compiègne in 1279, at the age of twenty-five.

From the earliest mentions of tourneying, it was the travel to and from tournaments which caused the most trouble to the rest of the population. In September 1139, the great ecclesiastical dignitaries of Hainault were gathering for the consecration of the new Premonstratensian abbey church of Vicoigne, near Valenciennes. They arrived hot and flustered having been mocked, and possibly threatened, by groups of knights from Artois and the Laonnais, who were gathering for a tournament nearby, presumably with the local Hennuyers. The offended clergy were grimly delighted to hear the next day, that the tournament organiser ('the chief of the rioters') had been accidentally killed in the mêlée.[10]

Knights on the road were at best raucous, excited and oppressively jovial; at worst they were bullying, high-handed, thieving and violent. Whether in a good or bad mood, they were a trial to the spirits of those they met, especially clerics who had a high idea of their own authority. Cardinal James de Vitry told a story to illustrate quite how independent a tourneying knight might be on the road. A knight had taken a ransom from a poor colleague on the security of his own word and 'in the name of the Lord'. Riding out to meet the poor knight for payment of the ransom on the appointed day, the knight was kicking his heels at the meeting place because the man was late, and saw a well-mounted monk approaching. As he trotted up, the knight grabbed the monk's bridle and demanded to know who was his lord. The alarmed monk replied that he had no lord other than God. 'Right,' said the knight, 'your lord, to whose household you belong and whose servant you say you are, is my pledge, so I am taking satisfaction from him'. He pushed the monk off the horse, forgave the poor knight his ransom, and rode off with it.[11]

That this was not much of an exaggeration is illustrated by a curious story of the English knight, William Marshal. Early in 1183, he was travelling with a small group of friends south towards Maine from Flanders. He stopped for a nap on a grassy verge by the roadside, with his squire sitting beside him minding his horse and arms. He was woken by a man and woman riding past, the woman complaining of the fatigue. Getting up, Marshal pursued and interrogated the pair under armed threat. He discovered that the man was a runaway clerk and the woman was the clerk's lover on the run from her family. Marshal took it upon himself to offer to arrange a reconciliation between the woman and her family, which he apparently knew, but when she was obstinate, he let the offer drop. What is most bizarre about the story is that he took drastic action not then but when he discovered that the clerk had £48 on which the two were proposing to live by usury. Shocked, as he maintained, Marshal took the money and left the pair penniless. The money he took he used to pay for meal and lodgings for his friends, dividing it up with them. His friends wondered at his leniency in leaving the runaways their horses and baggage, and one of them proposed to pursue the pair and take even those.[12]

By the end of the twelfth century, knights had an acknowledged rank which gave them privileges: for instance a French writer of the 1180s tells us that 'in virtue of the privilege of his higher rank' a knight did not need to ask permission before sitting next to a common woman. In the thirteenth century, if a man of lower status struck a knight, he could lose his hand at the wrist.[13] With the authority of their swords, and riding above the common herd, twelfth-century knights on the road might administer an entirely personal justice on those they met. They did so with impunity. Dukes and counts had long had the right to deal out justice to all who were within their 'peace', that is, all who they met and who were in their household and in the precincts of their houses and lodgings. Lesser barons too might claim the same right, and the knights that rode in their households and associated with magnates would see every reason to claim the right to intervene in other's affairs, as they shared the culture and privileges of the higher nobility. This happened even in England, a land where the idea of justice as a royal prerogative was stronger than anywhere else in medieval Europe. In August 1209, for instance, we hear of four Essex knights who heard that a lady had been robbed and turned out to track the gang that did it. They followed them by the impressions of their horseshoes first to the place where the gang had separated, then up to the doors of the houses where they were sheltering. The suspects were questioned, and an attempt made to hold the horses while the sheriff's officer was sent for, but the suspects slipped away.[14]

The way that knights on the road would assert themselves is plain enough from the tournament regulations promulgated by King Richard the Lionheart in August 1194 to enforce his peace on tourneyers. There we read the following:

> From the moment he leaves his home on the way to get to the tournament, no knight, earl, baron or any other tourneyer may take unlawfully without permission any food or supplies from anyone else: he ought to buy everything he needs in the market place. He should not confiscate anything from anyone on the road on his own behalf or on behalf of any of his men. He ought not to permit anyone within his power to be harassed unjustly either by himself or his men. If he should come across a criminal and can put his offence to rights by himself or by his men, he may do so. If he is unable to do so, he should explain it to the barons who have sworn to maintain the king's peace in the tournaments, and it should be settled by their judgement. The earls and barons of England, and all who want to go to tournaments, must swear that they are within the jurisdiction of the king and his chief justiciar, and will maintain the king's peace with all their ability, untroubled and whole, going to and from tournaments, particularly in the king's forests and markets.[15]

The regulations were drawn up for just such people as William Marshal.

They recognise that English earls, barons and knights on the road might feel called upon to intervene forcefully in situations that offended their sense of justice, and that they would do it with complete autonomy, whatever the king might think. They also recognise that the tourneying aristocrats might themselves be a source of trouble: that they and their servants might requisition food and goods, and not pay for them; and that they might trespass in the king's forest with their dogs and huntsmen without asking permission first.

The futility of King Richard's attempts to enforce a peace on his roads is indicated by the evidence of Joscelin of Brakelond, a monk of Bury St Edmunds, as to how knights and barons behaved subsequently. One of the first English tournaments to be held in 1194 was convened not at the permitted sites but at an unlicensed venue between Thetford and Bury St Edmunds, probably on the Norfolk-Suffolk border. The use of Thetford indicates that the promoter was the king's uncle, Hamelin, earl of Warenne, who had great possessions in the town and who had been one of the three earls who had petitioned the king to permit tourneying in England and who was supposed to be monitoring the peace. Abbot Baldwin of Bury, who had private rights of justice over the hundreds south of Thetford, attempted to forbid the tournament, but was completely ignored. To annoy him further another unlicensed tournament was advertised, probably in July 1195, and eighty young magnates and knights appeared at the abbey of Bury looking for lodging before the event. The enraged abbot attempted to arrest them as they stayed in his guesthouse. Deeply amused, the affable young men behaved reasonably well until Abbot Baldwin retired after lunch, but then they sent out for wine and held a loud all-day party, singing and dancing and disturbing the monastic siesta, before forcibly breaking out of the abbey and town. Baldwin, not amused, excommunicated them all.[16]

Not all tournament parties were quite so raffish and troublesome. At a certain social level the tournament became something of a state occasion. Prince Charles of Salerno, son of King Charles I of Sicily, made a visit to his native land of France in 1279, meeting his cousin, King Philip III, at Paris, and accompanying him to Amiens where they greeted another cousin, King Edward I of England. Charles was provided with a great retinue of scores of knights from Poitou and Anjou (his father's French domain). Two great tournaments were staged in his honour at Senlis and Compiègne, at which over thirty dukes and counts, and thousands of knights were present. There were banquets and receptions, and besides that solemn treaties were concluded and a high religious festival held, with the translation of the relics of St Firmin at Amiens.[17] We get a similar, if more coloured, picture from literary sources. Philip de Remy's king of Scotland landed on the coast of Flanders and then made a sort of state progress south into Picardy. Coming to the city of Bruges with his household he sent ahead his chamberlains to take lodgings and made enquiry as to where the count of Flanders was. He travelled eastward to meet the count at Ghent and there he enjoyed a civic reception. The count told him that he was on the way to a tournament at Ressons-Gournay, and the king decided to accompany him. So, with sumptuous households and hundreds of knights, the cavalcade travelled south through crowds of onlookers and came to Lille, another of the count's towns, where the king again enjoyed his hospitality. Their itinerary took them on into France, to the east of Artois and into Vermandois. We are told they took the road through Roye, east of Montdidier, and so they came to Ressons by easy stages along France's equivalent of the Great North Road, the modern route N17, that runs from Paris to the Low Countries.[18] Princes and magnates on tour could expect that sort of treatment, and find the civic fathers lining up to welcome them at the gates of the towns and cities they passed, jostling each other to hold the princely stirrups as they dismounted.

The Travelling Retinue

When magnates took to the roads, they did so in great and deliberate style. Since they lived an itinerant life, they took their servants, furnishings and plate with them. When Earl Richard of Cornwall crossed to France in 1250 to visit his cousin, Queen Blanche, he travelled with his wife and son as a prince should. He was escorted by a company of forty knights uniformly dressed in new and handsome robes, splendidly mounted, their harness glittering with gold. He was accompanied by a train of fifty pack horses, many great wagons and innumerable servants 'so that he might offer to the admiring French onlookers a sight as marvellous to them as it was honourable to him'.[19] Literary sketches offer us some further detail about these great cavalcades. Around 1180 Thomas of Kent, for instance, pictured a queen's household on the road: a column of mules and pack horses passed by first with their attendants, then the footmen, marshals, quartermasters and ushers who managed the column and found it lodging and stabling. Following these came the valets, the noble youths and the squires of the household, with the queen herself at the rear of the column, presumably with her guard of knights.[20] It was a commonplace social observation of the time that magnates rode around with far too many servants, just to emphasise their own importance. The magnates would have put it differently, that they were supporting their honour by riding out with an appropriate retinue.

These deliberately spectacular mobile households were expected of princes, counts and great barons. But knights on the way to tournaments rarely travelled alone, even if they were not in the company of other knights. We have arleady come across the early contract drawn up in the 1120s or 1130s for the Warwickshire knight, Osbert of Arden which mentioned his travel to tournaments in England and abroad. The other party to it was another Englishman, Thurkill Fundu. Osbert gave Thurkill a small estate within his great manor of Kingsbury, near Tamworth, sufficient for one plough, and in return Thurkill undertook to accompany him, carrying his lances, when Osbert rode home from tournaments at London or Northampton (presumably, Thurkill would have accompanied him there without a summons). Thurkill was also bound to accompany Osbert when he crossed the Channel to tourney in France. Osbert undertook to provide him with horses and meet his costs.[21] Thurkill thus became what a contemporary Frenchman would have called vaguely an *escuier* or *serjant*, a riding servant with a responsibility for keeping Osbert's arms. Whether Osbert would have called him that, or used some comparable English word, we do not know. But Thurkill would not have been what we would call today with too much precision, Osbert's 'squire'.

It was not until the middle of the thirteenth century that the word 'squire' (*escuier* or *vaslet*) became a social rank in France, acquiring the exclusive meaning of a noble youth in training for knighthood, or of a member of a knightly family who had not taken up knighthood. In the twelfth century all sorts of boys and men might be called squires. Squires might be no more than body servants, armed guards or riding attendants, working for their upkeep or for a small pittance, following after their lords.[22] Thurkill Fundu was one of the more prosperous sort of squire by this reckoning. But slowly the squire's status increased, as the status of the knight, his master, also rose in the twelfth century. William Marshal's biographer recalls that the squires of the 1170s did not expect too much from their masters, whereas by the 1220s squires insisted on not just a mount from their master, but also a pack horse too.[23] By 1200 squires had acquired a recognisable costume: short coats provided by their masters and a distinctive cropped haircut. When they fought or attended the tournament, squires were armed with quilted leather coats (*doublentines*), short swords (*coutels*), clubs and iron caps (*capeliers*), the same equipment permitted them by the English Statute of Arms in 1292.[24]

In the 1130s it was already the case that any travelling knight needed the minimum of one squire in attendance to support his dignity and manage his pack horse and armour. William Marshal on the road in 1183 was riding with a single squire, Eustace de Bertrimont, who minded his horse and arms while Marshal took an afternoon nap on the grass by the roadside. Earls and barons rode about with much larger retinues. The earl of Warwick in the 1170s rode with a crowd of body-squires, whose demands worried the earl's town of Swansea in south Wales.[25] In the same decade Bishop Stephen de Fougères felt obliged to warn aristocrats about travelling around with too large a retinue of servants, in fear of embarrassing their hosts.[26] The warnings, apparently, were not heeded. In 1226 Ulrich von Liechtenstein, one of the greater magnates of Styria, embarked on his great jousting tour from Venetia north to Bohemia escorted by a marshal and steward; three pack horses and three war horses, each with a groom; twelve mounted squires with his lances and arms; and a party of musicians, with trumpets, viols and flutes.[27] The consequence of squires increased as they began to claim noble status. By the mid thirteenth century, Henry de Laon saw the demands of squires for fees and equipment as ruinous. They were better horsed and armed than the knights who were their lords. Things had got to the state in France that they were riding on to the field with their lords as bodyguards, just as barons had ridden with knights as bodyguards. Squires were themselves taking horses as ransoms from other tourneyers they had overcome.[28] But Jacques Bretel in 1285 was inclined to rejoice in the large number of squires attending their lords in the grand French tournaments: six or seven surrounding their masters as they rode together on to the field, each carrying an item of his armour and weaponry.[29]

At the end of the thirteenth century it was also the case in England that knights were supporting ever larger retinues of mounted servants and footmen. By 1292 King Edward I of England had come to believe that the trend was a danger to public order. Knights were limited to taking three squires on the road to tournaments with them, and squires were forbidden maces or sharpened weapons. The statute assumed that crowds of armed squires, heralds, footmen and servants were a major nuisance and liable to cause trouble on the road and in the lodging houses. The limit stuck and in 1303 Aymer de Valence assumed as a matter of course that the knights he retained for his tournament retinue would bring only two or three squires along with them, whom he would also feed and lodge.[30]

The squires or valets of the late thirteenth century were retained in much the same way as Thurkill Fundu had been 160 years before. An indenture survives from 1297 when the distinguished Marcher knight, John Bloet of Langstone in Monmouthshire, took on a certain William Martel as his 'vallet'. Just as with Thurkill Fundu, the agreement was for life, and the liability for costs incurred by the squire was a major concern. There were differences. Whereas Thurkill was given a landed estate for his support by Osbert of Arden, Sir John offered William sixty shillings a year as a fee and robes for him twice a year, his food and drink 'proper for a gentleman', and he also offered to support William's own two servants. William was to attend Sir John on campaign and at the tournaments he entered, and he was to be provided with a suitable horse and arms.[31]

The Sites

Every sport needs space. Tournaments demanded the same sort of space as professional golf does nowadays. The bigger the tournament, the bigger the space that was needed. When thousands of men and horses were involved in a mêlée without many rules, manoeuvring in lines and squadrons, the tournament site had to be as big as a battlefield. The biggest sites were undoubtedly those in northern France, which attracted knights in great numbers from all over north-western Europe. As Sarrazin, the thirteenth-century author of the *Roman de Ham*, said, 'the whole world is accustomed to come to tourney in France'.[32] The northern French sites were sanctioned by long use and tradition. Patrons and knights could not just turn up anywhere and hold tournaments, they had to select where to hold them from one of over a score recognised fields. We do not know fully how these great French sites got to be regular venues, although we have already looked at some theories. One thing we do know is that they none of them were selected by the French king, because they were all outside his personal domain in

the Île de France. The sites also show a certain caution in the face of
the power of dukes and counts. The greatest of them were right on the
boundaries of duchies and counties, which may indicate that the tourneyers who first used them were seeking to hold their sport in a place
no prince could claim effectively to control.[33] It may also be, as was suggested in the first chapter, that the early tournaments were forced out
to the border areas because of the strictures of Peace legislation within
the various counties on the march of the Empire.

England was of course very different. Tournaments there, as in Germany before 1154, did not meet on sites set on political boundaries, but
next to towns. This would seem to indicate something of a relaxed attitude to tournaments in their early days in both England and the Empire.
But then tournaments outside the northern French heartland were not
the large and intimidating events that occurred in Flanders, Vermandois, Hainault or Brabant, and perhaps they did not at first cause the
same amount of disquiet. In England also the king had enough authority around 1155 to completely ban tournaments within his realm, and
during the reign of Henry II (1154–89) no known tournament occurred
in England, other than one promoted by Count John of Mortain, the
king's son, that met in the county of Cheshire in 1185, where the king's
writ did not run.[34] England's centralised government had sufficient
ambition in the later twelfth century to attempt to fix where tournaments might be allowed to meet, and also to make it necessary for
would-be promoters to buy a licence.

The custom in northern France was to define a tournament field as
lying between two settlements, at least one of which was usually a
medium-sized town. The reason for this, as later accounts make clear,
was that the two sides would gather and lodge in whichever town had
been designated as theirs, and use it as a base. When we look at the map,
there is often quite a distance between the two settlements. A famous
site, in use from at least the 1160s to the 1240s, was the great field
between the count of Flanders' town and castle of Ressons-sur-Matz and
the neighbouring town and castle of Gournay-sur-Aronde (Oise), which
belonged to the count of Clermont. The tournament field is actually a
long and gentle whale-back ridge in Picardy, some fifteen kilometres
north west of Compiègne. Ressons lies at the north-eastern end of the
ridge seven kilometres from Gournay. Both places were substantial
towns, offering markets, over a hundred houses for lodging knights, and
handsome stone castles to welcome the great princes who attended.[35]

Ressons-Gournay was easy of access in the middle ages; it was crossed by two major Roman roads and was on the main route from Paris to Flanders. It is even more accessible nowadays, since the six-lane Autoroute du Nord cuts right through the ridge on its way to Paris. Ressons-Gournay gave the tourneyers plenty of space to manoeuvre; it was good cavalry country, clear of obstruction and with no broken ground. If the whole ridge was used by the tourneyers, they had as much as 800 hectares (1976 acres) of open land to play with. In the great days of the tournament, the knights did not confine themselves to roped off enclosures. They roamed the landscape like armies at war.[36]

Other large northern French sites offered different sorts of terrain, and the challenge of differing terrains may have been part of the attraction to serious medieval tourneyers, much as it is to serious modern golfers. A major site in the later twelfth century was the southern bank of the River Marne, between Lagny-sur-Marne and Torcy, east of Paris, on the border of the county of Champagne. The site here included the flat-topped river bluffs west of Lagny above the valley, where a major Roman route to Paris reached the river crossing at Lagny. The Lagny-Torcy site has remained popular as a place for mass entertainment: part of it is now occupied by Disneyland Paris. Other sites were not on the edges of valleys, but right down inside valley bottoms. On the border of Normandy, the spacious flats of the southern bank of the River Eure between Anet and Sorel-Moussel hosted at least two tournaments in the late 1170s. South west of the town of Anet there was as much as 600 hectares (1482 acres) of river meadow and fields for knights to ride over. In the case of Anet-Sorel we know that the tourneyers took possession of the whole site for their sport: lanes, fields, hedges, barns, earthworks and woodland. Some knights even took their tourneying into the streets of the town of Anet itself, which they should not have done. The most eccentric site of all was that regular tournament ground between the Bretons and Normans, which John of Marmoutier said (c. 1170) was on the broad tidal sands under the towering islet of Mont-St-Michel, on the border of the two duchies.[37] In northern France, tournament grounds were usually a long way from the really big towns; no tournament is known to have been held near great cities like Rouen or Reims, and certainly not near Paris, but, as we will see, this was not the case outside northern France.

The practice in England, Germany and in other parts of France than the north was to locate tournaments next to large towns and cities and not to designate them as between two settlements. Where the site was close to a large urban centre it tended to be defined as on a 'plain' or 'fields', which implies that these suburban sites were deliberately constricted and limited. The tournament held at Toulouse between 1181 and 1185 was held outside the walls, on the count's extensive river meadows to the north west of the city. The fact that the count had called the tournament seems to have left him feeling obliged to site it on a restricted piece of land where only his interests could be damaged.[38] In England the same happened. The Chester tournament of 1185 occurred on a 'plain' outside the city walls, just like at Toulouse. In England before 1154 tournaments were known to have been held outside Worcester, Northampton, York and London.[39] In Germany the earliest tournaments we hear about in the 1170s and 1180s were also held next to largish towns, like Neuss, Ingelheim and Worms. The difference in tournament sites between northern France and the rest of these places can probably be accounted for by differing histories. France's great northern cities did not get the chance to exploit, or be offended by, the aristocracy's military games. England had external borders, of course, and indeed in 1242 the Anglo-Scottish frontier was the location for several tournaments between the English and Scottish aristocracies.[40] Within the realm, however, there was nothing resembling the French network of princely jurisdictions, with the debatable lands that were a consequence of them. Elsewhere, the later importation of the tournament into the Rhineland and the Midi happened at a time long after the need to use border sites to escape the men sworn to maintain the Peace.

In England tournaments were an imported pastime, and so they naturally gravitated to big towns where there were plenty of people and facilities. Locating them by the bigger urban centres made obvious sense. Towns offered plenty of accommodation and provisions, and the sorts of services that knights needed: armourers, saddlers, farriers and blacksmiths.[41] This closeness to towns also gave the English king a way to control them. When the government of Henry III of England wanted to discourage the tournament in 1220 it tried to intimidate the urban providers of facilities and supplies. It threatened with papal excommunication not just the tourneyers but those who gave them lodging, those who came to cheer them on and those who supplied them with goods and foodstuffs. In 1233 the king ordered the mayor and bailiffs of Northampton to close their gates against would-be tourneyers to prevent them from securing lodging and food. The citizens of Blyth were presented with a similar demand in 1241. In 1244 the sheriff of York was ordered to make a list of the names of those citizens who offered their inns for the accommodation of participants in a prohibited tournament, so that action might be taken against them.[42] The English measures were noticed abroad. When King Philip IV of France began to step up his measures against tournaments in 1304 he did not just threaten participants with arrest, he also threatened those who hired lodgings to them, and the merchants who travelled to the sites and sold them food, horses, fodder, armour and saddlery.[43] The English and French evidence of prohibitions allows us a glimpse of just how economically attractive and important the tournament could be to urban communities, important enough to tempt them defy royal mandates.

English tournament sites also seem to have been different in nature as well as location from those of France. The best identifiable example is the tournament site near York, as identified in the thirteenth century. This was Langwith Common, a stretch of woodland and heath three kilometres (1.86 miles) to the south east of the city liberties; now partly within the precincts of the modern university of York. As a tournament site it was comparatively large, containing (according to an inquest of 1270) four hundred acres of oak woods and a hundred acres of open ground with a tendency to flood; but it was still a lot smaller than the big sites of northern France and it was not on any significant boundary. Its significance was its closeness to York. Langwith is eloquent testimony to the difference in scale between the English and French events: less knights involved meant that smaller grounds were required. Langwith lacked the polar settlements to demarcate the site; they were unnecessary because of its relatively small size. The tourneyers needed no lodging on the field, they could have ridden out in the morning for their sport directly from the city. The nature of the site also meant that it did not involve manoeuvering across arable land and upsetting landowners. Langwith included no houses and the site was woodland in the keeping of royal foresters.[44]

Between 1154 and 1194 the tournament was banned in England, for whatever reason. In August 1194 King Richard allowed tournaments to be held once more. When he did he listed where the permitted sites were to be. Northampton, London and York are all absent from the list. Five sites were licensed: Salisbury-Wilton, Warwick-Kenilworth, Brackley-Mixborough, Stamford-Wansford and Blyth-Tickhill. There was a deliberate attempt to reproduce the French way of holding tournaments, for they offered polar settlements as team bases, with one pole being of moderate to large size in population. There is also some comparability in the selection of these sites with the French practice of tourneying on borders. Blyth and Tickhill lie on the very southern edge of Yorkshire, Brackley and Mixborough straddle the Northamptonshire and Oxfordshire border, and Stamford and Wansford are on either side of the Lincolnshire-Northamptonshire boundary.[45] Three sizable towns are mentioned amongst the designated sites in 1194: Stamford, Salisbury and Warwick. Stamford became a very popular location in the following decades, but no event is known to have occurred at Salisbury and the first mention of Warwick being used comes in 1245. It is perhaps likely that Stamford was willing to host the events as being a major market site on the Great North Road, but Salisbury and Warwick would seem to have resisted the dubious distinction offered them. Of the five, it was the sites at Brackley, Blyth and Stamford which had lasting popularity. It is a suggestion worth considering that they may perhaps have been traditional English tourneying fields revived in 1194, being popular because the local people were willing to put up with the periodic nuisance they caused. This would account for why, in default of meetings at Salisbury and Warwick, Northampton had resumed its traditional place as a premier tournament site by at least 1218.[46] But Bury St Edmunds and Cambridge soon joined the group of regular venues; the demand for the tournament may simply have outstripped the facilities King Richard had offered.

There were further sites used in England after 1194. In the early thirteenth century two further tournament fields were found in or on the edge of the Thames basin, near Staines and Dunstable.[47] They were probably selected as being near enough to London to attract tradesmen and supporters, but not too close as to annoy the city authorities. The site near Staines was the famous Hounslow Heath, the haunt of highwaymen in the eighteenth century. Like Langwith it was an area of coppices and clearings, away from more productive arable land. Langwith and Hounslow together are some evidence as to what some locals thought about the tournament in England. It may be that they resented dislocation and damage, and tourneyers in England had been forced to listen to their objections and those of the royal government, and find places to fight where they could not annoy agriculturists. In France, the tourneyers may have been less considerate about local opinion, secure in the protection of tradition and of the great princes who were themselves devotees of the sport. French critics like Cardinal James de Vitry and Huon de Méry demonstrate that tourneyers had a bad reputation. James and Huon were very fierce about the indifference of tourneyers to the damage they did to fields and vineyards. Huon was sarcastic about the way some participants pitched camp around the designated bases and cut down hedges and brushwood to make level areas for their tents, without so much as a by-your-leave from the locals. James talked of heedless knights trampling down vineyards as they pushed their way through the vines, looking for opponents. Tourneyers cursed the peasants who were unfortunate enough to get in their way.[48]

Things may not have been quite so grim in France as the critics of the tournament claimed. The long periods over which these sites were used tells us something different. The local landowners and their workers may not have been uniformly resentful, any more than nineteenth-century farmers necessarily resented the meetings of the local hunt. The tournament was part of their life and tradition, and there were ways it helped the local economy. Besides, to be at close quarters with dukes, counts, barons and noble knights added some colour and glamour to life. The locals may even have enjoyed watching the spectacle. There is only one known example of a local landowner objecting to a tournament, which was when Baldwin V of Hainault planned a tournament between Montbard and Rougemont in Burgundy in 1172. The tournament had been announced without the consent of the count of Nevers, whose personal estate of Rougemont was one of the poles of the site. The count of Nevers may have resented it for economic reasons, or because the foreign count of Hainault – a prince of the Empire – had presumed to make free with his territory. But it still went ahead despite his objections.[49]

Spectators

Knowing something about the sort of sites that were used allows us to speculate about whether the tournament was a spectator sport. The balance of evidence indicates that tournaments did indeed draw large crowds of onlookers of all sorts and conditions. English accounts that have survived talk of 'supporters' (*fautores*) gathering at the sites, and other accounts talk of 'hangers-on' (*lecheors*) and 'armchair warriors' (*parleors d'armes*) lounging around the site and gawping at the action.[50] These might have been fellow knights and squires, but people of lower social origins certainly flocked to the fields, people the Marshal biography calls the 'riff-raff', or 'the trash' (*la rascaille*).[51] A literary description of a mid thirteenth-century jousting field tells us that organisers expected all sorts of conditions of people to flock to the event. Stands were set up around the field for the knights, squires and their ladies, but the field lay in a deep valley and the 'common folk' (*communes gens*) were expected to watch from the hillsides.[52]

Onlookers were certainly noisy. Apart from the heralds, who made their living by shouting out the names and warcries of particular champions, we have descriptions of girls and ladies singing the latest songs in the stands; lounging lads shouting comments; and serving men and idlers urging men and horses on. This must have been the reason why signals and commencements had to be accompanied by flourish of trumpets and beat of drum.[53] The *Lancelot* cycle tells us of shouts going up when the crowd witnessed acts of physical strength or great skill. When a man went down in a welter of blood at Pomeglai, the crowd shrieked in horror: 'He's dead! He's dead!'.[54] Heralds acted as commentators to the crowd, they drew attention to the achievements of their patrons, or any act of valour that passed before their eyes.

From the earliest times when the sources allow us to see what was going on at tournaments, women were in the crowds. They gathered to watch the action at the tournament of Joigny in 1179. The countess of Joigny led a large group of married women and girls on to the field to view the opening matches, one of whom suggested that they and the knights dance while they were waiting for the other team to arrive. The author very much approved of the presence of women and believed that their support had been a factor in the Marshal's team's victory, commenting on the knights' part: 'They were convinced that they had become better men as a result of the ladies' arrival'.[55] This is an important social aspect of the tournament, and will be treated at length later in the book.

4

The Gathering and the Vespers

The classic tournament was usually a one-day event, and for good reason. As that seasoned French warrior and tourneyer, Sir Jean de Joinville, tells us, the gashes and breakages and bruises sustained in combat did not disappear overnight. Following a day's action in 1250 he was unable to bear the weight of his chain-mail hauberk or carry his shield the next day. The poet Jakemes explained the traditional two-week period of notice between tournaments as a necessary period for the knights to get over the injuries and exhaustion of a single day's fighting.[1] Two-day events were sometimes advertised. The only surviving twelfth-century tournament summons, composed by Bertran de Born in the early 1180s, was for a grand tournament to be held at Toulouse, and he notified those going that they would need to plan to be there for a stay of three nights.[2] In England there was a two-day event at Blyth in England in February 1232, Another, at Cambridge in September 1234, would, like the one at Toulouse, have involved a three-night stay.[3] But since the grand charge of the tournament (the 'estor') was not something that could physically happen twice in two days (outside romances and poetry), a tournament advertised as being over two days could best be explained as the organisers' desire to make time for extensive jousting on the first day before ending in style with the grand charge on the second. Literary tournaments could last several days, such as the one between Wallingford and Oxford described in Chrétien de Troyes's romance of *Cligés* and the tournament of 'Pomerglai' in the Lancelot cycle, but these extended events were simply a way of highlighting the great prowess of Arthurian knights. In reality, no twelfth or early thirteenth-century knight could have replicated that achievement.

During the thirteenth century the tournament did begin to spread out over several days. In part this was probably due to the Arthurian romances. After 1200 we begin to find knights enjoying 'round tables'. These were not mêlée tournaments at all but staged individual jousts, and they spread over several days. Jousting had long had its particular attractions for knights, and those attractions might be stronger than those of the tournament. Ulrich von Liechtenstein describes an Austrian tournament advertised to be held in Friesach in 1224 which was nearly abandoned because the knights present got caught up in the amusements of the preliminary jousting, which eventually spread over ten days.[4] The round table held in 1252 near Walden Abbey in Essex ran from Monday 16 September to Wednesday 18 September, and might have gone on a further day, had not an accidental death brought it to an end.[5] The attraction of multiple days of jousting seems to have had an effect on the classic tournament, which often, as at Friesach, became the concluding climax of several days' entertainment. So the tournament of Chauvency-Montmédy presented in great detail by Jacques Bretel in 1280 lasted four days, but when he goes into detail it is clear that the 'estor' (the grand tournament charge) was on just one of them. At Chauvency, Monday and Tuesday were set aside for jousting, the jousts were then followed by a day of rest and the full tournament happened as the grand finale on the last day, Thursday.[6] For all this, the invariable assumption in earlier sources, such as the *History of William Marshal*, is that tournaments lasted a day, even the festive coronation tournament at Lagny in 1179.

There is good evidence that, throughout the period dealt with by this book, a favoured day of the week on which to hold a tournament in England, the Netherlands and France was a Monday. In Germany in the thirteenth century 'fighting on a Monday' was a synonym for being to a tournament.[7] There are in fact a number of twelfth-century tournaments which can be dated to a particular Monday. For instance, a tournament was held in the Empire at Trazegnies on Monday 13 July 1170, according to Lambert de Wattrelos.[8] The Marshal biography mentions a tournament held at Maintenon whose preliminaries were held on Sunday 27 May 1179; the main tournament must therefore have followed on the Monday 28 May.[9] Monday tournaments meant Sunday travel for many tourneyers. This was frowned on for clergy in the late twelfth century and not necessarily thought proper for the noble laity.[10] The meeting at Le Fère in the Laonnais described by Jakemes was to be on a Monday, and it is perhaps significant that many of the competitors and their wives were already at the team bases by Saturday afternoon, although people were still arriving the next day.[11] Those who did travel on the Sunday may have enjoyed a certain frisson of subversiveness as a result. In the biggest sample of dated tournaments that we have – the fifty-seven listed as forbidden by the king and his ministers in England between 1216 and 1250 – twenty-five had been arranged for a Monday. In noble tournaments held in the Low Countries in the first half of the fourteenth century, Monday and Tuesday were still the days chosen for half of the recorded tournaments.[12]

The reason for the preference for Monday for tourneying is something of a mystery. A possible explanation is historical. Great royal or princely courts were held in the eleventh century to coincide with the greater religious feasts. William the Conqueror, for instance, made it a practice to wear his crown during the Christmas, Easter and Pentecost feasts, and Easter and Pentecost were always Sundays. The lavish festivities of a great court in England went on for several days after the religious celebration that began it: in the reign of the Conqueror's son, Henry I (1100–35), they lasted for a week after Christmas, and four days after both Easter and Pentecost.[13] It is certain that tournaments and military games were part of the extended festivities. The horseback exercise called the 'quintain' is well attested as happening at courtly festivals. When around 1136 Geoffrey of Monmouth described King Arthur's Pentecost court at Caerleon, he modelled it on the contemporary English royal courts, and he depicted 'horseback games ... in the manner of a battle' held in the fields outside the city following the religious feast, although he does not say that they happened on the Monday.[14] In Germany a tournament was associated with the knighting of the future emperor, Henry VI, at the close of the imperial Pentecost court of 1184 at Ingelheim on the Rhine, the day after the octave of the feast, the close of the religious celebration, that is, Monday 13 June.[15] If eleventh-century kings and princes got in the habit of sponsoring tournaments to follow on from solemn Sunday celebrations and so lighten the mood of the court, this would explain why aristocratic society adopted Monday or Tuesday as customary days on which to hold them.

In England between 1216 and 1250 Monday and Tuesday together accounted for five out of every seven of the total number of tournaments listed in the government records. But, despite the obvious preference for the beginning of the week, two in seven tournaments in the same sample were arranged for other days of the week, with the exception of Fridays and Sundays. In France, the tournament at Ressons-Gournay in 1183 was on 15 January, a Saturday, so Monday was not the invariable choice in the twelfth century on the Continent either.[16] The exclusion of Sunday would be because even the most enthusiastic knight would not compromise the Sabbath day peace. Friday was reckoned as a day on which the Passion was to be recalled in fasting, which also gave it a particular solemnity.[17] The exclusion of tournaments from Sundays and Fridays would explain why the four-day tournament described by Jacques Bretel at Chauvency happened between Monday and Thursday.

Lodgings

The prelude to the big day occupied an important place in the social life of the knights and magnates present. This accounts for why tournaments were sometimes called 'meetings' or 'gatherings' (*assemblees*), a word that refers to the social rather than the sporting side of things.[18] The first business on arrival at the field was to secure lodgings at whichever of the pole settlements was the advertised team base. Which base was to be used by which side was known to knights in advance, apparently, as Gilbert of Mons's account of the 1168 tournament at Ressons-Gournay makes clear. Gilbert also says that, at a riverside tournament between the city of Soissons and Braine-sur-Vesle in August 1175, it was arranged in advance that the men of Hainault and their allies were supposed to occupy Soissons, while the opposing Champenois and French were to take up quarters upriver in Braine. Huon d'Oisy says that tournaments held at Lagny-sur-Marne accommodated one of the sides at Torcy, several kilometres downriver.[19]

In his imaginary account in the late 1220s of a tournament between the real venues of Montargis and Château-Landon in the Gâtinais (the region south east of Paris) Gerbert de Montreuil described the frantic activity of squires and servants to secure lodgings for their masters in a particularly crowded tournament venue, with the losers obliged to take up quarters in the fields around the town.[20] Huon de Méry satirises the whole process. His narrator accompanies the Antichrist's chamberlain as he engages lodging for his master in the city of Despair with a usurer of the place who is obliged to house and provision him for his sins. The squires who had preceded the Antichrist's knights were not so lucky; many were so desperate to secure accommodation for their masters that they fought for lodging places in the streets.[21] This was by no means all satire and fiction. In June 1138 the fall from power in England of Bishop Roger of Salisbury was triggered by a fight between his men and those of Count Alan of Brittany over disputed lodgings in Oxford. The royal court was in the crowded town and the count's men had attempted to eject the bishop's men while they were dining; in the resulting street battle many were wounded and one knight killed.[22] At the Christmas court held by Henry III of England at York in 1252, the city was packed to bursting because the king was marrying his daughter to the young king of Scotland. The wealthy dowager queen of Scotland had arrived from France for the occasion with a huge retinue of French nobles and knights. The magnates' household marshals competed so fiercely for the limited number of lodgings left that fistfights broke out, which turned into a riot as the servants resorted to clubs and swords. One marshal died and several others were crippled by their injuries.[23]

The unlucky tourneyers who came too late to find lodgings were obliged to set up their tents outside the town. Huon de Méry describes such men needlessly slashing at vineyards and hedges to clear a space for their camps. With Huon we get a glimpse of the uncomfortable side of the tournament: the flapping of cold and draughty tents; the gymkhana smell of crushed grass, wood smoke and horse dung. Travelling aristocrats were philosophical about sleeping in tents in the middle ages, although they preferred to be under a roof, especially in the winter months. The complaints still survive of an English knight about being stuck in a freezing 'house of linen' in an army in Wales at the end of September 1245.[24] In the 1170s and 1180s writers expected to find big tented camps around the towns where tournament teams were based, and the Toulouse tournament of the early 1180s was explicitly advertised as being held under canvas in the city meadows, in a camp gathered round the gonfanon and pavilion of Count Raymond himself. Chrétien de Troyes described such a tented camp at his imagined tournament of Noauz (although its radius of fifteen miles is pure Arthurian hyberbole).[25] Most aristocrats travelled with tents, pavilions or larger structures called *aucubes* (which we might call marquees) in their baggage, in case they were caught out by night on the road. Sometimes they were erected simply to offer shade on a hot day when out hunting or when pausing at the road side. They were often constructed in luxurious style, made of fine embroidered cloth with carved and gilded tent poles and hung with tapestries. Some, so large that they needed to be transported in several carts, needed special winches and cranks to raise them on their poles, like the great marquee which Henry II of England sent as a gift to Frederick Barbarossa in 1157. In the summer, masses of

wild flowers were cut and laid on tent floors to add some fragrance to
the atmosphere, although woven carpets (*tapiz*) might also be laid down
over the ground.[26] Since the aristocratic lifestyle was so mobile, it was
not unusual for a knight or magnate to have to resort to sleeping in a
tent when no other lodging was possible. But even so, it was better to
be indoors by a fireplace in winter.

When a house was taken as a lodging, Philip de Remy tells us that the
lucky occupant's squires advertised the fact by fixing his shield at the
upper windows, or his banner, if he was an important enough magnate
to possess one. Huon de Méry meticulously noted also that the shield of
the Antichrist was fixed up over his host's door. A similar practice is
mentioned by Jean Renart around 1209. Chrétien de Troyes twice mentions the practice much earlier, in the later twelfth century. He has
Lancelot fixing his shield over the door of his lodgings before the tournament at Noauz, and in *Cligés* the eponymous hero displays his arms
outside his lodging for passers-by to see before each day's action. Jean
Renart says that the heraldic devices on the displayed banners had the
purpose of notifying knights where their friends were, and where the
drinking parties were going on.[27] They would also tell everyone who
would be taking part the next day, so the shields offered an ad hoc list
of participants in the tournament. All that was necessary would have
been to wander through the streets and note the banners and shields
above you.

It was by no means just knights and their squires who thronged the
tournament towns. Tradesmen and merchants came in great numbers.
The resident traders would never have been sufficient to provide for the
tourneyers' needs. Specialists like armourers, farriers and saddlers took
to the roads to follow the circuit, as we know from royal prohibitions
which tried to suppress the tournament by stifling its support industry
(see above p. 52). Tournaments were being called *nundinas* ('fairs') from
as early as 1130, a word which implies that swarms of merchants and
dealers were setting up booths wherever the tournament assembled.
Food, wine and forage for the horses must have been brought in by provisioners in cartloads. We can guess that one of the most important sort
of merchant present were the horse dealers, although they are only
rarely mentioned. They would be there more to buy than to sell, perhaps. The surplus of horses taken in ransom had to be converted into
cash by the winners, and the tournament field would be a fine place to
pick up bargains in horseflesh.

Other people turned up with an interest in horses, who did not want to pay for them. In 1179 William Marshal went to Épernon for a tournament and left his horse with a lad he found hanging around the streets, as he went into a reception. A thief grabbed the hair of the boy as soon as the Marshal was gone, and dragged him off the horse. The Marshal heard the boy's squeals and ran into the night after his horse which was clattering off up the dark street. Worried about being followed, the thief turned the horse into an unpaved sidestreet, where its hooves could not strike sparks and make a noise. But the Marshal heard his horse stamping and was able stealthily to sneak up on the thief, and strike him over the head with a club, so that he lost an eye. He prevented his friends, who had run after him, from lynching the thief, saying he had suffered enough already. The dangers of horse-thieving at tournaments were real enough and universal. In 1198 in Lincolnshire a character called Spainolle (the 'little Spaniard') and a lad accompanying him were arrested by the sheriff in possession of two horses stolen earlier at a tournament at Blyth.[28]

Heralds and their Kings

A particular specialist attracted to the tournament was the herald. One of the principal theories to account for the appearance in the twelfth century of a professional group of 'heralds of arms' is that such men made it their particular business to memorise, record and recall heraldic devices on such occasions. If there were normally hundreds of different devices on display on the eve of tournaments, the sense in this theory is obvious. The first firm evidence of this practice is Chrétien de Troyes's story of the over-curious *hyraut d'armes* who stumbled into Lancelot's lodgings at Noauz because he did not recognise the shield on display outside, and presumably wanted to add the identification to his repertoire.[29] So much depended on knowing the identity of the man whom you had captured, and this obliged knights as well as heralds to be proficient in remembering the arms of their opponents. Early references depict these heralds as little more than vagabonds trailing after the circuit, eking out a living by flattery and tips. The herald at Nouaz was barefoot and poorly dressed.

Such was the enthusiasm for the tournament and the need for specialised and knowledgable commentators that heralds had begun to establish themselves on firmer social ground early in the thirteenth century.[30] Henry de Laon, writing between 1220 and 1250, described heralds as being by then one of the major expenses of the circuit. Any serious tourneyer taking to the road for the season would be encouraged to employ several of them for their advice and expert knowledge. They had become tournament consultants. Henry thought they were a waste of money: posturing nobodies chattering jargon and nonsense as 'consultants' tend to do, and imposing on everybody around them. He found their fees exorbitant.[31] But the more talented among them nonetheless established themselves on firm social ground. The idea of the senior and expert herald appears as far back as the late twelfth century, when a few senior heralds had been given household positions. Bertran de Born believed that King Henry II of England employed a household officer called a *rei d'armar* as early as 1184. We do not know what were the duties at Henry's court of such a man. Since King Henry was hostile to tournaments, it is unlikely that tournaments were part of them, at least in England. Still, Bertran describes this early 'king of arms' as wearing a short tunic (*jupa*), like a squire's, featuring the device of the king, which would appear to make him the forerunner of the retained herald of the later middle ages.[32]

The appearance of 'kings of arms' has usually been dated to the later thirteenth century, but on this evidence they seem to have appeared much earlier. By the end of the thirteenth century the profession of herald had evolved a hierarchy in which 'kings of arms' had become supreme across France, Scotland and England. They had territories and long careers. Robert Small, for instance, had a career of over forty years as 'king herald' for the south of England from the 1270s to 1320. Scotland had its own king herald in James Cowpen in the 1290s, who later became a refugee in England on the fall of the Balliols.[33] In France in 1278 we find a chief herald called Corbioi, who had authority in southern Picardy around Corbie and Amiens. Jakemes, writing in the same area and at much the same time, called the chief herald at Le Fère-Vendeuil a 'king of heralds' (*roi des hiraus*).[34] It is not too fanciful to suggest that the king of arms got his name as a twelfth-century tourney field joke, because he was a retained herald who exercised some momentary organisational authority over the lords and knights as they were marshalled for the tournament, as opposed to the usual run of heralds, who appear to have been little more than entertainers, vagabonds and hangers-on before 1300.

All sports need their *Wisdens*, and heralds made their presence invaluable by offering the tournamenting classes a memory and a running commentary. It can only have been heralds and minstrels who disseminated bulletins of the doings at great tournaments. We hear of the report (*renons*) of the great tournament at Ressons-Gournay in 1183 which was brought to the court of the Young King by an unnamed individual, with details of teams and individual performances. He was listened to avidly.[35] In the mid thirteenth century Jakemes describes part of the minstrel's job as giving reports of recent tournaments to noblemen and women who could not get there. This included giving a list of those present and a brief word on their individual performances, and who it was who drew the attention of the crowds and won the prize.[36] The tournament roll of Lagny, preserved in the Marshal biography, was one way that such reports could become a permanent record. They reach their culmination in the account of the jousting at Hem in 1278 given by the herald Sarrazin, using his memories and his score sheets as sources. Heralds were able to exploit a world where there were aficionados of the tournament and joust. People really cared about who was the best knight of their day, and compared notes on performance. We see an echo of this in Arthurian literature, where knights like Bors got into fights over an argument as to who was the best knight of the Round Table, Lancelot or Gawain.[37]

Receptions

The social aspects of the tournament were very prominent on the day before it met. Gathering hundreds of knights and magnates in a confined space for an afternoon and evening must have produced some interesting social dynamics. Jean Renart gives a vivid account of the gossip and exchange of news when friends met at supper on such an occasion in his fictional account of a Franco-German tournament at Saint-Trond in Brabant (*c.* 1209 x 13). Here his hero, William de Dole, has adroit and knowing servants who take the best lodgings available overlooking the market place, despite the crowding of sightseers and servants in the town. Looking out of the windows into the main streets and square, he and his friends are able to see and comment on whoever passed by. Nightfall makes no difference, because torches and flares light up the teeming and noisy square and streets as though it were daytime.[38] Ulrich von Liechtenstein recalls for us the torches lighting up the streets of Korneuburg and the blaze of candles from the town's windows, which allowed knights to wander from reception to reception the night before the tournament with no difficulty.[39] Chrétien de Troyes in the 1170s says that by his days the night time din and bustle was made all the more intense by the activities of heralds running through the streets and announcing new arrivals at the tops of their voices. They would offer a flattering commentary on the abilities of champions (presumably hoping for money) and he notes the ultimate flattery they would at that time offer a select *preudomme*: 'The one who will take their measure has arrived' ('Or est venuz qui l'aunera'). The Lancelot cycle has a similar scene where its incognito hero is recognised on his way to the field of Pomeglai, because he was riding without a helm, and is embarrassed by a woman shouting: 'A mighty wonder has come about!'[40]

In Huon de Méry's allegorical account of a tournament, the Antichrist made a grand entry into the city where he was to be lodged, in the manner of a great magnate or prince, late in the afternoon, the city fathers jostling each other to hold his right stirrup as he dismounted.[41] Great preparations had already been made so that he could fulfil his role as dispenser of hospitality. His napery and plate were already unpacked and ready for him, and an enormous retinue sat down to dine with him. His servants had commandeered a hall and kitchens to prepare and lay out a sumptuous feast of several courses for their lord, although, since he was the Antichrist, he dined in style at ruinous expense to his host and the loss of reputation to his hostess. Songs of jongleurs and the music of viols and harps accompanied the feast, although the nature of the diabolic feasters meant that they drowned it out with drunken shouts.[42] We have what purports to be a contemporary description of a count of Namur throwing an expensive reception on the Sunday evening before a meeting, at his team's base at Vendeuil in the Laonnais. He invited all the Vermandisiens and Hennuyers who were on his side to come with their ladies. After an ample meal the merrymaking (*deduit*) continued with music and singing, the people sitting here and there and servants circulating with fruit and wine. One of the ladies present amused the hall with a song whose refrain was: 'Our side is by far the finest in the tournament'. The merrymaking went on so long that it had to be brought to an end by heralds announcing, 'My lords, go to bed, for we will soon be rousing you. There is little enough time to sleep as it is.'[43] To be invited to such an ostentatiously luxurious pre-match reception by such an eminent and wealthy nobleman would have been the dream of the lesser knights who came to join the event.

William Marshal was such a man in the 1170s. His biography gives a lot of attention to the eve of tournament. It comments not infrequently on the social side of the prelude, mentioning in its account of the Épernon meeting of 1179:

> The high-ranking men who had gone to the tournament were lodged throughout the town. It is the custom that in the evening they go and visit one another at their lodgings; this is a fine custom, and their conduct is courteous and polite when they seek to talk together, get to know one another and acquaint one another with the affairs which each has in hand.[44]

Not all these pre-match gatherings were quite so civil, as Huon de Méry's satire tells us. Boisterous claims, lies and story-telling was certainly a major part of the evening's pleasantries. The defeated French at an anonymous meeting of 1179 were mocked for deciding how they would split up the Anglo-Norman team's equipment in their parties of the night before.[45] The manner of a knight's reception by his fellows at these gatherings said a lot about his status, and the Marshal biography depicts its hero in the late 1170s and early 1180s on easy terms with some of the greatest men in western Europe: greeted, discussed, sought out and fêted.

At such a point the sporting metaphor naturally enough applied by historians to the tournament breaks down: it had a deeper social dimension. Business was done. It was allegedly at a tournament banquet in Flanders in the early years of the twelfth century that Arnold the Old of Ardres negotiated his marriage with a daughter of Baldwin of Aalst.[46] It was on the eve of tournament that employment was sought, important political knowledge was solicited and spread about, networks of relationships formed, secured or broken, and the aristocratic identity of both individuals and the social elite itself affirmed. Although he was a knight who lived primarily on his pay, it was a delight to William Marshal (and in due course to his children) to find that at Epernon in 1179, every prince who was present acknowledged him as friend and invited him to the pre-tournament receptions they were holding. It affirmed the Marshal as a man who had a claim to high status in his small world.

The Vespers

With many knights now assembled and the streets full of spectators, some fighting might very well take place on the eve of the tournament,

in the late afternoon or early evening. It would be before or after supper time (around 5.30 p. m. in summer). These preludes were sometimes
called the 'vespers', after the last of the canonical hours of the day.[47] The
choice of name was probably not intended to be facetious. Vespers concluded the liturgical day, and as far as the Church was concerned
Monday began after vespers on Sunday evening. This might have reas-
sured scrupulous tourneyers who were nervous about fighting on the
Lord's Day. Nonetheless, if the eve of a tournament was a Sunday, as in
Jean Renart's *Roman de la Rose*, some knights might still decline to participate in the tournament vespers because of the sanctity of the day.[48]
The term 'preliminaries' (*commençailles*) was also used for these exercises, as appears in the account of the arrival of the Young King at the
tournament at Eu in 1178 x 79. On arrival, most knights went to the
social gatherings (*assemblailles*) but the keener ones joined in the first
preliminaries (*premieres commençailles*).[49] The crowd that turned out to
watch the vespers was therefore likely to be a thin one, made up of
enthusiasts, idlers and the odd talent-spotter. It would not have been
unlike the sort of crowd that attends training sessions of professional
football sides, or reserve team fixtures.

What was the purpose of the vespers? Since a general onset was not
possible the day before the tournament, the vespers would satisfy the
very keen, or the very needy. It would also give aspirants to fame on
the circuit a chance to showcase their talents. There was an element of
the parade about the evening pre-tournament event; it did not so
much involve fighting as individual feats of swordsmanship and horsemanship, and the participants might wear lighter, padded armour, as
the Hennuyer knight Matthew de Walincourt did in the *commençailles*
at Eu in 1178 x 79.[50] William Marshal's first visit to the site at Ressons-
Gournay in the summer of 1176 tells us a little about what happened at
a vespers, because the author tells us that day was notable because
there were *no* preliminary contests, which the biography describes as
jostes (individual combats) and *plaideïces* (fencing).[51] Jousting was a
perfect activity for the vespers, as it was a public test of individual
skill. The fencing was called *plaideïces*, because it resembled what happened when two champions fought each other on foot in a trial by
combat (*plaid*), where the two fencers fought in a cleared grassy
space, perhaps roped off like a boxing ring. Both sorts of combat would
draw casual spectators, and some who were there to look for talent
for their own or their master's retinue. For the young knight who

excelled there would be an increase of reputation and the hope of a job offer.

The author of his biography no doubt has so much to say about the vespers because of their social importance for such men as the Marshal, who had to assert their market value at every opportunity. The Marshal was in fact still willing to engage in the jousting at the vespers as late as the end of the 1170s, when he had passed the age of thirty and had long found a profitable position in the royal mesnie. One reason for him to do this was that it was possible for the performers in the vespers to take horses and ransoms from their defeated opponents, and indeed the fact that they did so with talent spotters looking on added to the advantages to be gained in money. The vespers of the tournament at Maintenon-Nogent were held on the evening of Sunday 27 May 1179, and were particularly notable, as the Marshal's biographer explains.

> Once the young men (*li giemble home*) had reached the site, as was right and proper they commenced most keenly the preliminaries of the tournament (*les vespres del torneiement*). Each man strove to perform well, with the result that there were so many feats of arms that no one witnessed them without saying for a fact that it was chivalry that drove the participants on. But when all is said and done the barons and high-ranking men (*li baron e li halt home*) did not compete in the preliminaries; instead, they sent men on their side to join the contest. It so happened, according to the poem that is my source, that Sir Reginald de Nevers captured two of the king's companions and took them off with him that night.[52]

Reginald, like William Marshal on other occasions, was out to make a point in the Maintenon vespers. He had been turned down for membership in the Young King Henry's tournament mesnie, and his intention was to prove to the king how undeserved was the snub dealt out to him. He therefore refused to return the ransoms, which brought the Marshal's hand down on him hard in the main event next day.

It is important not to underestimate the importance of the eve of the tournament. For the younger knight out to gain reputation and employment, it was more important than the tournament itself. It was a magnificent showcase for emerging talent, although of course the penalties for abject failure were all the more severe. As has been said, it was because of the plotting and conspiring which happened on the eve of the tournament that some kings were keen to suppress them in times of crisis, not because of what happened on the day itself. One other thing that is alleged to have happened at the eve of the tournament also led to their condemnation. Alexander Neckam, a student in Paris in the 1180s, heard this about them.

> The form of those military games strikes one with horror, though it is a horror which fascinates. What that some knights sell their fellow-warriors to other knights on the opposing side, particularly the young bachelers who have not yet any experience in knightly gatherings? They allow their lately knighted colleagues to be led off to captivity in order to get a share of their ransoms! Shameful betrayal! Underhand rivalry! Damnable sale of a knight, no better than slave-trading! Selling into serfdom out of greed, utterly unworthy of the high name of knighthood![53]

Neckam's accusation is that amongst the more hardened participants, something of a pool-hall mentality developed. Messages passed in the night before the tournament between the two camps of the tournament, so that accomplices on the other side could be alerted to pick off the vulnerable and overconfident youngsters fresh on the circuit, and split the profits after it was all over. This was not merely Neckam's cynicism. The staging of special tournaments for new knights (*tirocinia*), which we hear of in the thirteenth century, may have been intended to provide a safer environment for the first-time tourneyers, where they would not be at a disadvantage against the more experienced and ruthless knights, like, indeed, William Marshal. We know from the Marshal biography that he and a Flemish knight entered into a profit-sharing agreement in the later 1170s, splitting each other's takings over a ten month period. There is no hint that either man set up members of each other's side, but the arrangement did sail very close to the wind in moral terms.

5

The Commencement

The town awoke well before dawn on the big day, with squires up and dressed in the dark, preparing horses and laying out the armour and weapons: such was the scene as described by both Huon de Méry and Jakemes, who both complain about the racket the turmoil of preparation made.[1] We may assume that breakfast was also being prepared by lowlier servants. But the first business, as the sun came up, was religious. The poets of the thirteenth century refer to knights attending morning mass before the main day's sport began. This may seem odd, for devotion and social respectability were linked, and the tournament was anything but respectable to a clergyman. Walter Map in the 1180s talks of a knight, en route to a tournament, who turned aside at the ringing of a bell in a wayside church and left his companions so as to hear mass, and who then was providentially saved from rejoining them by a mysterious confusion that obscured his path for three days.[2] Nonetheless Philip de Remy indicates that in the early thirteenth century it was usual for the participants to begin the day hearing mass; both Jean Renart and Gerbert de Montreuil say independently that priests customarily celebrated at first light a votive mass of the Holy Spirit.[3] This was a devotion associated with commencements because it was the Spirit's appearance at Christ's baptism that initiated his ministry, and the descent of the Spirit on the disciples that first energised the apostolic mission.

Gerbert de Montreuil describes heralds and pages shouting in the streets at first light rousing the combatants with the words: 'Knights, seek out the churches! God may grant that your sins will be obliterated if you hear a mass of the Holy Spirit. Get your shoes on! Now is the time for worship.' The urgent reminder about their sins tells us that the knights were conscious that fatalities were a possibility during the coming day, and were being offered the chance to put their soul in balance with God. There may even be some early evidence here of the fifteenth-century popular belief that witness to the elevation of the host might preserve one from sudden death that day.[4] Ulrich von Liechtenstein had less penitential thoughts on his mind in church: he says he was quite happy to pray for luck in the field that day.[5] By the thirteenth century at least French priests seem to have been willing to ignore the papal strictures against tournaments, even to the extent of offering a special weekday liturgy to suit the occasion. No doubt they expected a generous level of oblations from their knightly congregation. Later in the century the hierarchy was happy to celebrate mass for tourneyers. Archbishop Eudes Rigaud of Rouen was in Pontoise on Monday 25 January 1266 on a visitation of his diocese. In the morning he celebrated mass and preached for the feast of the Conversion of St Paul at the great collegiate church of St Melan, finding it packed with knights gathered for a special tournament for the newly knighted (*tyrocinium*) to be held outside the town later in the day.[6]

The Dividing of the Sides and the Review

The morning mass was followed by a quick breakfast and a gathering of the participants in their teams at both poles of the tournament. The *Prose Lancelot* preserves the advice to tourneyers that, however excited, they should eat a little to keep themselves going.[7] Tournaments (and jousts later on) required two nominal sides into which to divide the participants. The usual way it was done in the great tournaments of northern France, was by national groups. They were supposed to arrive by nation at one pole or other of the tournament on the eve of the tournament. The 'nation' was sometimes an obvious ethnic identity, like English, Scots, Bretons, Germans or Normans. Sometimes it was an identity which owed more to contemporary politics, as with the Brabazons, Limousins or Hennuyers. The idea that the ruler of a nation might lead the team of his own people was certainly established by the time of Philip of Flanders and the Young King Henry. The Young Henry led a Norman, not an English team, which led to questions about William Marshal's place in it. But the likelihood is that the idea of tourneying nations goes back to the amusement's earliest days, when teams from neighbouring counties challenged each other. It had certain advantages: for instance, no knight would find himself facing the embarassment of fighting against his natural lord.[8]

At this point, in some tournaments, a glaring inequality of sides might emerge when the traditional groupings of national teams produced an imbalance. An adjustment might therefore have to be made.

Ulrich von Liechtenstein tells us that it was then, after church and before arming, that the knights would be divided into two equal groups, as at Korneuburg in about 1226.[9] There were only 250 knights at Korneuburg, and it was a small event. But the same might happen at bigger events too. At Friesach in 1224 Ulrich says that the 600 Austrian knights in their various ill-matched companies were carefully arranged into two teams of close to 300. The Dunstable roll of 1309 shows us one way that it might be done. The heralds present had clearly listed the participating magnates and their retinues the night before, which must be the basis of the roll recording attendance that has survived. Analysis of the roll has proved that they went on to do their sums, placing the earl of Lancaster's large retinue on one side and balancing it against the opposing earls' retinues by adding to it a large proportion of the unattached independent knights who were there.[10] Sometimes it was the leaders of the tourneyers who organised the balancing. At Ressons-Gournay in 1168 the Flemings and Picards who had turned up much outnumbered the rival French. As a result, Baldwin V led his Hennuyers, who would normally have joined the Flemings, into the French camp to balance the numbers, much to the disgust of the count of Flanders. A similar story is told in the 1160s by John of Marmoutier of Count Geoffrey of Anjou at a tournament between the Normans and Bretons. Finding that the Normans – whom he had joined because he had married into the royal family – outnumbered the Bretons, Geoffrey led his Angevins to join the Bretons and balance up the numbers.[11]

Unequal tournaments were clearly not popular, for obvious reasons, but they happened. The Marshal biography mentions that the people at a tournament at Joigny found the side quartered at Joigny itself was much inferior to the other. The fact that the Joigny team eventually got the best of the encounter was thought therefore to be all the more remarkable. The author stopped just short of awarding the credit for the achievement to William Marshal.[12] Whatever and however it happened there would in the end be two sides. They were always called 'those within' (meaning those lodging at the principal settlement) and 'those without' (meaning those lodging at the other one). For many knights it hardly mattered much which side they were in. Arriving independently at Chastel de la Marche, Bors asked his squire on which team he should tourney, those within the castle or those outside it.[13] Bors's dilemma was probably not an unusual one for those independent knights who turned up unattached to a household. As we have seen at Dunstable in 1309, heralds might use them to balance out the sides, if they were unequal. The important thing was the fight, not whose side you were on.

The assembly of knights in their teams probably took some time, as the knights had to get armed, and then slowly gather in groups to move off jingling through the crowds to the lists. There could be quite a press of horses and men. The Prose Lancelot records advice to women to leave early for the stands before the crowd of horses and men became too difficult to push through. It also records that the greater ladies might arrive on horseback with groups of their attendants in an escorted procession, to minimise the discomfort of the crowd's jostling.[14] In the bipolar tournaments of northern France the team based at the town distant from the lists seems to have come in a formal procession, which might have taken some time. At Joigny in 1179 the team based at the town had a long wait for the opposition to turn up, and passed the time dancing and singing.[15] In 1280 the knights based at Montmédy, their ladies and a host of attendants were led by the heralds to the lists at neighbouring Chauvency. On the way, the ladies in the cavalcade rode in pairs and sang to the accompaniment of musicians, led by the countess of Luxembourg. They did not arrive at the lists till nearly midday.[16] When both teams were gathered at the lists, something like a formal review parade (*regars*) opened the event. In Philip de Remy's account of a tournament at Ressons-Gournay trumpeters, hornplayers and drummers struck up a stirring noise which echoed over the hill as the knights rode out unhelmeted on to the field. Jean Renart and Jacques Bretel describe similar scenes, knights riding out though the gates of the lists on their caparisoned horses, each escorted by several squires in new white gloves carrying their lances, banners, shields and helmets, some also flanked by minstrels and musicians.[17] Brave and colourful though this preliminary was, it was also a very practical way of commencing the day. The stirring music signalled to both teams that the day's work was about to begin, but while it continued the event was still pending.

In the review each company shouted its warcry, perhaps as they passed through the lists. The ritual told each side who was participating, and under what banners. Warcries (*enseignes*) were an old way of proclaiming a soldier's allegiance, and, under the guise of the watchword, were still in use up to the nineteenth century. But the way it was used in the tournament review was different; it was used like a team chant, to assert identity and team feeling. We have a fair sample of such chants from various twelfth-century sources. The most famous and oldest of all was the French royal warcry 'Montjoie!' (an apparent reference to the Iron Age earthworks and monuments which were characteristic of the landscape of early medieval Paris).[18] The English royal house had its equivalent in the cry 'Dex aïe!' (God our help), the cry which the Young King Henry employed, as also did his cousin, the count of Boulogne, son of King Stephen.[19] William Marshal eventually got in trouble with his young master for devising his own warcry 'Dex aïe li Mareschal!' (God for the Marshal), which was looked on coldly as being over-pre-sumptuous by his fellow-knights.[20] Some warcries were topographical: the noble poet, Huon d'Oisy castellan of Cambrai, shouted 'Cambrai!' as he rode on the field with his knights; the duke of Lorraine shouted 'Metz!'. Some warcries were simply the family name: 'Montfort!', 'Mello!' or 'Poissy!'[21] Others reflected local saints' cults: the Bretons, we are told, shouted 'Saint Malo!' and the Welsh Marcher lords in Ireland called out: 'Saint David!'.[22] One or two were more like haloos used in field sports, Guy de Châtillon's men bellowed out the unforgettable: '*Alom lour Chastillon!*' (Go get 'em, Châtillon!).[23]

Identification was all important when two temporary armies were formed out of a miscellaneous group of companies on the day. The *Prose Lancelot* mentions one way that one side could be marked out eas-ily (if expensively) from the other. One side at one of its tournaments hung the same distinctive leather barding over all its horses, 'so they would be distinguishable from the others'.[24] The usual way of marking and rallying a company of knights was by means of its banner, or gon-fanon. A banner was an ancient way of marking out a company, and banners had a continuous military history in western Europe from the time of the Roman imperial army. The word *banière* was Frankish and was drawn from the word *ban*, which meant 'command'. It was a reference to the way that banners were used to signal to columns of troops on the march and mark the presence of a commander. Banners were the prerogative of great men and high office; ordinary knights would not presume to use them, their lances being adorned with trian-gular pieces of coloured cloth, called pennons. The eleventh- and early twelfth-century banners were square panels of stiffened and embroi-dered cloth, to the fly of which were attached several long coloured streamers of silk. These streamers had become old-fashioned by the end of the twelfth century, and banners became simple rectangles for the dis-play of heraldic devices.[25] Stout gilded clips attached the banner to its staff so that it might be detached easily for use as a standard over a castle, or simply taken off and kept in a leather or canvas case.[26] The lord himself might carry his banner when leading his men, but in combat it was generally handed over to a gonfanonier to carry alongside him.[27] As early as the time of the conquest of England by the Normans, kings, princes and lords had individual banners by which their presence was recognised, and one explanation of the pre-tournament review was as a sort of 'trooping the colour', where the banners of each lord on the field would be displayed and ridden along the line so that every knight would be able to recognise its owner.

Numbers at Tournaments

We have some idea of the numbers of knights who might gather for a twelfth-century tournament. When writers of the time gave an opinion, they seemed to believe that thousands, rather than hundreds, of knights attended the great tournaments of northern France. Walter Map early in the 1180s believed that thousands attended the great meetings customarily held at Louvain in Brabant.[28] There is some solid backing for this generous sort of estimate. The great tournament of Lagny-sur-Marne in November 1179 was commemorated by a list of participants, which has survived by being incorporated in the biography of William Marshal. The list is not easy to interpret, and the biographer did not copy it word for word. He mentions eighty-seven individuals, of whom it explicitly says that seventeen carried banners; that is, they rode at the head of their own retinue of knights. But there were certainly a lot more names in his source than he repeated, because he says elsewhere that the Lagny list included the names of one duke and nineteen counts, and the names he gave include only four counts. The author says that there were over three thousand knights at Lagny, and when he does he may well be giving us the running total of names he had calculated from the complete roll. He says that the most impressive retinue present at Lagny was that of the Young King Henry, which he says included 560 knights. Of these, a subdivision of two hundred knights rode under the leadership of fifteen bannerets, including William Marshal. The splendour of Young Henry's retinue that day was enhanced by its inclusion as a banneret of Count Robert of Dreux, the nephew of Louis VII.[29]

Lagny was the greatest tournament of its age, and should not be taken as in any way typical in terms of numbers. The Young King Henry's huge retinue at Lagny was exceptional, but there is a glimpse in the

Marshal biography of some smaller and more representative ones, giving us some insight into tournament organisation on the field. For instance, when the Norman magnate William de Tancarville rode to the tournament between Sainte-Jamme and Valennes in 1166 he retained a company of forty knights, one being his cousin, William Marshal. Another great knight who rode out on the field at Lagny in 1179 was William des Barres the elder. He was the French counterpart to William Marshal: a man of the minor Parisian nobility who rose through his superb military skills into royal favour. Like the Marshal, he became a respected captain and royal officer and eventually attained the rank of count by marriage. He never had a biography written of him, but his fame was such that his name begins to turn up as a character in romances in the thirteenth century. He too was called by contemporaries 'the best knight in all the world'. Des Barres rode out with a retinue of sixteen French knights at Lagny, including his two sons, William des Barres the younger and Simon, and his nephew, Peter des Leschaus. Such companies of one, two or three dozen knights, recruited by family connections, friendship and cash, were the more typical tournament *conreis*, escorts of honour and also body guards, deployed to protect their lords and range the field in a body – if they were well disciplined – looking for ransoms.

The next chance we have to give a rough calculation of figures also comes from France, but not till a century after Lagny. In May 1279, Charles the young prince of Salerno, son and heir of Charles of Anjou, king of Sicily, was touring his father's native land on a state visit to his first cousin, King Philip III (1270–85). Two great tournaments were held in his honour, one at Senlis and the other outside the royal town of Compiègne in the north of the Île-de-France. A roll survives from the Compiègne meeting and gives a list of the princes, magnates and bannerets present in lavish heraldic detail. The kings of England, Navarre and France apparently witnessed the day's sport, Edward I being on a visit to the French court. The roll lists the names of one king (Navarre), five dukes, twenty-eight counts, and 295 other barons and bannerets on the field, including Prince Charles, giving a total of 330 names. Like the Lagny list, it was organised by nation: in this case, French, English, Rhinelanders, Scots, Champenois, Bretons, Limousins, Brabazons, Hennuyers, Normans, Burgundians, Flemings, Arroisiens, Tolosans, Picards, Poitevins, Berruyers, Beauvaisiens and Lorrainers.[30] Since, as at Lagny, each of those men would have brought their retinues of knights, whose numbers could range between a dozen and a couple of hundred, we have no way of assessing the total number who were there. But at the very least there must have been three thousand knights at Compiègne on that day, and there may have been a thousand or two more than that.

Further and rather more modest examples can be drawn from outside the tournament's heartland in the national meetings of the Empire and England. The tournament of Friesach in 1224 carefully described by Ulrich von Liechtenstein included only six hundred knights, divided equally into two teams led by the duke of Austria and the margrave of Istria.[31] A tournament was held at Dunstable at some time early in 1309 and a list similar to the Compiègne list was compiled to commemorate it. As with the 1279 list the Dunstable roll was compiled by a herald as a record of the devices on display that day, but, like the Lagny list, organised according to the retinues on the field. It records six large retinues (*retenaunces*) brought to the field by the earls of Gloucester, Hereford, Warwick, Lancaster, Surrey and Arundel, and also John Ferrers of Chartley, claimant to the earldom of Derby. The two largest retinues belonged to Thomas, earl of Lancaster, with seventy-seven knights, and Guy de Beauchamp, earl of Warwick, with fifty-four knights, and the smallest retinue was the thirteen knights of the earl of Hereford. Like the Lagny *conreis* the Dunstable *retenaunces* feature prominently the names of brothers and relatives of the magnates who led them. We know that by 1309 it was the practice of magnates to enter into written indentures with knights they wished to take into their retinues. But apart from these retained companies the Dunstable list records a further seventy knights *de la commune*, that is unattached knights riding as individuals. In all 235 knights participated at Dunstable, which seems to have been quite a large number for an English tournament. Obviously it could not compare with the great state tournaments of northern France; but, on the other hand, such a number might have been more comparable to the smaller meetings held across northern France during the season.[32]

Tournament Weapons

Apart from the bow and the pole axe, every weapon ever used by knights turns up in the tournament. Swords, lances, maces and knives all feature at some time or other, and they were the same weapons that knights used in war. William Marshal used his sword and lance in earnest on the tournament field. Nowhere is there any indication that during his career as a tourneyer in the 1170s and 1180s the sword edge was blunted and the lance was not tipped with a steel point. There is only one reference to blunted weapons at the time when the Marshal was tourneying, and it comes in the romance *Garin le Loherenc.* It portrays a French army on the road taking an opportunity to joust in some meadows they were passing. When the knights did so, they took the points off their lances, and just jousted with the staves.[33] This might have been a practice in jousting, where pointed lances could do terrible damage. On the other hand, it may just be the description of a bohort, an informal joust in which the knights did not bother even to put armour on, and used sticks, as King Richard did at a bohort near Messina in 1190. In the Christmas court festivities held at Camelot by King Arthur in the *Prose Lancelot* of *c.* 1220, it is in a bohort that Meleagant comes in for criticism for using a steel-tipped and heavy jousting lance where the opposing knights were wearing no armour.[34]

As the thirteenth century progressed, the good sense in moderating the possibility of injury by blunting weapons seems to have dawned on knights. The urgency must have been particularly strong in jousting matches, where the potential for serious injury was greater, especially as heavier lances had been developed especially for the lance by the thirteenth century.[35] The competitors in the Round Table jousts at Walden Abbey in 1252 were all supposed to have been carrying lances with blunted ends called 'sokets'. These were metal tips devised so as to curve around in a ring. On impact they punched the opposing shield, rather than pierced it.[36] Was the same restraint usual in the tournament by then? There is little evidence of it. The purchase roll for a tournament to be held in Windsor Park in 1280 has a famous reference to thirty-eight swords being constructed out of whalebone and parchment, with gilded hilts and pommels. But we are not told that these were to be used in combat. It is perhaps more likely that they were commissioned for display in trophies or in cavalcades, like the gilded and silvered leather helmets which were also commissioned for the same event.[37] The accounts of later tournaments still talk of the use of swords for battering opponents in the mêlée and the use of lances to run them down. The swords may have been given blunt edges, indeed, it is very likely that they were, but otherwise there does not seem to have been much difference between the arms used in war and those used in the tournament.

The Lists and Stands

While the review was going on the acclamations of the heralds identified individuals to the crowds of onlookers, gathered anywhere that was
safe, including the tops of carts. The companies were marshalled for the
beginning within 'safe areas' or *recets*, marked out by a barrier called the
lices (usually translated as 'lists'), as passages in the *History of William
Marshal* tell us. It would seem – since the same word is applied to pal-
isades – that the lists were marked by a line of painted and sharpened
stakes hammered into the ground. These barriers feature in the description of the tournament of 1166 at Valennes and at Ressons-Gournay in
1176, where the Tancarville company is depicted as assembling within
them with the other *conreis* (or companies) as the day began. From the
accounts of the tournament at Eu and Joigny in 1178 and 1179, it seems
that the *lices* might well be erected across the entrances to the towns
which were the team bases, for here the *lices* were said to be set out in
front of the *chastel* (meaning the bourgs of each town). In *The Tournament of Antichrist*, the narrator rides out of the Antichrist's city with
the tourneyers as they leave the town, and goes to where the lists begin,
('De la vile ovec li tornai et chevauchames jusqu'as lices').[38]

We have some clues as to how the lists were put up and what they
looked like. In some cases the lists were not just stakes hammered into
the ground. We know of one occasion in the 1250s where a tournament
patron mobilised a work force not just to set up lists, but to dig
ditches.[39] Lists could therefore be substantial structures. The account
books of Flemish cities which sponsored hastiludes in the fourteenth
century confirm the earlier evidence. Their lists were built as a palisade
of stakes, and soil banked up against one side. The cities used the inex-
haustible supply of horse dung from their stables for the revetment of
the lists, but more rural tournaments would have had to use ordinary
soil, dug out of ditches.[40] The use of ditches and banks further to mark
out the lists would not be surprising, as lists had to be defended from
overenthusiastic knights of 'those without' who might try to pursue
'those within' who were running for refuge.

When the tournaments were on sites defined as between two settlements, the review must have taken place outside the lists of the principal
base, rather than the two sides each holding its separate review at its
own base. Ressons, for instance, was seven kilometres and a hill away
from Gournay, and invisible from there. Holding the review at only one

1 Ulrich von Liechtenstein,
from the Manasseh Codex, thirteenth century.
For the items of knightly equipment, see pp. 137–48.
(*Universitätsbibliothek, Heidelberg*)

2 Rudolf von Rotenberg and his lady,
from the Manasseh Codex, thirteenth century.
For the role of women in the tournament, see pp. 156–9.
(*Universitätsbibliothek, Heidelberg*)

3 A lady gives a knight arms for the tournament,
from the Manasseh Codex, thirteenth century.
For the evolution of helmet crests, see p. 147.
(*Universitätsbibliothek, Heidelberg*)

4 Gueherset unhorses Agravains.
For the appearence of the joust, the one-to-one combat, see pp. 117–25.
(*Bibliothèque Nationale*)

5 Count Friedrich von Leiningen in single combat,
from the Manasseh Codex, thirteenth century.
For the question of the violent nature of knights, see pp. 153–6.
(*Universitätsbibliothek, Heidelberg*)

6 Knights charging. From the life of St Edmund,
Pierpoint Morgan Library, New York, MS 736, fol. 7v.
For the grand charge as the central part of the tournament, see pp. 89–92.
(*Pierpoint Morgan Library*)

7 A *mêlée* at a tournament.
(*Bibliothèque Nationale*)

8 Knights charging in pursuit. Enamel from Stavelot altar, twelfth century.
For the fight as the conclusion of the touranment, see pp. 102–3.
(*Pierpoint Morgan Library*)

base would account for the practice we find as early as the work of Chrétien de Troyes of describing the two sides in the tournament as the team
'from inside' and the team 'from outside'. Joachim Bumke makes the
point that this may reflect the circumstances of wartime tourneying outside besieged towns.[41] The inside team was the one at the principal
location of a bipolar tournament, and the outside team was the one
which had joined it by riding up from the secondary base. The lists were
the only thing approaching a focus that the day's entertainment would
have, for the review, the opening jousts and the grand onset of the mêlée
would have happened there. And it was at the lists that the stands to
accommodate women and other onlookers were placed. Women took a
very keen interest in the tournament, and, as James de Vitry mentions,
might hand over to a favoured champion one of their detachable sleeves
or other token to tie to a helmet or lance.[42] They would have wanted to
be at a place where there was the best chance of witnessing their
favourites' exploits.

Chrétien de Troyes tells us as early as the 1170s that structures might
be set up for the day which he called *loges*, and which we would call
stands. The fact that raised stands were necessary to observe the action
tends to confirm that the lists were substantial barriers that blocked the
view unless you climbed up on them. There is a good deal of evidence
about the tournament *loges* from the literary sources. The literary
accounts tell us that the stands were usually put up just within the lists,
in a long line if there were more than one of them. There was a clear
and convenient space between the lists and the stands where the heralds
and squires stationed themselves to observe the action, and unengaged
knights might sit on their horses and watch. To see the action, the heralds had to stand on top of the earth banks. There they shouted
comments to the ladies above and behind them, and urged on their
patrons on the field in front. Noble ladies could watch the day's spectacle from these stands in sheltered propriety, as in Chrétien's fictional
tournament at Noauz.[43]

Stands were built for the day, and later Flemish accounts talk of them
being built cheaply in unseasoned soft wood bought at the expense of
the patron. The carpenters who erected the stands dismantled them the
day after and kept the wood as their fee. The exterior was luxuriously
draped in cloth hangings so the cost-cutting in cheap wood was not
visible. Tapestries were hung on hooks within the stand to add to the
feeling of sheltered opulence.[44] In the early thirteenth century, the

author of the cyclical *Prose Lancelot* talks often of elevated, roofed timber platforms, to which he gives the name *bretesches* or *loges*, with wide windows for distinguished spectators. He also mentions that these stands were built on different levels, with the greater people up higher with a better view. King Arthur had to descend to a lower window of his stand to talk comfortably to Lancelot on his horse, and then to run down some more steps to embrace him.[45] The Prose Lancelot speculated that in Arthurian times the custom had grown up of building stands with windows (*fenestres*) and seats (*apoiaux*) because women in those days had been willing to travel great distances to accompany their husbands and lovers from tournament to tournament.[46] We might speculate more pragmatically that since the tournament met as often in January as in August, the stands also gave welcome shelter to the ladies and non-combatants. The only alternative would have been to stand around in the cold and wet for hours shivering in cloaks. Sometimes the accounts imply that the stand might be set up right in the centre of the tourneying field beyond the lists, like a bandstand in a park, perhaps so the ladies could get an all-round view.[47]

From these stands the ladies and non-combattants could watch the review parade and the opening jousting, and also catch the grand charge that commenced the tournament proper. This certainly was the case at the fictional tournament of Pomeglai, where the stands were filled by a great crowd of noble ladies and girls surrounding Queen Guinevere.[48] By the end of the thirteenth century, the stands seem to have become more elaborate and numerous. The fictional tournament at Montargis described in *Sone de Nansay* featured four 'rich' stands (*loges*), with the queen and three important noblewomen presiding as host over each.[49] The structures (*bretesches*) at Chauvency in 1280 were hung with silks and carpenters had provided shuttered windows and doors, which were folded open so that the people inside could watch the review.[50] Within the stands the ladies and young girls sat with their friends and 'chatted about this and that', as the *Prose Lancelot* puts it. But they also passed the time waiting like any group of spectators at a sporting event: comparing recent performances by knights, discussing their qualities, and placing them in order of excellence. When the teams were assembling the ladies might well become loudly partisan in their remarks about 'our men', excitedly identifying those knights whose arms they recognised.[51]

The extent and nature of tournament sites, even on the smaller scale of England, meant that only parts of the subsequent action could have been followed by onlookers. The view from the stands after the opening events must have been limited. In some case trees and broken ground would have frustrated any attempt to get a general view. The most that spectators could have seen at the wooded site at Langwith in Yorkshire, after the opening onset and mêlée, would have been the glitter of arms and helmets and the flash of the bright colours of surcoats as knights moved here and there through the trees in search of ransoms. Knights valued the cover, as it allowed them to stage ambushes on the opposing teams, but spectators who wanted a general view of the action would have found it frustrating. On the other hand, spectators may have approached the day in the spirit of hunt supporters: standing around in the hopes of seeing random encounters, but spending the rest of the time reminiscing, chatting, eating and drinking.

The Commençailles

Once the noise of music, war-cries and acclamations had stopped, and the companies were marshalled and lined up beyond the lists, a signal was given, usually, it seems, the cry of a herald or senior marshal on either side that the knights should arm up. Jakemes says the cry was 'Laciez!' ('Helmets on!').[52] It was now après prime, that is, an hour or two after sunrise, but it was still not yet necessarily the time for the main event, the general onset or estor.[53] There is plenty of evidence that joust-ing, under the name of the commençailles or bargaigne, might occur at this point too (which is why the estor was sometimes called the granz torneiement, as opposed, one imagines, to the 'lesser tournament' rep-resented by the jousts of the commençailles). New knights might – by prior agreement – offer to joust before the assembled companies. The one-to-one arrangement of these jousts might account for the name of li bargaigne, or la barcaigne, applied to them by the Marshal biogra-pher.[54] One knight from one side would ride with a lance against one from the other. Often, it seems, it was a privilege reserved for young knights riding out on to the field for the first time, but not always. The description of such an occasion given by Hermann of Tournai in the 1140s describes the accidental death of the seasoned knight Count Henry of Brabant in a joust in front of the ranks of his men and the knights of Tournai. This sort of preliminary was a transfer to the tournament of what happened in open warfare, when mounted champions out to make a name for themselves would commonly ride between the armies and defy the other side to put up an opponent. The preliminary combats staged between rival armies moving into battle are well attested, such as the joust in which Arnold of Raisse distinguished himself on the ground between the French and Imperial armies at Bouvines in 1214.[55]

It was by this sort of jousting that Huon d'Oisy's twelfth-century tournament of women began. Huon awarded his wife, Margaret, the literary privilege of jousting in front of the ranks as they assembled before Torcy, shouting his own warcry of 'Cambrai!'. A detailed account of a commencement joust by youngsters is offered in the late 1190s in the English romance *Gui de Warewic*. In this, the eponymous hero's first tournament, after all had assembled on the field, the Emperor Reiner's son rode forward out of the ranks to challenge any takers to an individual joust. Guy naturally took the challenge, struck the prince on the shield, knocked him to the ground and rode off with his horse, which he exchanged for his own and rode in the ensuing *estor*. A generation later Jean Renart offered a similar description of the prelude to his tournament between Montargis and Château-Landon: 'numerous new knights joust at the *commençailles* between the two lines of battle'.[56] These literary duels had historical parallels. The Marshal biography's accounts of the beginning of the Valennes tournament in 1166 and that of Ressons-Gournay in 1176 indicate that *jostes de pladeïces* ('individual jousts') might precede the general charge, although they did not do so at either of those occasions. But the individual jousts of the *commençailles* at Joigny in 1179 are described in detail, and are said to have occurred in front of the lists immediately before the main tournament began, as the companies were still assembling on the other side.[57]

Although the privilege of jousting might first be awarded to bachelors, the evidence of the *Prose Lancelot* is that knights might simply ride up and await a turn, as Gawain did at Chastel de Molin. Gawain rode up to what the romance called the *rens*.[58] In the time of William Marshal these really would have been the 'ranks', the space between the opposing battalions, waiting to charge. Two generations later things had changed. We know that by the end of the thirteenth century the word *rencs* had taken on a new meaning. In *Sone de Nansay* and the *Roman de Ham* the *rencs* were jousting courses, scattered with sand. Sometimes there were several of them in parallel so groups of knights could charge down them simultaneously. From the description of Gawain's jousting in the *commençailles* of Chastel de Molin, it would seem that by the second decade of the thirteenth century organisers were planning for extended *commençailles* jousting. They made arrangements for them to take place in the best possible place for spectators: on the other side of the lists from the stands, rather than in front of the ranks of their colleagues out on the field as in the Marshal's day.

Cheating

The Marshal biography mentions that Count Philip of Flanders had a particular strategy for winning tournaments in the mid 1170s, which was anything but sporting by modern standards. But then, Count Philip was more interested in winning than in respecting the rules, as when he ordered up infantry to deter the Hennuyers at Ressons in 1168. The count's special stratagem was to ride his men to the field with the rest of the companies, but then give out that he did not intend to fight that day. Then, when the sides were fully engaged without him, he waited until the companies were scattered across the field and knights were disoriented. At that point he launched his fresh and disciplined company through the lists and on to the field, sweeping up ransoms indiscriminately. The Marshal biographer was impressed by this trickery, which he called 'wise and proper' (*proz e sages*).[59] The strategy was adopted by the Young King Henry's team, after being the victim of it more than once.

Count Philip's strategy does not in fact make much sense without the existence of *commençailles*. They gave him the excuse of leading his men fully armed but unhelmeted to the lists, ostensibly to observe the jousting, perhaps even to let some of his men join in, but then grandly to decline to join in the main event, for whatever excuse. Sitting on horseback in the space between the lists and the stands, he could get his men to don helms and take up their shields unobserved, once the teams were engaged. This may well explain why some twelfth-century tournaments pointedly omitted the *commençailles*: their cover for the cynical cleverness of Count Philip and his imitators may have brought them into disrepute.

We have already seen several occasions when companies of infantry – bowmen and spearmen – might be marched up to the lists. Companies of footsoldiers were routinely raised by tourneying devotees to accompany them to the field. A series of charters issued by Picard lords to the men of their lordships survives from the mid thirteenth century. They all say that 'the lord may recruit his men to accompany him to join the army or to go with him on the road when he rides to war or to the

tournaments, without being accused of oppression'.[60] Able-bodied vil-
lagers had therefore to be prepared to take up bows and spears and
march behind their lord in the tournament season. They might also
have to dig the ditches for the lists, if their lord was the tournament
patron.

The Hainault chronicler describes conditions in the 1170s when the
princes involved in the tournaments of Lorraine simply did not trust
their rivals to keep the fighting at the level of mock combat. Duke Godfrey of Brabant at Trazegnies in 1170 was so angry with the Hennuyers
that he seems to have announced the tournament simply as a subterfuge
for a full-scale assault on Hainault, enticing the young Baldwin V into
a position where he could be trapped and destroyed with his knights.
Fortunately for Baldwin, the tension with Brabant was so great as to
leave him suspicious of the invitation and willing to march three thousand foot soldiers to Trazegnies, just in case. It turned out they were
needed.[61]

When Count Philip of Flanders summoned a tournament to the regular venue of Ressons in 1168 he came with a company of infantry,
which he called on to the field when the Hennuyers pressed home their
advantage against his side too enthusiastically. In doing this, Philip was
not exactly playing the game – or at least Gilbert of Mons thought not
– but his use of infantry was technically permissible if they were there
to police the lists, and the Hennuyers had driven the Flemings back to
Ressons.[62] This was how infantry were used at a tournament in the Norman marches at Anet-Sorel in 1178. Three hundred spearmen and
bowmen were stationed in the town of Anet under the command of the
local French magnate, Simon de Neauphle. The fact that the troops were
in the town means that they were within the lists, and they must have
been put there to police them and secure the town. Simon ordered the
troops to challenge the Young King Henry and William Marshal when
they strayed off the field, crossed the lists and rode into the streets of
Anet. It is a testimony to the great celebrity of the Young King that the
infantry refused to arrest him. The king and his William retaliated for
Simon's officiousness by seizing his reins and attempting to hold him
for ransom. Simon's only escape was to grab a low-hanging gutter as he
was ridden away by William Marshal, and so abandon his horse.[63]

Was it possible to cheat at the tournament? Some writers certainly
thought so. Philip of Flanders, as we have seen, came in for criticism
for wanting to win too much. Magnates who wanted to excel at the

tournament with little physical cost to themselves were a longstanding medieval complaint. For this reason, perhaps, Philip de Remy made quite such a big issue of the physical and personal excellence of his king of Scotland, who was able to demonstrate his capacity to give and take punishment at Ressons-Gournay before his bodyguards closed in around him. Henry de Laon takes up this theme. Of course magnates could deploy their knights and their retinue to protect themselves without being accused of cheating; that was only fair, he says. But they could hardly expect admiration unless they did something physically to earn it in the press of the mêlée, where Prowess, he said, took her fee in the number of blows of maces and swords. Then he went further and hinted darkly that some magnates were willing to pay to buy the treachery of knights in the field, and bribe the tournament marshals (*diseurs*) to look the other way when this was going on.[64] Sharp dealings at the level of the common knight were also suspected. Alexander Neckam talks of hardened tourneyers who collaborated with members of the opposing side to target and capture any new and inexperienced knights who came on to the field. The critics of the tournament certainly believed that it had a seamy underside.

6

The Grand Tournament

The *commençailles* seem to have gone on at the lists for as long as both sides had agreed beforehand. It is likely enough that around 1200 the pre-tournament jousting became so popular that some tournaments deliberately devoted an entire day to them. Indeed, the appearance of 'round tables' soon after 1200 indicate that some knights were quite happy to meet simply to joust. The Friesach tournament of 1224 was advertised as a mêlée tournament, but the knights got caught up with the *commençailles* jousting to such an extent that they were willing to postpone the mêlée indefinitely. Even in a one day event it must often have been mid-morning before the main event got under way.[1] The marshalling of the *conreis* or 'companies' would have taken some time. All the accounts we have talk of the two sides arranging themselves into two long and glittering lines of battle facing each other, close to the lists of the principal pole settlement, 'in front of the stands on the level ground' as was the case at Chauvency in 1280.[2] Onlookers watched from the upper windows of nearby houses if they could not get in the stands, or from the tops of carts if they were not people of any social importance.

Care was taken to match up the two sides so that the lines were roughly equal in numbers, as we have seen. It was hardly fair if one team swamped the other. It follows from this that somewhere at the heart of every tournament event there was a directing intelligence. In the mid thirteenth century we hear of 'adjudicators' (*diseurs*) who were responsible for marshalling the field beyond the lists and noting what went on during the action, whether good or bad.[3] Who were these adjudicators? At Chauvency in 1280 it was certainly the massed heralds who led the knights on to the field and gave the signal for the charge.[4] The Dunstable roll indicates that by that date in England the details of the show were also being managed by the heralds. How long had this been going on? The likelihood is that a species of herald had been specialising in the stage managing of the tournament for some time. The key to this might perhaps have been the figure known as the 'king of arms'. It was undoubtedly some such man who drew up the order of play for Friesach in 1224 or Dunstable in 1309, for he would have had the authority and the knowledge to marshal the lists. The accounts of tourney and jousting organisation given by *Sone de Nansay*, Sarrazin and Jacques Bretel confirm the key importance of chief heralds like Rommenalt, Corbioi, Maingient and Bruiant in advising, organising and communicating.

When the *diseur* or senior herald was satisfied a signal was given – a great shout or a bugle call – and the two long lines of hundreds of horsemen would ride at each other, shields up and lances in hands, taking their mark on the knight opposite them, as Lancelot did at Pomeglai.[5] This was what the knights called the *estor*, the 'charge' or 'combat'. It was the moment the spectators had come for, as the banners moved to the front and knights spurred their horses forward. Then there was the rolling thunder of hooves, the trembling of the ground, the jingle of harness and the shouts of excited men. We have some evocative contemporary sketches of this critical point in the tournament. We hear of the way that the strong colours of red, blue and white dominated among the linen and silk banners and trappings of the lines of knights and horses moving rapidly towards each other. At a certain point, some metres before the lines met, the lances were taken under the knights' arms and came down to the horizontal, allowing them to choose the point on their opponent where a blow would do most harm. Writers refer to the choking cloud of dust thrown in the air by the hooves of the horses pounding the field in dry summer months; or the reek of the steam rising from their coats in the cold winter; and to the loud crash as the lines collided, and the bursting of lances into splinters in the shock of the meeting.

The great charge was undoubtedly the most dangerous as well as the most exhilarating moment of the day. The knights charged in their companies in extended lines, so there would have been no rear echelon to ride over any fallen, although there was still the chance of falling amongst kicking hooves.[6] But when hundreds of horses and men rode at speed in close proximity, deliberately looking to strike or outmanoeuvre each other, there was considerable personal danger. Sometimes, as at Anet in 1178, one of the lines was poorly marshalled and collapsed into disarray. At Anet the French line was too crowded and knights got in each other's way, allowing the Anglo-Norman line to scatter and rout them.[7] Riders and horses alike would seek to avoid collisions, each having a healthy sense of self-preservation, but collisions and falls still happened. So when the teams came together with a great crash and shattering of spearshafts, accidents were likely, and it was at this point that fatalities could happen. This seems to have been the case in 1186, when Duke Geoffrey of Brittany, the son of Henry II of England, was trampled to death after he had been knocked from his horse at a tournament in the region of Paris.[8] Philip of Flanders in the *estor* at Ressons in 1168 likewise took a great blow to the chest which sent him over the back of his saddle. Philip was the victim of what Gilbert of Mons tells us was already then an established practice. The count's opponent had fixed his lance in a *feltrum* (Fr. *fautre*; Eng. 'fewter'), a spear rest attached to the front of his saddle furniture. It was intended to allow the knight to carry his lance aloft while riding, without having to bear its weight or balance it. But at Ressons, the knight had dropped the lance to the horizontal without taking it under his arm, keeping its butt in the fewter, which added power and solidity to the thrust, putting the weight of both horse and man behind it.[9] Count Philip was lucky to survive.

The two great charging lines of knights met with a shock and a crash. Medieval literature is full of this moment, whose excitement, colour and violence seized the imaginations of all who had seen it, even if they were not poets. This is how the historian John of Marmoutier described it around 1170:

> The charge commences and the lines meet; there is a great clatter of arms; trumpets sound and there is a chorus of horns of all sorts; the warhorses drown it with their screaming; shields sparkling with gold in the sunlight glitter all across Mont-St-Michel. Men are united in combat; ashwood spears are splintered; swords are notched. Now the fighting is hand to hand; shields clash; saddles are emptied; some horses are thrown down; others have lost their riders and run wild on the field with broken reins.[10]

The poet Jean de Condé provides quite as powerful a word picture, a century and a half later, describing a confident young knight taking his place in the line.

> He places himself there, where the line of the charge is deepest, as firm as any tower, like a veritable Gawain or Perceval, amongst the steaming horses and the dust as it climbs in the air, in the thunder of drums and the blaze of trumpets, in the press of attackers and defenders, in the clatter of sword strokes, where ventailles are slashed, where coats of arms are ripped; there where the press of men is pushed apart by the power of the strongest, where the heart of the young knight ever beats high.[11]

Some knights and their horses foundered immediately, and the less secure were sent flying from their seats. The knights who did not go down, but passed through the opposition, rapidly turned their horses to engage their rivals again. The French historian, Michel Parisse, suggests that it was this characteristic rapid turn that gave the 'tournament' its name. There followed what they called the *meslee* as groups of knights manoeuvered their excited horses for advantage, and others struggled to secure a capture, especially one of the richer sort. It was also graphically called the 'ironworks' (*fereïs*), presumably because the ring and clatter of maces and swords on armour sounded like the din of a whole workshop of blacksmiths in action.

But this too was only a phase of the tournament. Eventually the struggling mass of horses and riders would break up. While the mêlée lasted in front of the stands, knights could take additional lances held by their squires at the nearby lists, and attempt to find the space to charge down another opponent if they could.[12] So soon enough, knights must have begun to break off from the tourneying mass, looking for advantage and opportunities. As individual riders took off across the field, with others in pursuit, the mêlée itself fragmented, and very soon the people in the stands at the lists would have seen only isolated knots of knights moving across the landscape into the distance, and lesser mêlées called *presses*.[13] On a large field like Anet-Sorel in 1179 the tourneyers spread out across the hectares of meadow and woodland along the River Eure. The Marshal biography tells us that on that occasion the fight continued across ditches and through woods, with barns acting as temporary forts for embattled groups.[14] At this point the knights might be joined on the field by others. In the mid thirteenth century at least, squires would range across the field on foot. On the field of a tournament between Boves and Corbie in the Amienois Reginald the castellan nearly fell victim to an ambitious squire, who leaped up and hung on to his neck trying to drag him to the ground.[15] Whether the squires were risking themselves on their own or their masters' account is not clear.

Tactics

There was a choice of two or three tactics for knights in the *estor* and *meslee*. The most dramatic was the use of the spear to strike from his horse the knight immediately opposite in the line, which was in fact the same tactic the jouster used. Success depended on keeping a solid seat in the saddle when the spear struck the opponent's shield. It also depended on keeping a distance from your opponent. It was Ulrich von Liechtenstein's favourite tactic. He describes a good run where he had sufficient control of his horse to veer it away from the oncoming rider and miss his lance, but then to lean back into him as he passed and throw him down. He also describes a bad run where the horses did not follow their natural instinct to avoid each other, and the shields and knees of each rider collided, shattering the shields and badly damaging their legs.[16] A strike could have a variety of outcomes. As John of Marmoutier indicates and Ulrich von Liechtenstein confirms, when both warriors kept their seats and the lances connected, the spears that struck home would more often than not be shattered into fragments by the force of the blow. Ulrich seems to imply that there was then a danger that the sharp splinters might penetrate the chain mail of the hauberk, like arrows. Another outcome might be that the shield was ripped from the shoulder of the opposing knight; inconvenient for him, but not sufficient to unseat him. If the spear did strike home and burst, it, or what remained of it, would be promptly thrown down and swords could be drawn. The knight might ride around and grab another lance from the squires lined up at the nearby lists. Ulrich used up nine lances in the small tournament at Korneuburg around 1226.[17]

A second tactic was much more skilful, for it depended on horsemanship, timing and coordination, and the knights who could do it were much praised by their colleagues. Both Huon d'Oisy and William Marshal's biographer describe a practice where knights discarded their spears and instead made a bid to seize the reins or bridle of their opponent's horse as he rode past in the *estor* or the subsequent mêlée. It was William Marshal's favourite tourneying tactic, skilful and elegant. It drew the applause that William so much enjoyed.[18] William's contemporary, Huon d'Oisy, also admired that particular tactic. He has his female tourneyers encouraging each other by shouting, 'Let's get their reins! They're in our power!'.[19] Having taken control of his adversary's horse, the knight had to use his physical strength and his own mount's momentum to drag his capture away. Without reins, his adversary had no control over his own horse and could be pulled helplessly off the field. His only choices were to cut the reins or take a big risk and jump off the horse; most knights would do neither of those things.

A third tactic was a lot cruder. As a knight passed by an opponent, or caught up with him in pusuit, he might simply grab him and try to wrestle him from his saddle. The count of Chalon attempted to take

Edward I of England prisoner in 1274 by seizing him around the neck and wrestling him off his horse. It did not work, as the king was tall and strong enough to spur his horse and drag the count from his mount instead, dumping him on the ground.[20] Some knights, confident of their physical strength, apparently made a practice of grabbing the chain mail coif – the hood under his helmet – and tried to haul their rival off by the neck. Others tried to pull their opponent down by seizing trailing straps from the shield. These were the robust and decisive tactics that Huon d'Oisy admired in the 1180s. Lancelot at Pomeglai and Bors at Chastel de la Marche was depicted as doing just this to grab and to disable their opponents.[21] Usually such a tactic just ripped off the hood, but one imagines that it could lead to dangerous neck injuries. Once a man was down, the successful knight would leap on to him and force his surrender.

Naturally the great prizes of the tournaments were those kings, dukes and counts who had valiantly flung themselves into the mêlée. The reason so few kings actually rode in tournaments is demonstrated in literature. Lancelot plunged into the press of knights surrounding the king of Norgales and his guards, 'all endeavouring to capture the king from under the noses of his knights, for it was a great deed of prowess'.[22] Prowess was one motive, and profit was another. Philip de Remy's king of Scotland was at one point surrounded by a score of men grabbing for him, eager for the proverbial king's ransom, until his bodyguard rode up and dispersed them.[23] Princes and magnates knew the dangers and they rode into the tournament surrounded by a life guard of scores of their own knights, as Gilbert Marshal did at Hertford in 1241, although it did not do him much good, because they were ill-disciplined and broke up to run off after ransoms.[24] Chrétien de Troyes alludes to this practice in *Le Chevalier de la Charette* when he notes the practice of household knights assiduously clearing the way for their lords in the *estor* and the mêlée.[25] All too often these guards did their lords no good. Huon d'Oisy imagined the countess of Champagne swamped despite the efforts of her *gent*, her household, by a hundred would-be captors before she surrendered to Alice de Montfort who had seized her reins.[26] Historical sources say the same. For instance, there was a protracted and crowded struggle to capture, liberate and recapture the wealthy count of Clermont at the tournament of Maintenon-Nogent in 1179; it became so dangerous to the count that the Young King called off his household from the mêlée in fear for his safety.[27] The death of Geoffrey of Brittany in August 1186 occurred because he was knocked off his horse in just such a dangerous mêlée, as knights tried to grab him and his own men tried to protect him. In 1292 the Statute of Arms allowed English earls and barons to wear more elaborate armour than the knights on the field, presumably acknowledging the greater danger in which they were at tournaments.[28]

William Marshal's principal job in the mêlée was to act as minder for his king and make sure he was not taken; but, once it appeared that the Young King was looking after himself, Marshal seems to have been all too ready to ride across the field with his own henchmen to hunt down exposed groups of knights, a practice which brought much criticism on him.[29] Ironically, his son, Earl Gilbert Marshal, died partly because of his household's greed for ransoms. The young earl was not as accomplished or as sturdy a knight as his famous father, but he was determined to seek fame on the tournament field nevertheless. He rode with his large body of minders onto a field outside Hertford on Thursday 27 June 1241, but found himself struggling to manage a new Italian horse which was far too high-spirited for his limited abilities as a rider. As the more experienced knights of his household galloped off after ransoms, Earl Gilbert found himself unable to keep up, and as he spurred his mount and dragged at the reins, they snapped and he found himself being carried off helplessly on a wild and uncontrollable horse. His men were unable to get near him to help, and eventually swooning with the stress and heat, he lost his seat and was dragged along quite a distance bumping behind the runaway, his foot still caught in a stirrup, probably by tangling with one of his spurs. He died some hours later at Hertford priory from terrible internal injuries.[30]

The tournament field was noisy, not just because of the screaming of the warhorses and the shouts of their riders, but also because of the noise of the onlookers. The squires and other spectators shouted to encourage the riders. Drums and horns continued to thunder and bray throughout the action. Heralds were expected to flatter, to encourage and to praise at the top of their voices. They might try to alert their masters to a new threat: 'Here now! Noble knights! Help the men who need it more!' shouted one herald at Chastel de Molin, as a new company rode up to challenge his side.[31] Heralds would announce the arrival in combat of a particular favourite in words like those of the Prose Lancelot: 'Look out, it's my lord Gawain! Run for it! Show us your heels!'[32] Another sample of a herald's acclaim is given by Jakemes, basing it on the knight's own warcry: 'Coucy! Coucy! Here's to the bravest of men: his praise ought to the ring out as far as Rome! Here's to Coucy the brave knight! Here's to the castellan of Coucy! Coucy!'[33] There was certainly emotion in the stands. King Arthur and the ladies of Logres were so dismayed by the temporary rout of the Round Table at the tournament of Camelot-Montingnet by Lancelot and the men of King Baudemagus, that they were in agonies of humiliation and tears.[34] But when things went otherwise, and the ladies disapproved of a poor show by one side: 'then the mood went against them, and the ladies in the stands abused and heaped insults on them, calling them cowardly runaways'.[35]

Ransoms

The aim of the tournament, for everyone but the magnates involved, was to take ransoms and avoid being taken captive. That was the main aim of the tournament in the twelfth and thirteenth century for many knights. When in the *Prose Lancelot* Gawain and Yvain came unexpectedly upon a tournament in session, they asked a spectator why the knights were fighting: 'to win horses and capture knights', was the terse reply.[36] Not everyone was happy with the profit motive. Henry de Laon curtly dismissed it: 'Tournaments were not originally held as a way of capturing horses, but so as to learn who was manly in his conduct'.[37] Henry was writing in the middle of the thirteenth century, at a time when knighthood had become thoroughly aristocratic. By then the ransom system might be made to seem grubby and beneath the true nobleman, the devotee of free-spending Largesse. Henry could pretend that there was an earlier and purer age of tournaments where ransoms were unimportant, but we who are acquainted with William Marshal know differently, of course.

If they were secured before they could be rescued by their friends, the captive knights seem to have been kept in the safe areas within the lists, which would account for their name of *recets*. The key point according to the Marshal biographer was when the captured men offered their verbal good faith (*fiance*) that they had surrendered to him and acknowledged that they were subject to penalties. If the captives did this, and could be trusted, then they might even return to the field and seek better luck.[38] At Lagny in November 1179 the Norman, William des Préaux, had been taken prisoner, and should have left the field, but sneaked back on to enjoy the show, wearing a hauberk under his robes and a light iron cap on his head. At Épernon in 1179, William Mauvoisin rejoined the fight with perfect propriety after being taken prisoner earlier in the day.[39] Knights might well gang up to secure prisoners and share the ransom once it was pledged. William Marshal found himself at one time in his early career desperately trying to evade the clutches of five knights who were working to try to bring him down.[40] The mêlée of the tournament was not a place where combatants had immediate leisure and space for one-to-one combats.

For knights like William Marshal it was the taking of ransoms that mattered. From the Marshal biography, it seems that he generally took the horses of his victims as his prizes, as many as ten at Eu in 1178 x 79. At Valennes in 1166 he took a half share in a horse of a knight he and another knight both claimed as a capture.[41] There was a lot of profit to be had in ransomed destriers, but that sort of tariff showed a certain politic compassion too: all but the poorest knights could replace horses, and most rode to the tournament with at least three in their train, according to Jean Renart. The Marshal's known reasonableness in regard to ransoms may not have been entirely a matter of generosity, although his biography often asserts that he could be free-handed with ransoms. His reputation for generosity would make his job easier, in that everyone in trouble knew that he would offer them a liberal tariff. This may account for the choice of a group of fifteen beleaguered Picard knights sheltering in a barn at the Anet-Sorel tournament of 1179 to surrender to him, rather than to others from his side. They feared, as they said, the greed of his colleagues. The Marshal's colleagues in turn were aghast at his opportunism in taking what was offered to him and protested vigorously at their deprivation.[42]

Knights less confident than the Marshal that further victims would endlessly offer themselves would be less inclined to be generous to their prisoners. It was possible to find financial ruin on the tournament field. William, brother of Earl Richard de Clare of Gloucester, found nothing but disgrace and humiliation on the tournament fields of France in 1251. Philip de Remy, in his romance *Jehan et Blonde* (c. 1241) pictures Jehan's father as such a man: 'he had estates that were worth 500 *livres* if they had been not been burdened by the debts and assignments on them: in his youth he had spent freely in order to follow the tourneys, the expenses of which he would now gladly have rid himself '.[43] It is difficult to avoid the suspicion that Philip was recalling here someone in his own life. It would be unwise to think that William Marshal was quite as heedlessly generous as his biographer implies. He tells us of an arrangement made between the Marshal and a Flemish knight of similar interests, Roger de Jouy. The two men pledged to share out the profits they made in ransoms taken in one entire tournament year, from Pentecost to Lent. The biographer saw a parchment roll by which William and Roger reckoned up their profits from the 103 ransoms they took that year.[44] It was a canny arrangement for two reasons. It spread the risk to them as individuals of taking losses. Furthermore, as William was English and Roger was a Fleming, they would not have fought on the same side on the circuit, and so were not necessarily in direct competition. William seems happy to have contemplated profiting from Roger's captures of men on his own side.

Casualties and Fatalities

Dangerous the tournament assuredly was, but how common were fatalities? How common and regretted were human casualties? Ecclesiastical authors looked upon sudden death in tournaments as God's judgement on the violent men who attended them, and one of the earliest records of a tournament, near Valenciennes in 1139, dwelt on the instructive death of its promoter by a spear thrust to the chest.[45] But such sources were not unbiased, and might very well dwell too much on the dangers to body because they wanted to save the soul. In Baldwin of Hainault's first tournament at Maastricht in 1168, a knight called Walter de Honnecourt was killed.[46] The fact that a tournament was remembered because a death had occurred in it perhaps tells us that fatalities were isolated incidents and not necessarily as common as the critics of tournaments alleged.

Literary and historical descriptions of fatalities usually treat them as tragic accidents; but sometimes they allege that they were not accidents at all, but concealed homicides. In the tournament at Pomeglai, Lancelot rode directly at a knight who was opposite him in the ranks, and knocked him clear out of saddle by a spear blow which caught him in the throat. His opponent was mortally wounded and the fighting stopped around him when onlookers took up the cry 'He's dead! He's dead!' Lancelot was horrified, threw down his lance and was proposing to leave the field when he discovered that his victim was the seneschal of his mortal enemy. At this, his conscience stopped bothering him and he decided to fight on.[47] At Chauvency in 1280, when two young knights crashed together and horses and men went down in a flailing heap, the stands erupted as people shouted: 'They're dead! They're dead! Lord God what a tragedy!'[48] An historical parallel to the Lancelot story was the death of Ernaut de Montigny in a joust at Walden in Essex in 1252. His adversary, Roger de Leyburne, caught Ernaut in the space below his helm where he was unarmoured, and sliced through his throat with his lance. Again the knights and magnates present were horrified, and Ernaut's unwitting killer was distraught, pledging that he would go on crusade as a way of atoning for the blood he had spilt. But later gossip had it that Roger had a grudge against Ernaut and therefore Roger had contrived to commit a murder dressed up as manslaughter.[49]

Descriptions like this show that tourneyers looked upon accidental deaths as out of the ordinary and much to be deplored. If there was a large casualty list the reason may have been that sometimes knights deliberately played hard and dangerous. The tournament at Hertford in June 1241 was notorious because two men died, Earl Gilbert Marshal and one of his knights, and many others were seriously injured: personal grudges had caused the knights to treat the occasion more like a battle.[50] In May 1241 there had been another tournament across the Channel at Neuss in the Rhineland, where casualties had been exceptionally high; as many as sixty killed and seriously injured amongst the knights and squires present. Although the chroniclers say that this was God's vengeance for the contempt that the knights had shown for the friars who had attempted to halt the meeting, it may be that the friars had tried to stop them because they knew that personal hatreds made the tournament too risky.[51]

Deaths were regretted and exceptional, but they were likely to happen. Perhaps they were proportionally more likely to happen to the great men present at tournaments. As we have already seen, princes, dukes and counts were the objects of much unwelcome attention during the mêlées, as when Duke Geoffrey of Brittany died under the hooves of the knights who were trying to defend and to attack him in 1185. The mortality rate of counts in the medieval tournament perhaps parallels that of subalterns on the Western Front. For different reasons, they were likely to draw unwelcome attention from the enemy. There is quite a distinguished roll of noble casualties. In 1216 Geoffrey de Mandeville, earl of Essex, died as the result of a wound received in a tournament at London.[52] In 1234 Count Florence of Holland died after a fall from his horse in a tournament in northern France, as did his younger brother William not long afterwards. In 1251 Count William de Dampierre of Flanders died apparently as a result of a heart attack brought on by his exertions in a tournament at Trazegnies. In 1286 William son of Earl John de Warenne of Surrey died in suspicious circumstances at a tournament at Croydon.[53] A curious and unwelcome coincidence is recorded in an Alsatian chronicle which noted the death of Lantfrid of Hohen-Landsberg by suffocation in a tournament at Strasbourg in 1279, thirty years to the day after his father had likewise died at in a tournament at the same city.[54] The deaths of great men such as these on the tournament field were not readily forgotten and must have had a cumulative effect. It is not unlikely that the tragic death in 1293 of King Edward I's son-in-law, Duke John of Brabant and Limbourg, at the tournament held as part of the marriage celebrations between another of the king's daughters and the count of Bar, confirmed the old king in his determination to clamp down on tournaments in England.[55]

If deaths were out of the ordinary events in the tournament, injuries must have been common. Literary and historical accounts will talk generally of knights sustaining many hurts. Some of them were ugly. At the fighting at Arthur's Christmas court reported in the *Prose Lancelot*, Lancelot was run through the flesh of his left thigh and saddle with a lance, which then broke off in the wound, leaving the spearhead and the shattered and bloody truncheon sticking out. Lancelot, being Lancelot, pulled it out, bandaged it up without flinching and was able to pass himself off to his panicky friend Galehot as being unharmed. The queasiness of the onlookers and the fears for his life, however, were probably rather more realistic.[56] We occasionally get some indications of the nature of tournament injuries. Hands seem to have been vulnerable, despite the wearing of mailed mittens. A Rhineland knight, Gerard Wascard, had part of his hand severed in a tournament at Neuss in the 1180s, presumably from the slash of a sword. Ulrich von Liechtenstein lost a finger after a lance injury to his right hand in 1222, and a few years later wounded an opponent, Conrad von Nidecke, in the same way.[57] This may explain the adoption of more heavily armoured gauntlets by knights at the end of the century. Legs too were vulnerable, especially in a fall. The notable thirteenth-century English champion, Roger of Leyburne, sustained a broken leg in a tournament at some time before 1252, most likely from a bad fall.[58] The fact that lances might well strike knights full on the chest meant that bruising and mangling by the chain mail links of his hauberk was the very least a knight might expect. Ulrich von Liechtenstein's shield and hauberk were both pierced by Ottold von Graz's lance in a joust in 1226. Ulrich's chest sustained a deep cut which stained his white outfit with blood and which needed a surgeon to dress.

Smashed fingers and noses, broken limbs, bloody abrasions and heavy bruising were the least of what tourneyers might expect. Powerful warriors could dispense heavy blows that would do serious physical damage, because most tournaments allowed the use of unblunted swords. They would not hold back in a tournament where sword play with sharp edges was allowed. This is how Lancelot dispensed punishment to a knight after himself receiving a great cut from a sword:

> Lancelot closed with him sword in hand, and handed out such a blow on the left shoulder that he sliced through the mail of his hauberk. Lancelot's sword cut down through the flesh till it reached the shoulder bone, and he was borne to the ground by the agony that he experienced.[59]

The grand tournament demanded a huge physical effort from knights. Unlike the joust, it went on and on, sometimes for hours. In that respect it was far better training for battle. But for this reason, cautious voices from the beginning advised against new knights – who could be as young as sixteen in some parts of France – taking to the field, but rather that they should stick to bohorts and jousts. Henry de Laon talked of the stifling heat within the knight's great helm, and the drenching of sweat and blood that would soak a knight's body: 'this', he memorably said, 'I call the high bath of honour'.[60]

We have less indication of the casualty rate of the other chief participants in the tournament, the horses. The fact that horses were being protected by leather plates and chain mail as early as the middle of the twelfth century (see p. 143–4) is however grim evidence that there had been an unacceptable level of fatalities and injuries at an earlier period. More details begin to emerge in the later thirteenth century, and they are alarming. Henry de Laon scoffed at the lust for taking ransoms of horses, when even the winning side tended to kill three out of every four of its own mounts.[61] Maybe he was exaggerating, but in his tour of northern French tournaments in 1260–62 the Lord Edward, son of Henry III, ran up the large debt of around £70 for horses which had to be replaced. He had still not paid it off more than twenty years later. In 1309, Gilbert de Clare, earl of Gloucester, attended a tournament at

Dunstable and on that occasion his retinue lost two horses to fatal accidents and another to ransom.[62] Ann Hyland, the historian of horses, has
deduced that the mêlée was less likely to be a dangerous place for a horse
than the joust, which had '. . . the stupid aim of bowling over horse and
rider with the combined force of speeding horse and aggressive rider'.
But even so, equine behaviour dictated that when aggressive, trained
stallions came into proximity, they would fight with bites and kicks. The
injuries would perhaps rarely be fatal and could be ignored in the anger
and excitement of the mêlée, but we can easily understand why it was
that Duke John of Brabant in England in 1293 was spending fifteen
shillings on treating two of his horses injured in a tournament at
Northampton.[63]

The Ending of the Tournament

The day's sport might end in a variety of ways. If there was no decisive
outcome in the grand charge, even a small tournament could go on until
mid afternoon, or up till dusk.[64] In that case, it is not possible that the
fighting would have been continuous throughout the afternoon.
Descriptions such as those in the Marshal biography indicate that the
fighting broke up into knots of struggling men scattered over the many
hundreds of hectares of the tournament field, losing themselves in
woods, vineyards and plantations. As each mêlée was resolved, knights
could find themselves scattered further and further apart. Some groups
took shelter and rested in barns, or took up positions protected by
woods and ditches to treat their injuries in peace. Others scoured the
field for new victims as individuals or in groups, careful to avoid
ambushes. Others indeed took advantage of woods and hedges to set
ambushes for the unwary. In the lulls between fighting, parties of squires
undertook the dangerous task of trespassing on the field to secure loose
horses and help their masters if they could.[65]

A tournament could end decisively and sometimes rapidly. Huon de
Méry provides the best indication when he talks of the bulk of the
knights of one side losing heart and breaking to take cover within the
lists of its base, in this case because the leader of one party had been
taken prisoner.[66] In that sense, the tournament could end in the same
way as a battle, with a rout. The *Prose Lancelot* depicts examples of such
defeats. For instance, when Arthur's team was outnumbered three to
one, it was pressed back on the lists of its base through sheer weight of

numbers. In the tournament which Lancelot watched between the teams of the Chastel as Puceles and the Chastel as Dames, the team of the Chastel as Dames was driven back on the lists of its base through fear of the prowess of the knights Hector and Lionel. But in that case the defeat was not final, because Lancelot rallied them and led them out again.[67]

The survivors on the defeated side would ride hard to find protection. At Chastel de Molin, the defeated team scattered away from the stands and took cover in nearby woodland. At Camelot-Montingnet the men of Bademagus scattered, some taking cover in the woods and others riding hard for the lists at their base of Montingnet; Bademagus himself helped the disabled Lancelot to concealment in a grove of sycamores to investigate his injuries.[68] The best option was to head for the lists of the team base, where infantry would have been deployed to fend off pursuers who were too enthusiastic. This is what happened in December 1251 at a historical tournament fought at Rochester in England between two teams, the native born English and the king's foreign relatives and their followers. The 'aliens' finally broke under English pressure and began to flee towards the nearby city to seek safety, one presumes, within the lists. Unfortunately for them they came upon a force of English squires stationed on the road into the city. They were set upon with maces and clubs, badly beaten and many were taken prisoner.[69] Several of the Marshal tournaments ended in routs. As far as William Marshal and his like were concerned, this would not have been the ideal outcome. It limited the chances for taking profitable ransoms and displaying the skills that would have attracted the prize.

7

The Après-Tournoi

Following the departure from the field – which Philip de Remy describes as the bedraggled mirror-image of the morning's review, and Huon de Méry remembered as being a sweet release from the fatigue of the day – was a period of disorder. Physicians and others were on hand to treat and wash injuries.[1] Literary sources give some details of the limited treatment available. Agravain's serious wounds after his encounter with Bors were inspected by people in the castle, washed (rather sensibly) in wine as a disinfectant, treated with 'ointment'. Then he was confined to bed until he was fit to leave. Gawain's shoulder wound was inspected by a physician, pronounced clean, and then he was bandaged and put in a room to a heal for a month 'far from people so as to be quiet'.[2]

The Marshal biography depicts something similar to Philip's account of the confusion of the *après-tournoi.*

> Well, that was not quite the end of the day for them, for there was much still to be done and for each man to think about. The truth of the matter is that there was such a throng that there were more people than at a fairground. Some were looking for their friends, captured during the combat, whilst others were searching for their equipment. Others were making persistent enquiries of many who had taken part in the tournament as to whether they had heard news of their kinsmen, of their friends, and as to whether they knew who had taken them. And, for their part, those who were in pledge wanted a ransom or surety to be forthcoming through the offices of a friend or acquaintance. The reason why the throng was so numerous was that everyone asks in this way after any tournament for some indication of the losses he had sustained. In brief, it is for this reason that the high-ranking men were still there assembled, as I said before, whether on their own behalf or on behalf of friends.[3]

Twelfth-century ideas of customary justice generally involved appealing to the court of the most potent grandee available to hear a complaint. The disputes after tournaments were settled in just that way. The lodgings of the greater magnates present might become impromptu courts

of honour as knights argued over whether pledges had been given, and
who had given and received them. In such a way, the aggrieved Matthew
de Walincourt appealed to the Young King to get William Marshal to
restore the horse he had taken from Matthew at the tournament of Eu
(1178 x 79). Both men gave their evidence to the king in the hearing of
the other great magnates present, and the king was expected to judge the
complaint, assisted in this case by the dukes and counts at his side, and
supposedly influenced by the derisory hooting of Matthew's preposter-
ous claim by the onlookers.[4] When the Marshal pursued his own
complaints he was just as keen to enlist magnates, such as his appeal
against Peter Leschans, who with a companion deprived him of two
horses he had secured in the tournament of Anet-Sorel of 1179. The
Marshal took his case to Peter's uncle, the great French knight, William
des Barres the elder, and put pressure on him to restore one of the
horses, which Peter reluctantly had to do, after the Marshal evaded an
attempt at a compromise of offering half the value.[5]

The Award of the Prize

The other thing that was adjudged by one or more of the magnates in
the evening was the award of the prize of the tournament, if one had
been offered. The acclaim of the more intrepid participants by heralds
and spectators during the day would have provided a short list for their
consideration. We have a sample of the sort of acclamations that would
ring in the ears of the crowd's favourite as he rode off through the
lists: 'Welcome to the flower of knighthood! Welcome to the best of
the best!'. That was the way the ladies in the stands hailed Lancelot as
he left the field of Chastel as Dames.[6] The 'flors des chevaliers' is a title
we find awarded to elite knights in a whole range of historical and
fictional works of the late twelfth and thirteenth century, and it certainly
rang in the ears of William Marshal in his day. The point when the
prize was awarded seems to have varied. Famously, at Pleurs in the late
1170s, the Marshal heard the news that he had been given the prize of
a pike as a blacksmith was attempting to dislodge his helmet, which
had been jammed on his head by the great number of heavy blows it
had sustained.[7] The judgements in Arthurian romances were sometimes announced as the knights rode off the field and re-entered the
lists. At Chastel de la Marche they lined up in front of the stand for
the announcement by King Brangoire.[8] At Le Fère-Vendeuil the prize

was announced after a consultation during the dinner.[9] William Marshal, according to his biographer, was often awarded the prize, as at Ressons-Gournay in 1180 x 81, when the count of Flanders and the other magnates awarded it to him, despite the Marshal's known estrangement from his then master, the Young King Henry. The reason for the award would seem to have been the performance of notable feats of horsemanship and arms, as much as success in taking prisoners

Naturally, the award of the prize is prominent in romance literature. What better way was there to establish the physical pre-eminence of the young hero amongst his fellows? Guy of Warwick, Gerart de Nevers and Philip de Remy's king of Scotland all get the tournament prize. Guy of Warwick and the king get the prize in their first major tournament event, as an unarguable way of illustrating their military virtue. Establishing surpassing excellence was what this literary convention was about. In the *Roman de la Violette*, King Louis observes Gerart de Nevers preparing for the meeting at Saint-Trond and says to his entourage: 'This is the fellow who will get the honours in the tournament. If ever I was a judge of a knight, there will be no other today who will come near him in the fight', and naturally it was Gerart who was acclaimed as the winner of the prize.[10] The process of judging the winner is opaque to us. In Arthurian literature it was often left to the ladies. At Chastel de la Marche, the king's daughter and her ladies retired to the back of their stand to debate intensely the performance of each knight. They had to choose not just the champion, but select another twelve to honour as the next worthiest in valour and accomplishment. At Camelot, the ladies in the stand, who were not that day the judges, still debated fiercely the candidacy as champion of Gawain and Bors.[11]

Where the prize was awarded by a lady, she must have taken some part in the award. At Pleurs in the later 1170s, it was indeed the countess who had offered the prize who awarded it to her choice of winner, the duke of Burgundy.[12] At Le Fère-Vendeuil two prizes of a falcon had been offered by the countess of Soissons, one for those within and another for those without. Her part in the award was carefully choreographed. No announcement was made after the judges had consulted. The chief herald surreptitiously located the lucky recipient at the dinner, and the countess and her lady attendants danced and sang their way to where the herald indicated he was sitting, passing the falcon from one to another in a sort of figure dance. When the countess reached the prize winner, she stopped, pulled him out and solemnly awarded it with the words: 'My lord, of those within you most properly have the prize.' The winner of those without had to be visited more prosaically, as he was in bed in his lodgings, having been badly wounded, and could not attend the dinner.[13]

Like any sport, the tournament loved champions. People enjoyed telling tales of the exploits of famous tourneyers, and nothing charmed them so much as to compare the skills and capacities of the leaders of the tournament of their own day. Each no doubt had his favourite, whose virtues and accomplishments he would praise. So the tournament in every generation produced its elite. In the later twelfth century several men other than William Marshal were recognised as great on the field and in the assemblies. His master, the Young King, was praised as:

> ... the best king who ever took up a shield, the most daring and best of all tourneyers. From the time when Roland was alive, and even before, never was seen a knight so skilled, so warlike, whose fame resounded so around the world – even if Roland did come back, or if the world were searched as far as the River Nile and the setting sun.[14]

The Dinners

After the greater tournaments the magnates present favoured their men, friends and selected prisoners with lavish dinners, the counterpart of the receptions they had hosted in the vespers the previous evening. Dinners were offered at each of the pole settlements of the tournament, and they might continue from sunset to dawn on the next day according to Henry de Laon. There was a lot of pressure to get into dinners, with knights clamouring for an invitation from the host, and gatecrashers pretending to be minstrels and entertainers, hoping no one would ask them to perform.[15] Of course the dinners would be more joyous and hilarious in the lodgings of the winning team. The winner of the prize would reap further rewards, with a place of honour at the patron's table, the best food, the devoted attention of the ladies and universal acclaim.[16] Literary accounts of tournaments add that in the heat of summer the hosts might offer dinner in the cool of evening in brilliantly-illuminated marquees. This happened at Chastel de la Marche in the *Prose Lancelot*, in the Round Table held by the countess of Champagne at Machault in *Sone de Nansay*, and at the conclusion of the jousting at Le Fère-Veudreuil depicted by Jakemes, where dinner was laid out in the evening in the flower-filled river meadows between the woods and the green waters of the Oise.[17]

For a man outside a comital or ducal household to receive an invitation to these final events was to receive social patronage of a high order; and for his part, the tournament's prizewinner could choose which dinner to grace with his presence, where, like Gerart de Nevers and William Marshal, he would be courted and fêted by those who wanted to acquire the glamour of his acquaintance. Jakemes tells us that the guests would change into rich costumes and approach the tables in pairs, marshalled by heralds to the accompaniment of trumpets and drums. At Le Fère, he depicts each tourneying nation dressing in different coloured robes; the Flemings, for instance, were all in gold silk figured with little black lions, the livery of the count of Flanders.[18] Jean Renart depicts the glittering scene as the barons, knights and ladies came down into the halls of their lodgings in fresh linen:

> It was as if the lodging was alight from the number of torches that were burning there. This famous count and that famous baron came down from their chambers, and their entourages with them, each with a number of prisoners who were dressed in no more than their shirts and protective gambaisons. They found the tables laid out, and those entrusted to do the job had provided wine and food as fine as anyone could want. There was welcome hot water to wash the bruises on their skin where they had taken heavy blows and to cleanse their fair faces.[19]

Then there were – as the *History of William Marshal* portrays them – evenings of funny stories, much singing, dancing and recollections of the day's glories and humiliations by the participants, as the adrenalin drained out of their systems and left them exhausted. The standard of the entertainment may have been high, and Huon de Méry depicts sublime music of viols, harps and singers lulling the diners to sleep, even at the Antichrist's banquet. Huon d'Oisy's 'Tournoi des Dames' may even be such a song composed for the evening after the tournament, written to amuse both the male participants and the female onlookers with a topsy-turvy mirror version of what they had just been experiencing in the field.[20] The last word belongs to the knight, Philip de Remy, who tells us that everyone slept late the day after the tournament. We may well believe him.

8

The Rise of the Joust

Good evidence of the social impact of the grand mêlée tournament was the way that other groups besides knights attempted to share in something of its excitement. It may be that the eleventh-century tournament grew out of a field of related military sports and exercises, which ranged from simple horseback games and parades to the more specific training exercise of the quintain. But some amusements just as obviously grew out of the tournament, notably the 'tirocinium', the special tournament for tiros, or beginners. Then there is the way that the lower social group of the urban elite borrowed and copied the tournament and joust and played at them within their walls, town fields and market places, as was happening as early as the twelfth century.[1]

One of the earliest examples of this diffusion throughout society of knightly games may have been the event staged by the townspeople of St-Omer when they formally received William Clito as their count in April 1127. A mock battle was engaged in between the young count and his retinue on one side, and the armed youths of the town on the other, playing at being bowmen and cavalry. It ended in the count seizing the town's banner and entering the gates at the head of the young men of St-Omer.[2] We find something similar in England in the 1170s, a time when the knightly mêlée tournament was forbidden there by the king. The author, William fitz Stephen, describes in high-flown language the London play tournaments which happened on Sunday evenings in Lent:

> Every Sunday in Lent after dinner a fresh swarm of young gentles goes forth on war-horses, steeds skilled in the context, of which each is apt and schooled to wheel in circles round. From the gates burst forth in throngs the lay sons of citizens, armed with lance and shield, the younger with shafts forked at the end, but with steel point removed. They make war's semblance, and in mimic contest exercise their skill at arms. Many courtiers come too, when the king is in residence; and from the households of earls and barons come young men not yet invested with the belt

of knighthood, that they may there contend together. Each one of them is on fire with hope of victory. The fierce horses neigh, their limbs tremble, they champ the bit, impatient of delay they cannot stand still. When at length the hoofs of trampling steeds careers along, the youthful riders divide their hosts. Some pursue those that fly before, and cannot overtake them; others unhorse their comrades and speed by.[3]

As well as these mock battles and play skirmishes there were more individual contests in the twelfth century, which like the tournament must have emerged from an earlier horseback culture. A game persistently mentioned throughout the twelfth and thirteenth centuries was the 'quintain', usually in connection with court festivities. The mid twelfth-century epic, *Girart de Rousillon*, opens with Charles Martel holding a court at Pentecost in Reims, and Girart's knights amusing themselves by setting up a quintain as the focus of their recreation. The king, incidentally, was not amused. He was worried that the roughness of these games would lead to bad blood and real fighting. Anyone caught at them was threatened with the loss of his eyes.[4] A contemporary epic, *Raoul de Cambrai*, has a similar episode at a Pentecost court of Emperor Louis. The newly-knighted Bernier was invited to ride at a quintain set up in the meadows the day after the religious feast. The quintain was described there as a mannekin constructed out of posts hung with two hauberks and two shields. Bernier's lance blow on the shield was so effective that he shattered the counterpoised pole, and tore open the hauberks.[5] Early in the thirteenth century, the *Prose Lancelot* described the 'young bachelors' at the quintain at Arthur's Easter court 'as was the custom at the time'.[6]

It is not just the literary sources that tell us that the quintain was a popular courtly amusement. Count Philip of Flanders held his Pentecost court in his city of Arras in 1177. In the city in the week after the religious feast was the student, Gerald of Wales, making his way home from Paris. He took lodgings on the market square and woke one morning to find it a sea of people. The count had commanded that a quintain should be set up for the squires and new knights of the court to exercise themselves. So a great post with shields was erected in the middle, with a stout rectangular fence around it to keep back the crowds. The count and the nobility sat on their fine horses, dressed in their fine silks, and Gerald, in an upper window of his lodgings, had a good view of the impressive scene. The great square was packed and every window had faces in it, and great shouts went up as each youngster made his run at the post, and so it went on for over an hour, until the count rode off with his court.[7] In such circumstances, we can see why the quintain, like the tournament, was an object of aspiration for the urban elite, which found the amusements pursued in the royal courts to be irresistible, and which presumed to be quite good at them. In 1253 the household squires and young knights of King Henry III challenged the rich youths of London to a match at a quintain yard in or near the city. The Londoners won, but in winning caused bad blood with the king's household. The event degenerated into insults and fights, just as Charles Martel feared it would at his fictional court.[8] From this we can assume that the quintain was not necessarily regarded as a safe amusement for the young male.

One of the most intriguing of these parallel horseback amusements, participated in by urban youths and noble squires, was the one called the 'bohort' by the mid twelfth century. This obscure word is rendered variously (*bohort, behordicium, buhurdicium, boherd*) and there is no standard spelling for it. The word is frequently used in the twelfth century, and there is a pattern to its use which is revealing. The mid twelfth-century *Romance of Thebes* pictures the Greek army camped outside the city, with its squires watering the horses and amusing themselves in the fields by the bohort. From the same time the epic *Raoul de Cambrai* describes the son of one of its heroes as being trained up in the use of arms and in the bohort.[9] It is tempting to put the bohort down as being the *Homo habilis* to the *Homo sapiens* of the tournament: an older and more primitive pre-tournament species out of which the tournament grew, and for a while continued alongside, but that may not necessarily be the case.

Bohorts were the spontaneous amusements of the young. They were not in general formally arranged and organised; most bohorts just happened. As well as William fitz Stephen, Wace of Bayeux expected such games to be carried out with blunted weapons, and German sources describe bohorts which took place with no weapons at all.[10] As a result, bohorts were not generally subject to royal and ecclesiastical restrictions. The Knights Templars, for instance, were unable to tourney because of the papal ban, but their Rule permitted them to participate in bohorts, provided they did not get carried away and start throwing lances about.[11] There was one occasion in 1234 when the squires of two noble English households were forbidden to hold a *buhurdicium* at Sherborne in Dorset because of the evident danger that the fighting would become serious and deaths would result.[12] Probably the fact that this meeting of squires had been advertised and organised lifted it out of the class of bohorts in any case.

Bohorts were generally put on impromptu for fun, and were not serious amusements, although bad temper could surface in them. Perhaps the most famous example of this was the bohort which happened at Messina in Sicily on the evening of 2 February 1191. King Richard was out riding with knights of his household and some French knights after dinner. Feeling like some fun, they commandeered a stack of canes from a passing peasant and held a bohort in the road. Unfortunately the celebrated French knight, William des Barres – who had the bad luck to tear King Richard's hat – was subjected to vigorous retaliation by that mercurial and egotistical monarch. He had the further bad luck of possessing the skill and adroitness to evade the king's attempts at vengeance. Utterly enraged, the king swore and struck at William, and vowed mortal emnity with him, leaving the French knight no choice but to flee Messina.[13] Things were not supposed to get so serious, and elsewhere bohorts are found rated with dancing as appropriate amusements for wedding festivities, or as part of the leisure activities around great courts held by kings.[14] Even so, they remained notorious for getting out of hand.

Perhaps the best image we have of a court bohort is that literary one held at the Christmas court of King Arthur, imagined in the early thirteenth-century cyclical Prose Lancelot. After the Christmas dinner, which would be mid afternoon, a quintain was set up, 'as was traditional', so that the knights could show their prowess with the lance and, no doubt, burn off some calories. The king was then asked for permission for an informal tournament in which the knights carried only swords and shields, 'with no more armour that that', which was allowed on those conditions on the holy day. Even so, some were unhappy that it was allowed, forseeing casualties. There were two sides, as in a tourney: three hundred young bachelors of the king's household on one side and an equal number of Galehot's men on the other. The bohort was carried out in the meadows, and a charge brought the companies together. Unfortunately the restriction on arms and armour was not respected, and Lancelot and his colleagues fought with lances as well as swords in too much earnest, causing serious injuries. In the end Meleagant charged down Lancelot with a heavy and steel-tipped jousting lance 'as he should not have been carrying'. Lancelot was distracted by a combat with another knight and was not on guard, and Melea-gant ran him through his thigh with the lance, which broke off in the wound and embedded itself in the saddle. It was that which brought the knights to their senses. Horrified and alarmed, they threw down their weapons, 'and said they would skirmish (*bohorderont*) no more that day'.[15]

A variant of these courtly amusements was the scaled-down tourna-ment called the *tirocinium*, which seems to have reproduced tournament-like features but was restricted to recently-made knights (*tirones, tyrones*). Contemporaries did not regard them as serious events, judging by the evidence of Alexander Neckam's late twelfth-century word lists, which equates the *tirocinium* with the 'bohort'.[16] As we have seen already, young and inexperienced knights were, according to Neckam and others, easy victims of more experienced knights. *Tirocinia* gave them a chance to acquire experience in a restricted version of the grand tournament. There are few details surviving about *tirocinia*, but they were clearly associated with the passage into adulthood of young princes and magnates, and like the other sorts of bohort they were not subject to state or Church restrictions. In 1266 the archbishop of Rouen happily celebrated mass for knights at a *tirocinium* near Pontoise, although tournaments had by then been forbidden in the Capetian domain by Louis IX as well as by the pope.[17] Following the ceremonies of knighting and equipping, the prince or magnate and the young men knighted alongside him might skirmish in a bohort-style conflict, where they could be seen to advantage rather than be crushed by more experienced knights. So in Walter of Arras's *Eracle*, the emperor knights the eponymous hero along with thirty other youths, and the new knights spend the next day exercising their *chevalerie* to good effect. That this *chevalerie* was demonstrated at a bohort is evident from the similar knightings in the later twelfth-century epic *Garin*, after which the new knights 'go to a bohort'.[18] We have portraits of knightings at historical great courts which are very similar. So John of Marmoutier in the 1160s described the knighting in great style of Count Geoffrey of Anjou at Rouen in June 1128 alongside thirty other young Angevin hopefuls, which was followed by their 'exerting themselves in warlike games'.[19] In Germany in 1184 the Emperor Frederick Barbarossa knighted his sons, after which the court held a bohort, which could not have been much more than a cavalcade, as they were armed only with shields.[20]

The Round Table and the Lure of Pageantry

Bohorts were amusements for the young and the relaxed, and as such were a welcome variation on the great event itself. They were not by any means challenges or alternatives to the dominance of the grand tournament, but a challenge eventually emerged. When it did, it emerged from within the tournament itself. As a sporting event, the tournament, as we have seen, was a complex creature, involving team work, ceremony, parade and an element of individual competition. It was that last element, the joust, which developed into a separate devotion and cult at the cost of the main event.

The joust was an amusement which was as old, and possibly older, than the tournament itself. Jousting, as we have seen, was related to the ancient practice of champions engaging in single combats between armies. In Middle French the verb *joster* can simply mean 'to encounter'. The earliest reference to what we mean by a 'joust' comes in the context of a tournament, when Count Henry of Brabant was killed in the preliminary jousting at a tournament at Tournai in 1095. But there is no reference to knights gathering simply to joust for sport until the thirteenth century. The likelihood is that jousting long remained a tournament preliminary and sideshow, in the vespers and the *commençailles* we have already looked at. But in the thirteenth century the joust and the grand tournament began to part company.

There is no hint in the Marshal biography that jousting in the 1170s and 1180s had at that time sufficient favour with knights to seduce them from the grand tournament. They clearly valued the jousts that sometimes preceded the tournament, but did not prefer them. By the second decade of the thirteenth century this had changed with a vengeance. The Marshal biographer himself notes around 1224, in an aside, how in his day noblemen preferred hawks, hounds and jousting to serious tourneying.[21] The generation of Ulrich von Liechtenstein in Austria apparently amused itself in the 1220s with meetings devoted to joustings as much as to tourneying. When Ulrich made his first great tour in 1226, disguised as 'Queen Venus', he spent twenty-nine days jousting his way from Venetia north to Bohemia.[22] The new preference for jousting comes out in a number of ways. First, there was an extended amount of time and a greater importance given to the *commençailles* jousting. Instead of taking an hour or two over them before the charge, organisers were willing to devote a whole day to jousting before the tournament.[23]

Then from somewhere came the idea of a 'Round Table'. The obvious source of inspiration was the literature generated around the legendary King Arthur in the twelfth century.[24] Arthur's Round Table first appeared in the *Roman de Brut* of Wace of Bayeux, composed around 1160, and soon became an accepted feature of the Arthurian world. By the time of the composition of the prose Lancelot cycle soon after 1215, the Round Table was perceived as the elite military household of the king, almost what we would call an 'order of chivalry'. It had by then been joined at the Arthurian court by a second household order, sponsored by the queen, called the 'Knights of the Watch' (*l'Eschargaite*) of which there were one hundred and fifty members.[25] Medieval society had a powerful taste for drama, pageant and display, and it is not surprising to find that the idea of the Round Table as the highest expression of knightly virtue took a fierce grip on the aristocratic imagination.[26]

The first known event that might be described as a Round Table met in the kingdom of Cyprus in 1223. It was recorded in the autobiographical memoranda of the learned moralist and statesman, Philip de Novara. The occasion was the knighting of the two eldest sons of John d'Ibelin, lord of Beirut, and Philip says that: 'At this gathering of knights was the greatest and most extended festival that anyone on that side of the Mediterranean could ever remember. John gave many gifts, he spent much, he staged bohorts, and enacted the adventures of Britain and the Round Table, and many other sorts of games.'[27] The Round Table at Cyprus seems to have been a sort of dramatic knightly pageant, but we get no other clue as to its nature, other than that it was not a bohort. Round Tables are mentioned in England, Austria and France before 1240. The references are brief and generally unrevealing but indicate that some sort of military game was definitely intended, and in retrospect it must have been a joust of sorts. A royal prohibition was issued against one in 1232 in England, and another was held at Hesdin in Picardy in 1235, but all we know of it is that many of the barons of Flanders who had gathered there were inspired to take the cross.[28]

We begin to get a more detailed idea of what Round Tables were in the 1240s and 1250s, and when we do it is clear that we are for the first time seeing a serious rival emerging to the grand tournament. Matthew Paris provides us with the earliest details of a Round Table when he describes one held in fields next to Walden Abbey in Essex in September 1252. Whatever the Arthurian associations of the name, he gives no clue as to how that the Table evoked in the event, which was clearly an

organised series of jousts between a large number of knights.[29] The
Walden Round Table was perhaps sponsored by the earl of Gloucester;
it gathered on a Monday and was still continuing on Wednesday, when
an accidental death brought it to a halt. It may have been expected to
go on for a further day. The knights present jousted individually and
there is some reason to believe that the contests involved elimination
rounds to find the best jouster, for by the Wednesday only the acknowledged experts were left in the field. The weapons in use were supposed
to be blunted lances, a mistake over which caused the fatality. One other
clue as to the nature of the English Round Table is the brief reference
to one held at Warwick in August 1257: the reference says that it 'sat'
(*sedit*). This would imply that chairs, or at least stands, were actually
involved at some stage of the amusement.[30]

Paris's description of the Round Table in England is complemented
by other descriptions from the Continent. In 1240 Ulrich von Liechtenstein had organised a Round Table in his native Austria. This involved
his riding through the province in the guise of King Arthur challenging
knights to joust with him and prove themselves worthy of joining his
Round Table. The final event of his circuit was a meeting of all the
Round Table knights at Katzeldorf, where a great pavilion was pitched
in a field to represent the Table. The knights defended the tent in five
days of jousting.[31] This compares well with the French Round Table
described in the later thirteenth-century romance, *Sone de Nansay*. The
Franco-German hero, Sone, attends four events called Round Tables
during the course of the romance. Two of them, at the real locations of
Chalons-en-Champagne and Montargis in the Gâtinais, were jousting
events associated with tournaments, but the others were independent
meetings. Sone attended his first Round Table at Chalons as an attendant squire. It was an event where a 'table' of some sort was certainly
used as the focus of the sport, as at Warwick. His second, not long afterwards, was a Round Table held exclusively for squires. Before Sone left
home to join it, his patron, the count of Saintois, tutored him in what
he would see there. The 'Table', he said, would be set up in the middle
of an enclosed ground, and a hundred participants would be designated
as members and would hang their shields within the enclosure. The rest
of them, who were the majority, would be outside the table and would
challenge those within it to joust. Around the field, in the manner of a
stadium, were set up wooden stands where knights looked on as judges
and the participants' ladies watched, having handed the lances to the

squire they were sponsoring. As each squire fell in the joust, so his lady was disqualified too. In the end the victor would emerge and award the prize of a gold crown to the lady of his choice. The competing squires got to keep the horses of those they defeated in their jousts. Significantly for us, the count said that this was the way that the Round Table was organised in many countries.[32]

When Sone arrived he found it much as it was described. In the middle of the field he found (just as at Katzeldorf in 1240) a great marquee, with its hangings raised high so that what was inside was visible, but there was no table inside, just a great chair set on a dias on which the lady whose champion had won would sit to be crowned.[33] The 'Table' was plainly only a notional one, a designated group of knights, like Liechtenstein's Arthurian society. The knights of the table 'within' hung their shields on the lists surrounding the enclosure and retired to the stands to await the call. Those 'outside' the table, of whom Sone was one, were called up by heralds to use a staff to strike the shields of those within as a formal challenge. Then courses were run in front of the stands until one of the two riders was thrown down. The event lasted two days and Sone was left in the elite group of survivors. It was he who was chosen as champion, crowning his patron's daughter as queen on the third day, after a great banquet provided by the prince who was the sponsor of the Round Table.[34]

Round Tables were exclusively jousting events, and there is no doubt that they were very popular and widespread from the 1220s onwards. They were popular for a number of reasons. They were not much safer than the grand tournament, perhaps, but at least no one had to risk the crush of the mêlée. Fatalities could still occur and limbs could be broken, but the deadly scramble for ransoms was avoided. Jousts were popular because individual skill was more easily recognised and acclaimed than in the turmoil of the tournament. Courses were run immediately in front of an audience, which had leisure to comment on the performance of each rider. As we have seen from the example of *Sone of Nansay*, there was still also the possibility of profit, as horses could be acquired from the losers. The popularity of the Round Table must also have resided in the possibility it offered for parade and pageant. The old tournament always had something of this, but jousting offered far more opportunities. Pragmatically, jousting events were perhaps also to be preferred as they could be confined to much smaller sites and would cause less social and economic disruption. But most importantly, perhaps, Round Tables were useful as a response to criticism of the tournament from outside authorities. They were not stigmatised by kings and the Church as politically undesirable or unwelcome distractions from the defence of Christendom. They were seen as innocuous courtly festivities. This meant that organisers could stage Round Tables without transgressing the royal prohibitions regularly imposed on tournaments in England from 1217 and in France from 1260.

There was an exciting and satisfying formality and splendour about the Round Table that the old tournament could not offer. It is true that, as early as the 1170s, the grand tournaments had demanded a certain amount of staging. Someone had to organise the posting of the lists around the principal settlement, and rows of stands were often erected for spectators of the *commençailles* and grand charge. But Round Tables demanded more expense and effort. *Sone de Nansay* gives us an insight into the developments in elaborate staging that jousts demanded in the 1250s. In the two-day Round Table for knights sponsored by the countess of Champagne at her town of Machault on the Seine, on the border with the Capetian Gâtinais, the field was laid out with care and expense. The combat area (called 'the Table') was closed off by lists, described as a rectangle of ditches with a revetted palisade within. Shields were hung on the lists. The Table was surrounded on all sides by elevated stands for the spectators, along the front of which stood upright and waiting the lances of the competitors with their pennons or favours, ready to be handed on by squires to their masters. Also embanked was a neighbouring enclosure, where singing, dancing and dining was to take place: the *esbanoie* or 'merry-making' associated with so many thirteenth- century noble gatherings. The social enclosure was expensively equipped with luxurious tents and (one assumes) field kitchens for the banquets which were to be held under canvas. The golden stag which was the prize was exhibited there and guarded by armed serjeants. The entry to the 'table' was marked by a narrow gate and guarded by a company of infantry. These 'guards of the table' were charged by the countess to police the lists and break up any fights that broke out among the jousters. A great bell was installed to be rung at the end of the day's jousting. We are told that the countess had a principal herald, called Rommenal, on hand to organise things, to offer advice and to execute her commands, and other lesser heralds were present to offer commentary and announce results.[35]

Round Tables continued to be popular throughout the thirteenth century, and it is no exaggeration to say that their popularity, and that of similar jousting events, gradually eroded the dominance of the mêlée tournament. As early as 1224 the young author of the Marshal biography was commenting morosely that the mêlée tournament had noticeably lost ground in his day to single combats (*pladier*).[36] As has been pointed out, some very good English evidence of this decline of the tournament is the way that from the 1250s the royal Chancery began issuing occasional prohibitions of jousting as well as tourneying.[37] In the early fourteenth century, the poet Jean de Condé was to say that there were three distinct arenas of arms: the battlefield, the tournament and the joust; and the last two were devised to support the first.[38] By that time, tournament and joust had clearly parted company in the aristocratic mind.

Prohibitions and the Rise of the Joust

Later thirteenth-century writers give us a number of reasons for the growing importance of the joust. The historical meeting described by the herald Sarrazin in October 1278 at Hem, on the river Somme near Péronne in the Vermandois, is a case in point. Sarrazin explained that the Hem meeting was solely made up of jousting because of King Philip III's odious prohibition of tourneying in the Capetian domain. Sarrazin's regrets demonstrate that the rise of jousting in France followed the pattern already seen in England.[39] Round Tables had for a time been a way for knights to avoid Henry III's capricious prohibitions of tourneying in England from the 1220s to the 1250s. After Louis IX's first prohibition of tournaments in France in 1260, French knights apparently went down the same route, jousting because there was nothing better on offer. Sarrazin bemoaned the economic losses to northern France at the ending of tournaments, since foreign knights no longer came to spend their money; he sympathised with the loss of trade to armourers, farriers, harness-makers, provisioners and saddlers, and particularly (of course) to entertainers and heralds; he also made some worried comments about the decline in French knightly skill under this restriction. He worried particularly about the consequences for the Crusade and the danger from the fact that the tournament was still flourishing in the Empire.[40]

The elaborate nature of the jousting at Hem was in part in compensation for the loss of the honour that a tournament would have brought.

If we are to believe Sarrazin, its sponsors (two related seigneurs of Vermandois) had the joust proclaimed across northern France, in England and in the Empire. Sarrazin made a particular point of England's inclusion, since he wanted to honour King Edward as being (unlike Philip III) committed to deeds of knighthood. Edward had of course suspended the prohibitions of the tournament in England in 1267.[41] Sarrazin tells us that the Hem jousting was to commence with an abundance of Arthurian pageantry, which, if we trust his account, amounted to full-blown amateur dramatics. A lady, a sister of one of the sponsors, rode in the role of Queen Guinevere in a cavalcade of participants to Hem, arriving on Sunday 9 October. One of the sponsoring knights escorted her and her entourage in the role of the satirical Kay the seneschal. There followed at the first dinner the dramatic staging of an episode from Chrétien's *Yvain*, and the elaborate arrival of the count of Artois, acting the part of Yvain and appropriately accompanied by a courteous lion, although it is unlikely to have been a real one. Kay freely insulted Yvain, just as in Chrétien's romance. On the Monday, jousting began in the lists, which like those of Machault had a single gate and were surrounded by stands. Guinevere presided with her ladies from her own elevated box (*escafaut*) sitting with the greater magnates present, the counts of Artois and Clermont. The knight acting the part of Kay also hung around the box, keeping up his fierce repartee over both days, to the amusement of all. The knights present also made an effort to get into the swing of things. Enguerrand de Bailleul ran his first joust dressed up as a devil.[42]

As at Machault, announcements were entrusted to a principal herald, this time an officer by the territorial name of Corbioi (which would indicate that he was a king herald from the region of Amiens). Sarrazin is full of the comments and shouts which accompanied the charge of the pair of knights down the *renc*. His contemporary, Jakemes, gives more details of the 'great noise' at each joust. The drums beat, and horns and trumpets blared, the heralds shouted out the names of each rider, and the young lads at the sides jumped up and down and yelled.[43] There were so many knights within the lists that the fence was broken down in some places. But apparently there remained sufficient space cleared in front of the queen's stand that several courses could be run.[44] The jousting continued for two days, interspersed with episodes of Arthurian dramatisation.

Was Hem-sur-Somme therefore a Round Table? Despite the lavish

Arthurian play-acting it seems that it was not. There was no 'Table' in the lists by which knights outside could challenge others within. There was something comparable, in that the account says that the participants were paired off based on whether they had won entrance to Guinevere's court (as symbolised by sitting in her box). 'Those outside' had to seek entry to her court by jousting with her knights. But that was not sufficient for people to call the event a Round Table, which was (as they would have known) Arthur's mesnie, not Guinevere's.[45] As in the jousts in *Sone*, each pair of knights had three lances to run with, which indicates that they could make three attempts to unseat each other. The jousting courses (*rens*, or *rencs*) seem to have been laid out immediately in front of Guinevere's box, and it has been suggested that there were six of them in parallel. At the end of the second day, so as to speed up the sport, more than six were used.[46] There is little doubt that the bulk of Sarrazin's *Roman de Ham* is derived from the lists of jousting results he kept on the day, as a way of keeping track of each knight's performance.[47]

Hem in fact represents another sort of manifestation of the formal joust, devised as a substitute for tournaments, meant by its expense and elaboration to attract back to northern France the foreign knights who had been absent because of the ban. Sarrazin rejoiced in the large numbers who flocked to the event, claiming that over three thousand knights, ladies and other people of quality were present, but he records few non-French names amongst the jousters, other than that of the Franco-Scottish baron, Enguerrand de Bailleul, who had lands in the nearby county of Ponthieu. An anonymous German 'landgrave' arrived late and, as if to point out the importance of his attendance at the event, the lists were cleared so that he and his French opponent could joust undistracted.[48] The likelihood is that he was just another French play actor. In fact by Sarrazin's own figures there were 180 jousts run, which indicates the presence of a maximum of only 360 participating knights at Hem and most were local men.[49]

Sarrazin would no doubt have been delighted that the year after the Hem meeting the prohibition was lifted and grand tournaments were announced by the objectionable King Philip himself at Senlis and Compiègne. There was a great influx of kings, magnates and bannerets from Italy, Germany, Spain and Britain, and it must have seemed that the good old days were again come. But the popularity of the joust had by now had its impact. When the late thirteenth-century poet Jakemes portrayed the northern French aristocracy at play, he had them meeting for elaborate individual jousts not mêlée tournaments, as at a great assembly he describes as happening on a Monday and Tuesday between La Fère and Vendeuil on the river Oise, on the border of the Laonnais. Even when it met, the new sort of tournament would have been unrecognisable to the generation of William Marshal, and that was because of the new emphasis on the joust even at tournaments. We see this demonstrated by another detailed account of an actual tournament, this time an extensive description by the poet Jacques Bretel of the four days of festivities at a winter tournament held between Chauvency-le-Château and Montmédy in the duchy of Lorraine, where there was no question of royal prohibitions (which Philip III in fact renewed in that year).

The jousting at Chauvency was announced to last several days, beginning on Monday 14 January 1280.[50] Since the main event was eventually to be a tournament, the elaborate rectangular enclosures introduced for Round Tables were not needed and what we find is the old-fashioned arrangement of elevated stands (*eschaufaus, loges*) being laid out in a line immediately behind the lists, for viewing the jousts and the final mass charge of the tournament.[51] The lists had been posted around the castle of Chauvency, and it seems that the castle towers (*berfrois*) were also used for spectating by the greater ladies, notably the countess of Luxembourg. Again echoing tradition, jousting on the first day was (in the manner of *commençailles*) for younger knights. But since all Monday was devoted to it, the jousting did not begin till mid morning (*tierce*), long after mass was finished. There had been a little rain overnight, so the jousting run (*cours, renc*) would not be kicking up dust.[52] Attention was given to detail with a procession of young knights out of the lists headed by pairs of heralds and trumpeters, the heralds taking their places in a crowd beneath the stands.[53] Bretel gives detailed descriptions of the jousts, the heralds' commentaries, the injuries and the reactions of the crowd. When one pair were badly bloodied, the ladies commented how the jousting that day was 'impressive and fine', and when two lances simultaneously burst into fragments that 'it was jolly well done'. Before each pair of knights hurled themelves down the run, some sympathetic and agitated ladies would burst out with prayers for their safety.[54] The enthusiasm and fearlessness of the young knights probably accounted for the fact that there were more casualties that day than in the rest of the week. The swift sinking of the winter sun put the

lists in shadow in mid afternoon, and the kings of heralds brought the
jousting to an end with the repeated cry: 'Lower your arms!'.[55]

The second day's jousting at Chauvency was similar to the first. The
jousts were 'terrible and harsh', and saw some further casualties. It carried on right up till nightfall, and in the dinner that evening, the count
of Chiny agreed to the proposal made in a 'parlement' of knights that
Wednesday's jousting should be suspended so as not to take the edge off
the tournament on Thursday. The heralds sent to announce this at
Montmédy developed the argument further. The tournament, said
Maignien, a king herald, was after all the more absorbing event, and he
described with the enthusiasm of the connoisseur the excitement of flashing weapons, the neighing, the shouting, the chases and flights, the
dust kicked up by the horses and the bodies of the fallen lying across the
field.[56] The tournament, since it had no *commençailles*, did not assem-
ble in front of Chauvency until nearly midday, when the cavalcade
arrived from Montmédy. We find the usual drawing up of the two
teams: the French, Lorrainers, Berruyers, Burgundians, Champenois
and miscellaneous others (*cil dedens*) at the Chauvency lists; and the
Luxemburgers, Flemings, Ruyers, Hennuyers, Germans and Brabazons
from Montmédy opposing them.[57] We find the grand review still being
acted out, knights riding in pairs unhelmeted and without shields.
Unfortunately wintry weather had by now returned, the sky was grey
and a cold wind was scything across the meadows; people were shivering.[58] The grand charge was arranged in the river meadows to the east
of Chauvency, at the foot of the hills which loomed over the town.
Heralds cried out for the knights to ready themselves, helmets were
laced on and the peasants and idlers hanging about in the meadows scattered out of the way as the opposing companies rolled toward each
other. They were in full armour, but had discarded their lances in favour
of swords and wooden clubs.[59] Bretel proceeds to give the most detailed
eye-witness description ever of a mêlée tournament, but for us its
importance is that it is also one of the last such accounts.

The Long Evening of the Tournament

Since the early twelfth century, and the first papal prohibitions, there
had been a concern that the tournament distracted knights from their
true vocation, which was to protect Christendom from its enemies. The
military classes had occasionally agreed with this view. There was a

tournament prohibition in force during the Second Crusade (1145–47) across France. It was this religious objection to tourneying that in the end produced the total ban on tournaments that Louis IX imposed on the Capetian domain between 1260 and 1262, which was the measure which did most perhaps to undermine it in the long term, for it was eventually repeated by his son, Philip III, in anticipation of further crusades in 1278, and again in 1280. The French aristocracy was divided on the measure. As we have seen, the aristocracy of Picardy had a grievance against the ban at Hem in 1278. On the other hand, the great Parisian poet Rutebeuf in 1266 and later, in the mid 1270s, directly harangued French tourneyers about the wickedness of amusing themselves and seeking 'vainglory' while other noblemen were expending their blood heroically in Palestine.[60]

In this troubled situation in northern France, England for the first time came by default to be the premier tourneying nation. The martial Edward I came to the throne of England in 1272 and his reign was a watershed for the tournament both in England and on the Continent, where he was duke of Aquitaine. Edward had begun to have an influence on the government of England following the traumatic years of the Baronial Rebellion (1263–65) and his influence favoured the tournament, of which he was a great patron. He had ridden on to his first field in a padded coat at Blyth in 1256, and tourneyed – rather unsuccessfully – on the Continent from 1260 to 1262. In the latter year he got badly beaten up and wounded on some foreign field, most probably in Flanders or the Empire, since Louis IX had by then banned the tournament in his lands.[61] After 1267 there were no prohibitions of tournaments or jousts issued by his father's chancery until the time when Edward announced his intention to go on crusade in the East in 1270. Worcester sources mention that during this time Edward, his brother Edmund of Lancaster and his cousin Henry of Germany lifted the ban his father had imposed and enthusiastically patronised a whole series of tournaments in England.[62]

The reign of Edward I saw a renaissance of the mêlée tournament in England, due to his enthusiasm and celebrity as well as the situation for tourneying in France. His celebrity is evident, both from the plaudits of Sarrazin and from what happened at Chalon-sur-Saone in 1274. On his return to England from the Middle East, the king arrived in Savoy. While there, the count of Chalon sent a pressing invitation for the king and his English knights to meet him in a tournament. The king agreed, proposing a little unwisely himself to field one team against that of the count, the count's knights and any others who turned up on the day. Despite the fact that Edward sent home (and perhaps to Gascony) for more support, the English were outnumbered two to one on the day. The general charge on that occasion must have seemed a golden chance to the count to achieve fame and honour. He and fifty of his men headed directly for the king, and after some vigorous exchange of sword strokes, the count in frustration attempted to take Edward by grabbing him around the neck and forcing him off his horse. But Edward was too powerful a man to wrestle down so easily. He shouted 'What are you up to? You can't think you're going to get my horse!', spurred his mount and used his great strength to tear the count from his own saddle and throw him to the ground.

This was not so far unusual in tournament practise, as we have seen. But Walter of Guisborough says that what happened next was commonly called the 'Little Battle of Chalon' for good reason. He maintains that the Burgundians cheated from the outset, by sending in infantry with the cavalry to force a rout. It is possible that something like that could have happened without premeditation. The Burgundian infantry would have been drawn up in the lists when the charge began, and some greedy and drunken elements could well have followed on the heels of the count's charge, believing that the English had no chance and wanting a headstart in the collecting of ransoms. At this point things must have got out of hand, for the English chroniclers allege that Edward's infantry saw what was happening and retaliated in earnest, bloodily driving off the Burgundian troops, and then getting among the French knights and cutting their saddle girths to bring them down and capture them. The Burgundian knights were pushed back into the lists. The action seems to have concluded when the remounted count of Chalon was cornered, and was ordered by the enraged king to surrender to one of his knights. He would not do him the honour of accepting his surrender personally. Rishanger says the count had been wounded in the hand. The soldiers retreated into the safety of the city hoping the citizens would protect them. The king summoned the authorities in Chalon to surrender, and ordered the mayor to apprehend and punish the rogue Burgundian soldiers or have his city burned and levelled.[63]

Apart from the over-enthusiastic engagement of the infantry reserve, the affair of Chalon-sur-Saone in 1274 seems not to have been much different from any other tournament of the previous centuries. But it might have had long-term consequences in demonstrating to King Edward the lack of regulation on the tournament field, and the disadvantages that flowed from that fact in a large and ill-managed field. The jousting enclosure was a model of good order by comparison. Edward was apparently just as keen on Round Tables as on tournaments. Both were often proclaimed during his reign in England. With tournaments in decline in France, other than in its marches with the Empire, it was in Germany and England that they were now principally pursued. Conclusions based on the English evidence can only be impressionistic, but it seems that they were fairly frequent events there, particularly between 1274 and 1281. While Edward was on crusade from 1270 to 1274 the Chancery had begun issuing prohibitions of tournaments once more, and we find that twelve were issued during that period, which indicates a still high level of aristocratic enthusiasm. The Dunstable annalist chose to record three tournaments held around his town between 1278 and 1281, and Dunstable was only one of many customary sites.[64]

The enthusiasm for the tournament was slow to dim in France despite all the pressure to which it was subjected. A long-lasting view amongst aristocrats, which we saw reported at Chauvency in 1280, was that the grand mêlée was more honourable than any other sort of knightly game. The tournament was believed to be the best proving ground for the knight, despite its obvious dangers and unpredictability. It is true that there were medieval people who would have disagreed with advocates of the glory and excitement of the tournaments – King Henry III of England for one. In 1279 Philip III's enthusiasm for it must have waned when one of his sons received irreversible brain damage at a tournament where his helmet failed to offer protection from a flurry of heavy blows. Then there was the long-standing crusading objection. But it was not that which perhaps turned the minds of Philip III and Edward I against them, but what went on when people travelled to them. Even enthusiasts for the sport had to admit that it was a social problem. No less a man than William Marshal had suspended all tournamenting in England during his regency from 1217 to 1219, because civil order was so precarious that riotous tourneyers roaming the roads could not be tolerated.[65] Philip III repeated his prohibition on French tournaments in 1280 after his son was disabled by injuries in one in 1279.

We do not know the specific reasons Philip gave for his 1280 ban, but the legislation of his cousin, Edward of England, may tell us what they were. Edward on other occasions took his cue from what his French cousin did in government. In 1292 in England it was agreed by king and magnates that the disruption caused by armed young aristocrats descending in gangs on towns had to be curbed, once and for all. The problems in June 1288 at Boston Fair where a bohort held for squires degenerated into a riot and looting must have had an influence on the mind of the king and his council. The bohort should have been a harmless and good-natured enough masque, with one side dressing up in monk's habits and the other in the robes of regular canons. But a certain squire called Robert Chamberlain used it as a cover to attempt to plunder valuables being displayed in the great fair. He was caught and hanged by the town authorities, refusing to the end to name his accomplices.[66]

Setting up a committee of earls armed with draconian powers, the king issued a series of regulations aimed particularly at restricting the younger and irresponsible elements of the tourneying world. Armed squires were particularly targeted, and a limit of three allowed as attendants to any knight, however wealthy and distinguished he was. Full military equipment was not allowed to any participant other than the earls and barons who were at particular risk on the day. The fringe element was also curbed. Spectators were not allowed to ride armed to the event and neither were servants. To discourage numbers, the magnates present were not allowed to offer hospitality to all comers, but only to their squires and households. The 'Statute of Arms' of 1292 seems to have been strictly enforced, and if any development led to a major shift in the way that aristocrats organised military games, it was the statute.[67]

Mêlée tournaments continued in England and some parts of France into the 1340s, but they were in general smaller events than they had been in the thirteenth century. The joust rose inexorably to take the tournament's place, initially in the shape of the Round Table, as we have seen. Two of the most celebrated and sumptuous events of Edward's reign were not tournaments. The first was the Round Table held at great expense over four days at Kenilworth in 1279 under the patronage of Roger de Mortemer, starting on Monday 25 September and lasting till the Thursday. 'Innumerable' knights and their ladies attended, according to one contemporary source, but only a hundred knights according to another.[68] The other great event was the Round Table the king himself sponsored on meadowland above the Menai Straits at Nefyn in Gwynedd at the beginning of August 1284, as part of the celebration of the conquest of north Wales. We can glimpse some of the arrangements from the brief chronicle accounts. It was widely publicised, and even knights from overseas came. Just as in the *Sone de Nansay* Round Table, a big feature was the *esbanoie*, the singing, music and dancing, which was staged near the lists. One of the main events chronicles noted was the collapse of the dancing floor in the temporary accommodation built for the event.[69]

The venerable tradition of the grand mêlée tournament ended in the 1340s, both in England and France. They continued to be held in the first decades of the fourteenth century, despite Edward I's irritable prohibitions during the Scots wars. Edward II (1307–27), and Piers Gaveston in particular, were enthusiasts, at least during the early years of the reign. We have the attendance list of a tournament at Dunstable in 1309. We find a sizeable number of knights were present, over three hundred, and we also find that it was very well managed, with the heralds apparently firmly in control. A period of prohibitions followed, due to the aristocratic unrest of the reign. Prohibitions were lifted under the young and ardent Edward III (1327–77) and his tournaments were splendid affairs, but courtly ones. The tournament under Edward III more than ever before was an event under royal patronage. Quite a number of tournaments were held in the late 1320s and 1330s, judging from the incidental survival of references.

Edward redefined the tournament as a courtly festivity, and defined it away from the tournament towards the joust. This might be seen in the Stepney and Cheapside festivities of 1331, which were organised apparently on the lines of the Chauvency festivities, with several days of jousting.[70] The Cheapside meeting seems to have copied those of the great Flemish cities, with stands erected against the houses of the wide market street, just as at the contemporary Epinette jousts at Lille. The queen's stand unfortunately collapsed. The last mêlée tournament in England was held in 1342 at Dunstable, where there was a large field of knights, including the young king himself. But the review and the *commençailles* must have lasted so long that the mêlée only began as the sun was going down. Under ten horses were lost and won. This was not a tournament of the great age, and demonstrates how parade and individual combat had now more appeal than profit.

Things were no different in France. In 1296 King Philip IV imposed draconian sanctions on tourneyers in the Capetian realm, with imprisonment and confiscation of lands for would-be participants. They were forbidden also to travel abroad to tournaments. The king's purpose was, he said, to concentrate the military power of his realm on his wars against his enemies, the English and the Flemings.[71] He maintained his hostility to the tournament to the very end of his reign in 1314, and it was continued in turn by his second son, Philip V, under the excuse of his contemplating a crusade.[72] Both kings made the same point as Edward of England about the disorder that travellers to the tournament caused. There is no doubt that these prohibitions were flouted by aristocrats. But the anger that these defiances inspired in the king, when they came to his notice, is good evidence that he intended his ban to be observed.[73] As a result, the enthusiasts from within the Capetian realm moved out to the fringes of the Empire, to Lorraine, Hainault or Brabant, in pursuit of sport. The tournament survived in Flanders amongst the urban elite and nobility until 1379, when a last Flemish mêlée tournament was staged at Bruges by the count of Hainault and duke of Brabant. The same year the citizens of Ghent rioted when the count of Flanders announced a tournament there, complaining of the expense. None was ever held in Flanders again.[74]

PART TWO

The World of the Tournament

9

Knights, Technology and Equipment

Without the knight and his lord, there would never have been a tournament, and the knight and the tournament may well have grown up together. What a knight was, and where he came from, are therefore important questions for anyone studying the tournament. Horseback warriors have existed since the bronze age, and several cultures before the middle ages had experimented with the idea of a heavily armoured horsemen as shock troops. In early medieval cultures, horseback warriors were naturally of higher status than foot soldiers, simply because of the cost of purchasing the horse and the intensive training needed to learn to use it. Indeed, a variety of medieval European cultures assumed that any man of status would be a rider. We see this in poverty-stricken Wales, where, even before the Normans, its noble warriors rode horses and used horses as marks of status.[1]

Aristocrats need not necessarily be warriors, but in the troubled medieval world there was no option. The identification of the aristocracy with the values of horseback warriors had certainly happened in the Frankish Empire of the ninth century. The aristocracy of Charlemagne and Louis the Pious was a military and horseback one. But nonetheless most modern historians do not believe that knights were in any way identifiable as a self-conscious group in society until the very end of the tenth century. It has been demonstrated that it was around the 980s that the Latin word *miles* (pl. *milites*) changed its meaning. It had been a general word for 'soldier' since the time of the Roman republic. In the land of the Franks in the generation of writers at the end of the tenth century it shifted its meaning to that of 'horseback soldier'. A major theme of French scholarship since the 1950s takes it as fact that these *milites* became not just a military but a social group early in the eleventh century. Free landowners of any consequence in their neighbourhoods – the social group which produced knights – made a point of taking the title *miles* as a way of distinguishing themselves socially.

There is as yet no generally accepted explanation as to why knights should have emerged as a social and military group in society at the end of the tenth century, but there are a number of suggestions. Historians are increasingly linking the appearance of knights with the contemporary growth in the number of seigneurial castles across northern and central France, something which was happening throughout the tenth century. Military historians point out that these early castles were expensive and pointless structures unless they housed a permanent and mobile garrison. What this suggests is that, for a few men from a particular sector of free society, it became possible after the tenth century to find a full-time career as a horseback warrior. The lords who recruited them rewarded them, sometimes with just bed and board, sometimes with money and sometimes (if they were really pushed) with land grants. So a new class of men appeared who lived more or less permanently at the court of great lords or in garrison in their high-status castles. Their circumstances gave them a social distinction that had not previously existed. The name they were given in Middle French was *chivalers* and in Latin, as we have seen, *milites*.

This is undoubtedly the sort of world we find in early eleventh-century sources. For instance, in a famous document called the 'Conventum' composed on behalf of a Poitevin lord in the 1020s to record his troubles with the count of Poitou, we find a world defined by castles and the skirmishing between their knightly garrisons. In the biography of Abbot Herluin of Le Bec in Normandy, we find a similar picture. The Norman counts of the 1020s were employing mobile households of knights recruited from among the members of free landed families, as Herluin was in his younger days. These early Norman knights lived in the household of the noble lords, and some of their lords' status rubbed off on them. It would go too far to suggest that these early knights, just by being knights, were noble. The knights of the 'Conventum' might be treated as savagely as peasants if they were captured. In the Empire, many of the early knights were indeed unfree peasants in status.

Possession of land and control of the people on it were the great and lasting definitions of status in the middle ages, and probably the bulk of the household knights of north-western Europe before 1100 did not possess land. For this reason, when the English became forcibly acquainted with French chevaliers after 1066 and had to find a name for them in English, they used the word 'cnihtas'. A 'cniht' before 1066 was simply a household servant or functionary. Nonetheless, even the least of these early knights had a measure of status from their skills and their daily association with the great. They were self-evidently a social group to their contemporaries, particularly to the eleventh-century clergy, who blamed them for the social disorders of their times. They developed a group ethos of sorts, with a powerful ethic of service and loyalty, and, as we have seen, the knights of Picardy, Hainault and Flanders found a common meeting ground and hiring fair in the tournament fields of their region, perhaps as early as the 1030s.

The Knight of 1100

A knight in the early tournaments rode out armed in the same way as if he were riding to war. Although hardly any items of armour physically survive from that period, we do know how he would have looked. Because the aristocracy was a military aristocracy, the image of the mounted knight became an image of power. It featured in religious art and it served as a stock design on aristocratic seals and on the coins issued by dukes and counts. The earliest surviving image of the sort is the obverse of the great seal of King William the Conqueror, as devised for him by English goldsmiths in 1067. It shows William as duke of Normandy, riding armed to war bearing the gonfanon of a commander and prince. It may be that it copied William's earlier seal as duke, in which case he had been using the image since perhaps the late 1040s or early 1050s. A few years after the creation of the Conqueror's seal, the embroidery known as the Bayeux Tapestry was created to commemorate the Hastings campaign, and its famous, cartoon-like knights in a wide variety of pose and equipment are for us nowadays the standard image of the early knight. This was an image of such seductiveness in its day that even outsiders to French culture borrowed it. The first surviving seal of a Welsh king from the 1140s shows Cadell ap Gruffudd, king of Deheubarth, unexceptionably dressed as a French knight riding to war.[2]

The equipment of the early knight included these essential items: a helmet; a padded coat, over which was dropped a chain-mail hauberk, often with a hood of mail; spurs; a large body-length shield; and of course his weapons: sword, spear and often also in early days a club and a bow. The equipment was more or less standard, so much so that clergymen of the period could write treatises dwelling on the symbolic theological significance of each item of the knight's equipment. Not long after 1109 an English clerk, who may perhaps have been associated with the household of Archbishop Anselm of Canterbury, composed a tract called 'The Likeness of the Knight' (*Similitudo Militis*). Taking as his inspiration a passage in Paul's first Letter to the Corinthians (13: 4) in which a symbolic meaning is given to each item of a first-century soldier's equipment, the author of the *Similitudo* updated the idea for his own times. He defined the standard early twelfth-century equipment as a hauberk of chain mail, helmet, shield (worn on the left side), spurs, lance and sword.[3]

Although early knightly equipment was standard it was not necessarily uniform. The Bayeux Tapestry gives a number of representations of knights all wearing the same basic equipment but showing different details. With one exception, the hauberks worn all have short sleeves, down to the elbows, which was perhaps a way of cutting labour and cost for this expensive item of equipment. But some knights were clearly protecting their lower arms with additional inner sleeves of mail, and the higher status knights have male leggings of some sort to protect their legs. All the hauberks have coloured bands of cloth or leather around the edges, no doubt to prevent the mail chafing skin or underclothes. The skirts of the hauberk are divided at front and back to allow the wearer to sit astride a horse. The breast area of some hauberks have a curious rectangular arrangement of straps and rivets, which is most likely to represent a mail face-guard (*ventaille*) hanging down from the neck, around which it was usually fastened, like a muffler. It is noticeable that they only appear in depictions of armed knights after the battle, and on the hauberks being carried to boats with the stores.[4] The helmets are all conical with a nasal piece to protect the face against slashing sword blows, but they vary in design. Some are riveted together from plates of iron, or perhaps leather, and reinforced with metal hoops. Others were solid, one-piece, iron caps. Some seem to be painted.[5] We may be seeing here in this variety some regional variation in armour, as well as poorer knights wearing already outdated styles. Wace of Bayeux tells us that in the twelfth century you could tell the region from which a knight came by his manner of arming himself.[6]

From early seals and illuminated manuscripts we see that by 1100 there were already changes to the sort of arms worn at Hastings.[7] The knights in the Bayeux tapestry all carry great, flat kite-shaped shields of wood bound and bossed in iron, some four feet in length, meant to protect the length of their bodies when mounted, and to serve them equally well if they were dismounted. By 1100 these great shields were already shrinking, flattened at the top to improve visibility. By the 1130s they were deliberately curved around the body to deflect lance thrusts. Literary descriptions talk of them having gilded ornamental metal fittings, bosses and floral strapwork. We can see here perhaps the influence of the tournament on encouraging technological change and increased display. The hauberks too had changed; all the sleeves are found hanging down to the wrist. Helmets are described as being 'laced on', which indicates they are heavier and more solid, and perhaps that some hauberks no longer featured an integral hood of mail, but have separate 'coifs', looking like knitted balaclavas, as well as the mail ventailles which could be laced to the helmet rim and veil most of the lower face and cheeks.[8] The appearance of these hoods stimulated a tourneying tactic of grabbing the hood of a passing knight and yanking him from his horse. The helmets of counts and dukes are referred to as flashing with gems with gilded nasals, and some artistic depictions show them increasingly fashioned not in a cone, but as imitations of the Phrygian-cap style of civilian headgear which had become fashionable around 1100.[9]

Fashion continued to have an influence in the armour that each generation adopted. It is clear enough that the tournament was responsible for many of the subsequent changes and for their rapid diffusion throughout Western Europe. It is worth noting here that the tournament heartland in northern France was also a technological centre. The recognised industrial focus for the making of quality chain mail hauberks was Chambly, in the Beauvaisis, from where Henry III of England obtained his mail coats.[10] The generation between the 1130s and 1150s was industrious in introducing striking new features, some of which became permanent and others were transitory. Seals and literature tell us of a characteristic fad of the time by which thin leather straps or cords were tied to the knight's wrist or the back of his helmet, designed to fan out and crack behind him as he rode at speed. Literary knights used peacock feathers or their ladies' sleeves in a similar way, fixing them to the back of their helmet to stream out in the wind of their passage.[11] This can only have been a tournament fashion. Grand cavalry charges were very infrequent events on the twelfth-century battlefield, where knights more often than not fought on foot. So the fashion for streamers is far more likely to have arisen amongst the avid tourneyers of northern France.

More permanent new features of knightly equipment related to heraldic display, and they too must have been inspired by the needs of the tournament field. The obverse of the seal of Count Waleran II of Meulan, adopted by him in 1139, shows him wearing a long trailing sur-coat figured with his chequy arms, carrying a much smaller triangular armorial shield and an armorial gonfanon. The same generation found another new fashion. Waleran's niece's husband, the young Earl Simon II de Senlis, covered his horse front and back with cloth hangings, according to the seal he adopted when he came of age in the 1140s. Another example of this is the seal of William (died 1160), the younger brother of King Henry II, which was devised almost certainly in 1155. His horse coverings were armorial, exhibiting an Angevin lion device. Although images of barded horses are rare, there is a reason for it. Mid twelfth-century literary sources also mention them, and indicate that horses hung with covers or trappers of silk were limited at that time only to princes or great magnates. There were new surfaces on which to display heraldry, and there was a particular need for magnates and princes to seek to extend this sort of display, so as to stand out more on the tourney field.[12]

It is likeliest that the explosion of magnate heraldry on banner, shield, robes and horses was a development inspired by the needs of the tourney field rather than the battlefield. As we have seen, personal heraldry appeared late in the eleventh century in Picardy and Flanders, the area which was the nursery of the tournament. It was initially the preroga-tive of great magnates and barons. Knights did not take up individual devices peculiar to themselves until the early thirteenth century.[13] What knights did do was to identify themselves by the colours and sometimes the badge of the magnate they served. Twelfth-century literary and his-torical descriptions of companies of knights make it clear that they were uniformly equipped by their lords in robes, saddles, shields, horses and arms.[14] It was the practice for a lord to give arms and horses to new knights when they retained them into their household, so this happened naturally. So we find that although no one knew William Marshal's name when he attended a tournament on his own for the first time in 1166, he was recognised as a household knight of the lord of Tancarville from his colours or the badge on his shield.[15] It is a reasonable conclu-sion that in the mid and later twelfth century the lord alone possessed a surcoat and horse trapper with his full personal device. Such trappings allowed the lord to stand out and be identified by his men in the charge and mêlée so that they could rally round and protect him from would-be captors, just as William Marshal guarded his Young King. Royal heraldry was slow to develop in both England and France in the twelfth century, and that may well be because most kings did not go on to the tournament field and so had less need of it.

The Knight of 1180

It has been often said that the essentials of knightly equipment remained much the same for a century after Hastings, and there is truth in that statement. But the appearance of knights was by no means static before 1180. There were technical improvements and moves to distinguish magnates in their equipment from the knights whom they retained. As we have seen, the stimulus for much of this can only have been tournament culture. By 1180, however, the essential equipment too was beginning to change. In part this was because the status of the knight was shifting upwards in society. Knights were becoming recognised as the lower level of the aristocracy, and were being expected to equip themselves accordingly, both in the trappings of war and peace. The knightly group in society began to shrink in numbers and the required level of wealth to be a knight increased. As part of this, knights began to assume the heraldry, surcoats and horse trappers that their lords had previously possessed.

Around 1187, Ralph Niger, a graduate of Paris and canon of Lincoln, another cleric, composed a moral treatise based on a knight's equipment. Niger was probably a former chaplain and certainly an associate of that great tourneying celebrity, the Young King Henry. He was a man therefore who knew France, knights and the tournament circuit very well indeed he must have been at present at many of the great tournaments of his age. His catalogue of knightly equipment is rather more elaborate than that of his predecessor eight decades earlier, and it is thoroughly up to date for the 1180s. He said:

> It is the custom for the knights of this world firstly to fix their spurs to their shoes, and then to protect their feet, legs and groin with mail leggings. After that they throw their hauberks over the rest of their body and arrange it around their bodies and limbs with a belt. After that they put on their helmets and lace them up to their hauberks and their heads, and finally belt on their swords. After that they take up their lances and shields ...[16]

The mail armour on a knight's lower body (*chausses*), devised like metal mesh tights, was not of course a new feature, as some of the knights in the Bayeux Tapestry can be seen wearing them. But it is new to find that it is a standard item of armour, and it also appears universal in the illustrations of knights in the Winchester Bible of *c.* 1160 x 80. The Winchester Bible knights also possess hauberks whose arms terminate in mail mittens. Niger mentions that there were laces to tie the mail sleeves and mittens (which he calls *fines manicae*) to the wrists and other laces and a belt to keep the rest of the hauberk taut to the body.[17] Niger mentions flowing embroidered linen surcoats as being normal for knights in the 1180s, and describes the boiled leather (*corium excoctum*) plates that the knight would put on under his mail. He also alludes to leather leg pieces worn with the mail chausses to protect the knees and thighs (*genicularia*), and this would explain why the upper part of the chausses are depicted as bunched above the knees in some contemporary pictures of knights.[18]

Niger mentions something else apparently new to the 1180s in that the helmet he describes has a visor (*viseria*), saying that 'from the helmet a fixture pulls down a short way, which covers the nose and protects the face, and shades but does not obscure the eyes'.[19] We get some visual evidence of these visor plates, looking rather like the Sutton Hoo face mask, on the reverse of the first seal of King Richard (1189) and on pictures of the now lost late twelfth-century tomb effigy of William Clito at St-Omer. These mobile visor plates were a technological improvement which must have come from the tourney field, in that they offered protection from the splinters thrown out when lances burst on impact in jousts. They were also less stifling than the alternative, which was a mail ventaille that hung from the helmet and was draped round the mouth. There is some visual evidence stretching back to the 1150s that these visors were preceded by helmets with fixed face masks, a sort of development of the nasal piece found in the Bayeux Tapestry. But such masks were not very common.[20]

By the 1190s the visor-mask was to develop a step further into an enclosing helm, like an inverted iron bucket. The seal of Count Baldwin IX of Flanders and Hainault (1195) featured a flat-topped helmet with visor attached, which completely enclosed the count's head. Again, we can look to the tournament as the inspiration for these new enclosing helms. The earliest direct reference to such an item is when the Marshal biography describes its hero after a tournament held in 1179 with his head on an anvil as a smith prised just such a helm off it; it had been crushed to his head by the force of the blows it had absorbed that day.[21]

Not everyone wanted a great helm but preferred to leave their faces open. Henry de Laon tells us that the *hiaume* was the most troublesome item of military equipment, yet the most useful: 'despite the heat and lack of air within, [it] resists the belabouring and dents falling on it'. The best knight was the one who could wear it as lightly as a cap.[22] But the discomfort of a helm would explain why seals and illuminations show that in 1200 open helmets were still common. We still see the helmet with nasal guard at the turn of the century, although new helmet shapes appeared around this time in illuminations and on seals. Sometimes they were a tapered cylindrical style, and sometimes a solid and deep metal cap rounded like a basin. This was the sort of helmet which began to be called appropriately a *basinet* in the early thirteenth century, and which became in the end the standard headgear in the fourteenth century.[23]

Horses and Horse Armour

Niger has much to say about the harness and furnishings of the knight's horse in the 1180s. He gives one of the first indications that horse armour was by then in general use. He talks of a horse's armour, front and back, over which was cast the silk or linen armorial trappers. Niger talks of the 'tester', a protective mail or leather head piece; a 'collar' to protect the horse's neck and breast; and a similar 'crupper' to protect its rear.[24] Niger does not tell us what was the material of which these front and rear pieces of horse armour was made, and he does not tell us what size they were. However the *couvertures* on the warhorse of Duke Naimes in the contemporary *Chanson d'Aspremont* (c. 1189) were said to be leather, by which was no doubt meant tough moulded plates of *cuir boulli*, and the use of the word 'covering' implies they were not inconsiderable pieces of armour.[25]

Niger talks of leather horse armour, but were others of these 'coverings' chain mail at this time? The existence of mail horse armour (*coopertoria ferrea*) is well established in the 1230s, and when Wace of Bayeux refers c. 1170 to a baron whose horse was armoured in iron he may be referring to even earlier mail coverings.[26] The mention of 'bardings of leather' thrown *over* the 'coverings' of the horses of the knights of the Round Table in a tournament depicted in the *Prose Lancelot* (c. 1215 x 20) is then perhaps a further indication of the amount of protection afforded to horses.[27] It would imply that both mail and leather armour might be deployed together when horses were at risk of hurt. But it is clear from what Niger says in particular about horse armour that the knight of the generation of 1180 had already reached the level of equipment standard in the romances, illuminations and seal portraits of the first half of the thirteenth century.[28] If this is so, then the cause may have been the tournament, where, as we have seen, commentators tell us that the casualty rate in horses was high. Knights were fond of their horses, however, and those who could afford it would be very likely to want to protect them with armour in the same way that they protected themselves.

The Armour of Squires

A growing development in the later twelfth and early thirteenth century was the awareness of a range of lighter, secondary armour, used by knights but appropriate particularly to soldiers of lesser status, like squires. Here it is the English Chancery which provides us with the first such inventory. In 1181 King Henry II issued an assize, defining the weapons that every landed free man and urban citizen should possess, so that they could be summoned by the king to serve as an effective knight or by the sheriff to serve in the county or town militias. The arms and armour a knight should have is standard, and rather less detailed than the list in Ralph Niger's inventory. What was asked of the landed free man who had moveable property worth more than sixteen marks is more interesting. Every such man should maintain in his household, it was said, a haubergeon (*aubergel*), a broad brimmed metal hat (*chapel de fer, capellet ferri*) and a lance, while a burgess should have a gambaison (*wambais*) rather than a haubergeon.[29] The haubergeon was a lighter, tunic-shaped hauberk, and the gambaison was a quilted, thick leather tunic.[30] The assize says nothing about horses, but since lances are specified for both, it is possible that the freeholders and burgesses were meant to serve as mounted serjeants rather than infantry. An analysis of the judicial records of the reign of John (1199–1216) and the early years of Henry III reveals that items like chapels de fer, haubergeons, pourpoints (a padded woollen version of the gambaison) and mail chausses were frequently to be found stored, as the assize insisted, in the homes of freemen.[31]

Lighter armour such as this features in accounts of twelfth-century tournaments. It seems that it was commonly worn in the vespers on the day preceding the main event. The Hennuyer knight Matthew de Walincourt is said to have worn lesser protection than full armour at the vespers at Eu in *c.* 1178 than he did the next day in the grand tournament.[32] When William Marshal went scouting for the enemy at Le Mans in 1189, he wore only a padded tunic (*porpoint*). Richard the Lionheart was known for wearing only light protection, perhaps from bravado. He must have done it a lot, because he was caught out by the habit on two known occasions. The first time was also at the fall of Le Mans in 1189. During the taking of the city and later in the pursuit of his father's household Richard wore a *porpoint* and a *chapel de fer*. It was because of this that Richard was ridden down by the Marshal in the rearguard, who had in the meantime fully armed himself.[33] On the second occasion, Richard had gone forward to view the siege of Châlus-Chabrol in April 1199, carrying a shield and wearing for protection only a *chapel de fer*, when he received his mortal wound in the shoulder from a crossbow bolt.[34] Literary descriptions of squires in action confirm that they wore this sort of gear. So Philip de Remy describes Robinet, the squire of Jehan, as protected by a pourpoint in the shape of a doublet (*qui fu doublentins*), with an iron hat (*capelier*) and armed with a long knife.[35]

Edward I's Statute of Arms (1292) gives a similar limited range of armour as appropriate for the squire. We find the equipment of non-knights in attendance regulated as no more than a padded jacket (*corsteler*), mail cuisses, shoulder plates (*espaulieres*) and a bascinet.[36] This restrictive list parallels the fullest description we have of the appropriate arms for a squire. This is in a curious allegory of the human condition composed anonymously at some time around 1300, which takes as its text the items of military equipment appropriate to the 'damoysele', that is, the young nobleman who had not been knighted. The squire should wear an 'aketon' a belted jerkin padded and quilted with woollen wadding (*cadaz et cotoun*). The squire, like the knight, should wear mail *chausses* strengthened with leather armour strapped over it: *cuisses*, boiled leather thigh pieces, and leather knee protectors called *muscelers*, Niger's *genicularia*. Over it all was worn instead of the hauberk a quilted leather doublet, the *gambeson*, embellished with coloured silk piping and a strengthening of small metal plates.[37] The tract does not mention a head covering, but the bascinet or chapel de fer would have been most likely.

These English statements on armour and behaviour appropriate to the squire may already have been more than a little out of touch by the 1290s. In France in the 1260s and 1270s noble squires had begun deliberately to adopt knightly armour, trappings and weapons. We see this in the romance *Sone de Nansay*, which depicts Round Tables held for adolescent and adult squires. The depictions of these jousts make no distinction in their organisation and equipment from knightly jousts, and indeed a squire who rode a joust without full knightly equipment would be taking a dangerous risk. At about the same time, the polemic on the tournament by Henry de Laon says that many squires were wearing equipment better than most knights, and were actually riding on to the tournament field with them to fight. Although Henry did not approve of this presumption, nonetheless it happened. French seals indicate that the same generation of squires had adopted heraldry too. The English court here seems to have been mounting a rearguard action against the rise of the squires it had observed in France. In the long run it failed. English squires began to adopt heraldry in the reign of Edward II (1307–27) and, once that boundary was breached, there was nothing to stop them equipping themselves as knights, other than crossing the final boundary of the knight's golden spur. The participation of squires in English tournaments is known for certain to have begun to occur by 1313.[38]

The Knight of 1280

There were some further small changes in the nature of knightly armour between 1180 and 1250, and many changes of style. The great helm developed the shape that became familiar throughout the thirteenth century, with its eye-slits and puncture holes for ventilation. It gradually lost its cylindrical shape and by 1280 was more tapered and pointed at the top. The great helm never seems to have been hugely popular with the knights that wore it. It was stifling inside, and it hindered both vision and hearing. On the other hand, it was certainly prudent to wear one in tournaments and particularly in jousts. It deflected the blows of lance heads, and the only danger was that spearheads might lodge under the lower edge of the helm and either tear it off by bursting the straps, or rip into the mail armour ventaille below: this was how Ernaut de Montigny died at Walden in 1252.

The later thirteenth-century great helms were often elaborately decorated. Already in the 1240s literary sources note that the tops of the helmets were being circled with twisted silk wreaths, or 'torses'. A variety of contructions might be placed on top of these. In the later equestrian seal of King Richard the Lionheart his helmet seems to be topped by a fan of plumes. Ulrich von Liechtenstein describes in detail exactly such a construction which he claims to have worn in 1226: a gilded metal crest laced on top of his great helm, in the sockets of which were secured a great fan of peacock feathers.[39] Even more elaborate crests appear later in the century. At Hem in 1278 Sarrazin saw the helm of Gerard de Canle decorated with the crest of a bird in a cage.[40] This fashion had certainly crossed to England by then. In 1280 crests were made to decorate the helmets and the horses of the thirty-eight members of the royal retinue participating in the tournament at Windsor; presumably they were identical.[41] Seal depictions of knights and barons begin in the 1290s to feature all sorts of decorations: small models of dragons and wyverns, animal heads – all presumably of boiled leather – wings and more fans of plumes. The back of the helmet acquired hangings of cloth, or 'cointoises', which must have had the principal purpose of deflecting some of the summer heat that made the interior of the helm so insufferable to its wearer.[42] As with the mid twelfth-century enthusiasm for streamers, these hangings would whip out impressively when their wearer was in full gallop and make a brave sight. The same generation began a fashion for 'aillettes', stiffened squares of fabric or leather painted with a knight's arms, fixed high on the shoulders. What practical use they were is hard to say, but they were quite the fashion in Edward I's reign, and it has been suggested that they helped identify teams in belonging to a particular lord.[43]

The main change in knightly armour was the gradual appearance of pieces of iron plate in the mid thirteenth century. There was an early inventory of armour attached to a testament of a provincial English knight called Robert of Wichford, dated 1257. Although some of the words are obscure it is clear enough that, as well as his mail hauberk and chausses, he had iron, not leather knee pieces (*mustelers*) and shoulder pieces (*strumelers*).[44] Iron shin guards (greaves), thigh pieces, gauntlets and neck plates (gorgets), breast and back plates all begin to appear by the end of the thirteenth century.[45] The decisive move towards plate armour lay over half a century yet in the future. Nonetheless, the knight of 1280 was beginning to move away from two centuries of trusting in flexible mail towards a more expensive and solid carapace, and so find a new way of distinguishing himself from his social inferiors. In all this, and the other changes, it was quite clearly the tournament and joust which initiated such changes.

Aristocratic Violence and Society

How violent was the aristocratic society that amused itself with the violence of the tournament? Was its simultaneous pose of mannered restraint and civilisation no more than posturing? How far did its passionate Christianity counter the sort of behaviour which Christ condemned? These are questions that have engaged historians for many years, and which are not likely to be settled easily or, indeed, here. We expect knights to have been what we call 'chivalrous', and as a result their tactics in the tournament may come as a surprise. As we have seen, it was not by any means thought unfair for several knights to attack one. Princes in the field thought no less of themselves because they employed life guards of select knights to avoid the danger of capture. William Marshal, the 'flower of knights' entered into several dubious arrangements. He struck up a tournament partnership with a Flemish knight, the result of which was that he could indirectly profit from the capture of knights on his own side. He deliberately undercut the ransom demands of his fellow knights so as to encourage opponents to surrender to him. He was so blindly focused on his own profit that he was known to forget that his principal task was supposed to be the protection of his young master on the tournament field.

Noble Conduct

Clearly, chivalry was a more complicated idea than simply 'fair play'. But there was an ideal of conduct amongst knights and barons, and it did surface on the tournament field. This conduct was not, however, called 'chivalry' in the twelfth century. The ideal of a medieval male was then generally called the 'preudomme' (ultimately from the Latin *probus homo*, 'upstanding fellow'). We find what the idea of this sort of admirable man was established as early as the *Song of Roland* (c. 1100). He was hardy, that is he was tough and uncomplaining. He was loyal to his master, but not subservient. A preudomme was valued for his independent and sound judgement, and he would tell his lord precisely what he thought in any situation. Since a baron or a knight attended the courts of greater men, they had to be what was called in French *cortois*, or in Latin *curialius*. This meant that they had to have a confident and amiable way with other people, great and small alike, and not needlessly antagonise their fellow courtiers. To avoid envy, they had always to be modest about their talents and achievements, however great they were. Such was the preudomme, and his virtues can be recognised in literary heroes like Count Oliver, William of Orange and Gawain. They were also just as evident in the real-life preudomme, William Marshal, who was born to be a courtier as much as a soldier.[1]

The way of the preudomme only became 'chivalry' in the thirteenth century. During the two generations of men between 1180 and 1220 the status of the knight, the 'chevaler', rose so that by 1220 simply to be knighted was to be acknowledged as noble. This had not necessarily been the situation in 1180. To call noble conduct 'chevalerie' in 1180 would have seemed odd, as nobility belonged to a higher social sphere than many knights occupied. But by 1220 almost all knights were men of birth and means. The work which signalled this change of attitude was written around 1220, when an anonymous writer in north-eastern France wrote a tract which has much to say about the preudomme, a work he called the *Ordene de Chevalerie*. The *Ordene* opens by announcing that 'it is a good thing to talk of preudomme, for one can learn much by doing so', and he talks about the 'preudomme' on several occasions as a man given general respect amongst his peers. Hugh de Tabarie, the principal character of the work 'molt fu sages et preudom' (was a very wise and accomplished man). But the most significant thing about the *Ordene* is that it is a book which assumes that the preudomme is also a *chevaler*. The *Ordene* might have been intended to mean 'the Ordinal of *Chevalerie*'. In the Church, the principal ranks of clergy, the deacons, priests and bishops, were admitted to their orders by use of a book called an 'ordinal'. To use the word 'ordinal' was to say that knighthood was a rank within society, a rank which brought with it certain moral duties.

The imaginary story behind the *Ordene* is that the great and admired Turkish leader, Saladin, was intrigued by Christian knighthood, and wanted to learn more about it. So he called up one of his Christian prisoners, Hugh de Tabarie, crusader prince of Galilee. He obliged Hugh to instruct him in what a knight would undergo during his initiation.

Hugh consented under pressure, so Saladin was told that the knight had to be a preudomme who was wise (*sages*) and not indiscreet (*fols*). Hugh himself had outstanding qualities: he was full of bravery (*hardement*) and knightliness (*chevalerie*). As a preudomme he was the sort of man to instruct others in the qualities of a knight. The preudomme Hugh was self-evidently a courtly man and, as the author says, King Saladin 'honoured him much because he found him to be a preudomme, and caused much honour to be done to him'. But the *Ordene* is about *chevalerie*, and not *preudommie*. Its basic assumption is that the chevaler is the noble man, not the preudomme. The preudomme is simply a standard of virtue to which the new knight must aspire. The *Ordene* was popular and influential. People quoted from it, and its inspired several later and larger treatises, which were all written as essays on *chevalerie*, and so it was that *chevalerie* came to give its name to codified noble conduct.

The tourneying knight of the twelfth and thirteenth century was praised for being practical and sensible, and that is the reason why William Marshal's biographer tells us details of his career that would seem hard-headed to anyone with romantic ideals about knightly conduct in the middle ages. It was to the Marshal's credit when he showed himself a preudomme, just as it was when he showed himself tough, brave and accomplished. But he was never foolish. When he found himself outnumbered by a group of knights at an anonymous tournament in northern France, he pulled back and let them take the prize he was pursuing, rather than risk capture himself. He knew that he who fights and runs away lives to fight another day. He had also been taught as a young knight by his betters that a man who neglects opportunities to enrich himself when they present themselves will be poor and despised. The Marshal could also nurse a grudge for years. As a young knight he had been beaten hard by a Hennuyer called Matthew de Walincourt. A decade later, when he was famous and wealthy, he could not resist the temptation publicly to humiliate the older man in a tournament vespers.

What of romantic and religious chivalry, as nineteenth-century writers understood it? Twelfth-century noble conduct had its own ethics. At a pragmatic level, eleventh-century military society had come to a quiet agreement among its members that it was better to capture and ransom fellow knights than to kill them. This was true as much on the battlefield as on the tournament ground, where the ransom customs of war were duplicated at a more modest level. The tournament itself, as I have suggested, may have been one side-effect of the powerful move within society to moderate the widespread and continuous warfare characteristic of politically fragmented France. Noble conduct was influenced by the Church in other ways. Churchmen had developed during the eight and ninth centuries an ethical template for a just and moral nobleman who was pleasing to God. This was by adapting a verse in Psalm 145 to say that his power was moral when it was used to protect the defenceless, the widow and orphan, and to bring down the wicked and arrogant. This was the message that Pope Urban II adapted in 1095 in his call to the military aristocracy of his day to leave behind their sins as regards widows and orphans and to protect the defenceless Church by fighting its enemies in the East. William Marshal must have registered this because, when his army set fire to Le Mans in 1189, he and his squires helped an old lady and her daughter drag out their smoking possessions from their burning house. Even that well-known noble quality of largesse or generosity had a religious and moral aspect. By giving away your goods, knights were told, you showed how little store you set by the ephemeral things of this world.

It has been the custom since the nineteenth century to regard knights as hypocritical because they did not live up to their professed ethics. The hypocrisy and decadence of chivalry was a major theme in the great work of Johan Huizinga *The Waning of the Middle Ages* (1924) and it is a theme that continues to surface in historical and literary scholarship. However, to attack an ethical system because its practitioners did not pursue it systematically and wholeheartedly verges on being adolescent. Some medieval knights, like Geoffrey de Charny, unmistakably believed that there was a type of conduct which was noble, and that it should be pursued in a passion of idealism. Some medieval bishops, like Stephen de Fougères of Rennes, believed with equal passion that knightly conduct could be ethical and pleasing to God, and taught this with some courage directly to the knights' faces. When we meet a medieval knight like William Marshal, who tended to adopt conduct that was to his interest, and call that noble we might wonder whether a code of noble conduct could actually work. But his biography reveals that Marshal was not untouched by the prevailing ethics of his class. He adopted poses of liberality and modesty because it helped him at court; but he was nonetheless liberal and modest. He was profoundly loyal and long-suffering with regard to his lords, even though one of them was as insufferable as King John of England. The noble ethic of mercy to the poor and undefended touched that part of his character which was well-disposed and kindly, and affirmed it. Where he was hard-headed and pragmatic in his dealings he was responding to the old idea that a man should be circumspect and shrewd to be worthy of respect by his fellows. To that extent Marshal always tended to the ideal of the preudomme than the preu chevalier.

Violence

Medieval knights were armed men, and they were at liberty to use their arms as and when they saw fit. There is a certain fascination about this medieval freedom to commit violence, which resembles the fascination with the Hollywood depiction of violence in epics and space operas. The slaying of orcs and aliens in great numbers and without any call for a troublesome conscience about it has a cathartic appeal to people labouring under the stress of modern manners and controls. Were medieval knights equally devoid of a conscience about dealing death and mutilation? Was there any limit to the violence they would contemplate? A recent trend in writing on knights and aristocracy has been to concentrate on the violence of their culture, and contrast that with their failure to respect the widow and the orphan.

Medieval knights and noblemen could be sickenly violent, although they could not escape condemnation for it. In 1124 the very noble count, Waleran II of Meulan, found that his peasants had been taking advantage of the siege of his castle of Vatteville-sur-Seine to take wood from his forests, so he rounded up those he could find and had their feet severed. The reason we hear of this act of violence against the unarmed is the condemnation of it by a Norman monk, Orderic Vitalis. Orderic's condemnation was not entirely because of the criminality involved in mutilating the poor and unarmed, he was also unhappy that the count had done it in the penitential season of Lent.[2] Orderic had a lot of Norman aristocratic violence to condemn at various times in the 1120s and 1130s. Neighbouring castellans led their knights to set fire to bourgs and churches, wasted fields, attacked monastic precincts, looted, robbed and plundered. Orderic did not see ideals of noble conduct as a way of combatting these outbreaks, he set more store by there being powerful dukes of Normandy to crush the castellans who were responsible for the violence. Orderic's jaundiced view was understandable. If aristocratic power could not be contained by an ethical system or intimidated by greater force, then there was nothing to stop the reign of terror if an aristocrat turned out to be a conscienceless killer. The hideous tortures and casual brutality inflicted by Thomas de Marle (died 1128) on the peasantry of the Amienois and on his hapless captives may have been exaggerated by his clerical enemies, but they cannot have all been invented.[3]

A question that cannot be answered with any ease is how many aristocrats were as violent and abandoned as Marle apparently was. For if there was a Thomas de Marle there was also a Geoffrey de Mandeville (died 1144). Geoffrey was an English baron and a loyal bureaucrat who was undermined by his enemies at court and lost his castles in East Anglia. Angry and aggrieved he gathered his followers and waged war on King Stephen in the region between Peterborough, Cambridge and Huntingdon. To do so he had to sack towns and pillage churches to raise money. To make up for his lost castles, he had to seize and fortify undefended abbeys. Geoffrey was certainly violent, but was he without conscience and ethics? Even the monastic writers whose abbeys he victimised do not say so. A source from Waltham abbey in Essex noted how distressed Geoffrey was at the damage his men did to their town in pursuit of his enemies at court and goes so far to say that he was a good man and a Christian. The chronicler of Ramsey Abbey, which he occupied and whose gatehouse he turned into a keep, resented what he did but concedes that Geoffrey was not proud of the straits to which he was driven.[4]

Writers on chivalric violence turn to literature to look for indications of shared medieval attitudes. A witness often called is the poetry of Bertran de Born. Bertran was a baron of the Dordogne and an intimate of the courts of the young Plantagenet princes in the the 1170s and 1180s. He was a tourneyer and a troubadour, and he must have been an acquaintance of William Marshal, his contemporary. His poetry is often autobiographical. A lot of it is more to do with violence than love, and he describes the prospect of imminent war with relish and anticipation. The screaming of the dying and the sight of torn corpses are things his poems contemplate with real and unashamed satisfaction.[5] Bertran could therefore be read as a Thomas de Marle with a turn for verse. But how much of it is a testosterone-fuelled pose adopted to appeal to his fellow warriors? Is it bravado and machismo designed to impress others and set him apart from them as a man tougher and more fearless, and of course also more honest and idealistic? It is clear that he did like to think of other aristocrats as feeble backsliders, compared with himself. His love poem *S'abril e folhas* attacks other aristocrats who – unlike him – waged war with caution and scientific sieges; who designed attractive castles and staged elaborate banquets; who enjoyed hunting in style in their forests; and who took to the tournament fields solely in pursuit of profit.[6] We can imagine that this was directed against the likes of the Young King Henry's circle, and indeed against the more restrained majority amongst the nobles of France. A prominent theme in his poetry in the 1180s is that prowess is dead, honour is in decline in France, and that the aristocrat is now tainted by money, luxury and greed.[7]

The biography of William Marshal is the exact opposite of Bertran's poetry, yet it comes from the same world. Here there is a rejoicing in deeds of horsemanship and hardiness, but little if any praise of violence. Indeed, the biography fails to say whether the Marshal actually killed anyone in his long military career, despite the number of tournaments, sieges and campaigns at which he was present. Its graphic description of the murder of Earl Patrick of Salisbury in 1168 is certainly violent, especially in the way the young Marshal is brought down by being stabbed in the thigh through a hedge, and it dwells on his indifferent – if not exactly cruel – treatment by his captors. But it has Earl Patrick's murderers claiming sheepishly that it was all an unintended accident, not glorying in a bloody feat of arms. When it came to the crunch Bertran de Born also abandoned his rhetoric of death and glory. The lament he composed when his lands were attacked by, and lost to, Richard of Poitou early in the 1180s, and when he found that he was abandoned by his craven allies is nothing if not pathetic. Heroic death with honour was not then for him so attractive, for he was the desperate victim of another's violence.[8]

No one would deny that violence was widespread in medieval society, but it was not necessarily conscienceless violence. The knights of England for instance, regarded themselves as superior in their restraint to the barbaric warriors of Wales. William de Briouze, the lord of Brycheiniog and Buellt, once commented to the clerk Walter Map in the 1180s that he knew of a Welsh lord whose professions of piety and spiritual exercises in fasting and prayer were little short of angelic. But in war, there was no act so diabolical that the same Welshman would hesitate to commit it.[9] The implication is that the Anglo-Norman baron, however hard-bitten, recognised limits to his violence. If so, then it was a recognition of limits only in violence towards other Anglo-Normans, as the barbarity of the colonisers in Wales to the native aristocracy is well attested. When they committed and endured violence, it was not without consequences for these knights. Jean de Joinville's description of the battles between Turks and Christians around Damietta, in which he participated and was wounded, is deeply moving and astonishingly vivid. The pain, the horror, the fears of imminent death, the pitiful massacres of Christian prisoners, are all painfully reproduced for us. The point of it is that he did not write it all down until fifty years after the event. His prose is so very vivid because Jean has to have been playing and replaying those desperate hours in his mind for decades, and never had shaken off the memories. Violence could traumatise the medieval warrior, for all the ideals of hardihood and aggressiveness he embraced. His freedom to commit mayhem and even kill came with a price: memories he could not escape; wrongs he could not entirely rationalise.

Women and the Tournament

Historians have in general concluded that a woman's lot in the twelfth century was not good, and that she was a lot worse off than her grandmother in the eleventh century. This idea of a worsening position for women in the middle ages has a lot to do with the nineteenth-century belief that ideas of family and property changed in the eleventh century. Family property, says the theory, was increasingly concentrated after 1000 in the hands of eldest sons. The extended early medieval families with liberal attitudes to sharing property between sons and daughters gave way to the lineage, where only one son got the lot. Wives began to lose control of the lands they brought into their marriages to their husbands. The 'feudal' form of society in any case, so says the theory, tended to exclude women because they could not ride in arms with their lords.

All of these views are now contested. The prevailing belief is that less changed than was once believed. Certainly there was no push towards primogeniture in medieval families, and no sudden appearance of lineages. What did perhaps change was the ambition of kings and courts to control successions, and the ambition of lawyers to meddle in them. What the tournament reveals about women's status in the middle ages is in fact something very different.[10] The tournament was far from being an entirely male affair. As early as our sources permit us to see them, many noble women were attending at least the greater tournaments. As we have seen, stands for the spectators were being erected as far back as the 1170s, and these were principally for women. From their elevated stands and draped benches, the ladies present could look over the lists and observe the opening jousts of the day. Then in late morning or at midday they could marvel at the main event, the grand charge of the tournament, when two teams of hundreds of knights thundered towards each other across the open ground and then fought in a great mêlée.

The role of the spectator is not necessarily a passive one. Women on the day of the tournament were expected to be quite as vocal an audience as in any modern sporting event. They would sit for hours in their sheltered seats and reminisce about past encounters; in many ways they were the memory of the tournament, and possessing its memory, they were necessarily its arbiters.[11] They would comment loudly and sometimes sarcastically on the performance of the day. They would shriek when a knight went down in a welter of blood in a dangerous fall. They would consult together with the heralds and decide who was to be honoured, and they would offer prizes. The heralds loved to draw them into the action. Leaping on to the banks of the lists at Chauvency in the duchy of Lorraine in 1280, a king of heralds extemporised a speech to the ladies above, who had just watched two knights and their horses knocked on to their backs by a fierce joust. They had imperilled their lands and their bodies for you, he said, their wounds were suffered to earn your love. He lyricised for several minutes over the groaning bodies behind him, that they were there entirely for the sake of love, for from love derived all the great chivalric virtues. The ladies had tears in their eyes as he begged them then to be tender to those poor men behind him, and their like.[12]

What was going on at Chauvency and many hundreds more such places in the twelfth and thirteenth century? Literary sources for the tournament betray a world of considerable social interaction between men and women. In the evening receptions and dinners, women mingled and chatted with the men, they sang and danced. This was not a society where women were cloistered away from men. They rode with them, sang with them and danced with them. It is clear that the tournament would have been a pretty barren event without the society, the criticism, the memory and the praise of women, much more so than in the rather more masculine world of nineteenth-century sport.

Yet John Baldwin notes that the tournament world of William Marshal's biography appears to be as masculine as a rugby club on a January afternoon, with women appearing on only two occasions at the beginning and end of different meetings, with no hint that they were present in between.[13] An earlier source tells a very different tale. What else was Huon d'Oisy's *Tournoi des Dames* but a knowing and good humoured extension of the perpetual banter and flirtation that went on between twelfth-century men and women? There were power relationships going on there, but they were muted and the participants of either sex were equal.

Some relics of that equality of male and female standing survive. The *Tornoi des Dames* ('The Women's Tournament') was written by the noble poet and tourneyer, Huon III d'Oisy, castellan of Cambrai, late in the 1180s. Huon's poem imagines that the great ladies of northern France have assembled and decided to fight a tournament in place of their husbands. Huon gives a straightfaced and knowing account of their meeting at Lagny rather in the manner of a trouvère describing a conventional tournament.[14] It is so very knowing a song that he must have given a performance of it to their faces, and the most likely occasion for doing so would have been as an amusement in one of the post-tournament dinners that were such an important feature of the event. The *Tornoi des Dames* is very good evidence that tourneying magnates made a practice of bringing their wives and female friends with them to the greatest of the meetings. But it merely complements what the romances of Chrétien de Troyes tell us, for he assumed as a matter of course that his heroines and his female audience alike had a consuming passion for the tournament. The tournament was clearly a sport for all the noble family. The fact that the Marshal biography tends to ignore women in the tournament world is all of a piece with its pragmatic fixation on success and prowess. The Marshal was a single-minded careerist and social climber; kings and counts, not countesses, could give him what he wanted most. Huon d'Oisy, Hennuyer magnate and sometime count of Boulogne, was much more relaxed and urbane.

In the tournament we see a world of fun and remarkably free association between the sexes, perhaps increasingly so after 1200.[15] The thirteenth-century poet Jakemes takes it as a matter of course that competitors 'had with them their wives, their lovers or their daughters for companions, and they brought with them whatever fair ladies they might, for their better enjoyment. Because of this the knights were themselves more vivacious, full of fun and flirtatious, and also more resolute.'[16] It was fun-filled perhaps, but probably not a relaxed world, because there was danger in free association between men and women. Cardinal James de Vitry spelled it out:

> There is plenty of the seventh deadly sin, called Lust, since the tournament goers are out to entice shameless women, if they achieve prowess in arms; they are also accustomed to carry certain female tokens, as it they were their banners.[17]

The entire plot of Jakemes's romance of the *Castellan de Couci*, a historical novel set in the tourneying society of Richard the Lionheart's time, is about the adulterous passion between Reginald the castellan and the wife of a local lord. It was only possible because the two could meet frequently under cover of the the 'lonc sejour', the tournament season in the north east of France.[18] It was just the same sort of world where Andrew the Chaplain's courtly and sexually charged dialogues between men and women might occur in reality. It was the world where Count Alfonso of Poitiers, the brother of Louis IX, might organise gambling sessions in his palace at Acre in 1250, and invite *gentilz homes* and *gentils femmes* to crowd in and join the fun.[19] However, it is equally likely that unattached noblemen rarely went beyond flirting, even if they went that far. The social and physical penalties for proven adultery were not pleasant. William de Lorris gives sound advice for men and women in such social situations in his *Roman de la Rose*:

> Serve and honour all women; take every care to be at their service. If you hear some slanderer (*mesdisant*) who is putting down a particular woman, rebuke him and tell him to keep quiet. So far as you can, behave in a manner which is pleasing to ladies and girls, so that they hear and speak nothing but good about you. That is the way your reputation will increase.[20]

PART THREE

Documents on the Tournament

1

Osbert of Arden of Kingsbury
Retains Thurkil Fundu to Attend him
to Tournaments (1124 x 1139)

The form of this charter is unexceptionable in everything but its existence. It is unusual for such an early conveyance to survive, if not unprecedented. The others that do survive tend to be awards by abbeys of offices, but this is a grant of layman to layman. There was, however, an Anglo-Saxon tradition of committing land transactions between laymen to parchment: the old practice of 'bookland'. Both the parties here are English by descent, and it might be that what we are seeing here is a continuing indigenous tradition of written conveyances.

Osbert of Arden to all his men and friends, now living or yet to come. Know that I have granted and conceded and confirmed by my charter one carrucate of reclaimed woodland to Thurkill Fundu in Ashbrook, with everything that belongs to it, and also meadowland beneath Kingsbury, at Bradford, which is called Longlands, to hold in fee and inheritance in return for his homage and service, himself and his heirs, to hold it of me and my heirs freely and exempt, with all its liberties, in open countryside and woodland and everywhere else. He will hold it for this service, namely, that when I request it in due form he will carry my painted lances on my horses and at my expense, from London or Northampton to my house at Kingsbury. When I wish to go overseas to the tournaments, I will take him and bring him back completely at my own expense. Witnesses: Edric the priest, Ralph son of Alegot, Thomas of Arden, his son, Thomas the clerk, Godwin, Hoviet, his father, Roger of Hurley, Swein of Bickenhill, Robert Waleis, Morin, Osbert my son, Philip his brother, and many others.

Translated from British Library, Cotton Charter xxii, 3.

2

Count Geoffrey of Anjou's Adventures
at a Tournament on the Border of Normandy
and Brittany (Supposedly *c.* 1128)

There are a number of objections to the acceptance of this anecdote as in any way a historical account of Geoffrey of Anjou's youthful tourneying. It was written by John, a monk of Marmoutier, some time after Geoffrey's death in 1151, most likely around 1170. The date of the supposed tournament is an immediate obstacle. Geoffrey's father, Count Fulk, left France to become king of Jerusalem in June 1128, immediately after the marriage of Geoffrey and Mathilda, the daughter of King Henry of England. But Count William Clito of Flanders, supposedly at the tournament, had in fact died the previous year in the course of a war with his uncle, King Henry. A further objection is that the exploits of Count Geoffrey on the tournament field and in combat with the giant Englishman belong to the world of the romance epic, and some such influence clearly lies behind John's prose, especially when it shifts from the past to the present tense. The incident in fact parallels one described earlier in the work in relation to an earlier count, Geoffrey Martel, and the intention here may be to demonstrate how Geoffrey is the equal of his great ancestors. The fantastic and pseudo-Arthurian tinge to this story can be seen particularly in the way that John is led away at times to suggest that Geoffrey is in fact directing killing strokes against the Normans. Like David, Geoffrey is made to behead his Goliath, despite the fact that in the circumstances of a tournament that would be murder: he has clearly forgotten that he is writing about a tournament, not war. It may also be that John has some idea that ancient tournaments were more violent than those of his own day. Another part of John's inspiration may be an inaccurate recollection of the jousting that Wace of Bayeux mentions as happening on the sands of Mont-St-Michel between the armies of the brothers Robert Curthose, William Rufus and Henry in 1091, but that happened in war time. On the more positive side, there is nothing unlikely in John's assumption that the young Count

Geoffrey had a tourneying career in the late 1120s, which must rely on some historical tradition. There is nothing unlikely either in finding Normans and Bretons regularly tourneying on the sands of Mont-St-Michel, which lay on the border between both duchies.

When his father Fulk was raised, as we have said, to the throne of Jerusalem, Count Geoffrey devoted himself to the exercise of arms and the pursuit of celebrity. Not very long afterwards a day was fixed for a tournament between the Bretons and the Normans on the level sands of Mont [St-Michel]. Count William of Flanders, Count Theobald of Blois and his brother Stephen, the lord of Mortain, appeared on the Norman side, as all three were nephews of King Henry of England. Count Geoffrey came with them as an addition to their numbers. Opposite them were drawn up the ranks of the Bretons, remarkable for their courage and skill indeed, but fewer in numbers. When Count Geoffrey of Anjou saw that the Breton side was unequal, he rode away from the Normans, and just before the beginning of the event he lent his support and that of his men to the underdogs.

The charge commences and the lines meet; there is a great clatter of arms; trumpets sound and there is a chorus of horns of all sorts; the warhorses drown it with their screaming; shields sparkling with gold in the sunlight glitter all across Mont-St-Michel. Men are united in combat; ashwood spears are splintered; swords are notched. Now the fighting is hand to hand; shields clash; saddles are emptied; some horses are thrown down; others have lost their riders and run wild on the field with broken reins. Geoffrey attacks his enemies, a formidable sight to the other side; he has his hands full riding here and there to rally his men. He throws down many men with his lance and then redoubling his efforts he finishes off others with innumerable strokes from his sword. The Bretons pursue victory behind their leader, dealing out all sorts of mayhem to the Normans. The count of Anjou closes in, fiercer than a lion, the Breton squadrons close in, scenting victory. The Normans, exhausted by so hard a contest, turn their backs and run and are forced to retreat to their base; the many routed by the few. Demoralised by unexpected opposition, the Normans are conceding this extraordinary tournament to the Bretons.

Enticed by the spreading popularity of the tournament, an English knight (*miles Saxonicus*) of great stature has come from across the seas. The Normans put their hopes of winning in his great strength and fearlessness. So out of their camp comes this knight, beyond the measure of any normal man, and standing on raised ground he challenges the Bretons to put up whoever they like to meet him in single combat. Those who hear him go pale and their strength drains away. Everyone is naturally intimidated by the idea of a duel with a man of such size. Geoffrey, realising how such a challenge has reduced courageous men to feeble cowards, rallies his spirit and, careless of any doubt and obstacle, spurs on his horse. He takes up his arms and, with the men looking on from every side, begins a single combat with the gigantic knight. It is a hard fight. To the Englishman, who is far beyond the normal man in strength, a lance is no more than a weaver's spindle. He attacks the count of Anjou, breaks his shield and hauberk and draws blood. But Count Geoffrey, as if he were rooted to his horse, stands unmovable, and thrusting with his lance overthrows his enemy, and standing over his fallen opponent, he cuts off his head with his sword. He leads away in triumph the horse of the defeated knight, to the humiliation of the Normans and the glory of his own men, and he retires as the glorious champion, taking his prize with him.

The envious counts are jealous of Geoffrey but they say that he, as the king's son-in-law, may now tourney with them with no fear, as there is no danger that he would be taken captive. Because of this Geoffrey, a shining example of a knight, stoking up his own reputation and keen for further contests, began to engage in tournaments within the borders of Flanders and even further afield, and, eager for celebrity, began to receive the reward for his success in his own day.

Translated from John of Marmoutier, *Historia Gaufredi ducis Normannorum,* in *Chroniques des comtes d'Anjou et des seigneurs d'Amboise,* ed. L. Halphen and R. Poupardin (Paris, 1913), 181–83.

3

Huon d'Oisy III, Castellan of Cambrai, Composes a Fantasy of the Noblewomen of his Day Tourneying at Lagny-sur-Marne (*c.* 1187 x 1189)

The date of this fragmentary poem must necessarily precede the departure of Huon d'Oisy on the Third Crusade (1190) but must also broadly post-date 1160 when the young Ida became countess of Boulogne. The best potential for dating the poem is an apparently historical reference to the 'year when the knights were away'. Knights foresook the circuit for only two reasons, crusade and real war. The most likely occasion for this would be the campaigning of the 1180s when France and the Plantagenet realm were at war, and most likely the period in 1187 x 1189 when war was almost continuous.

c. 1   In that year that the knights were away
and the valiant did no feats of arms
the ladies went to tourney instead at Lagny.
The tournament was organised by
the countess of Vermandois and the lady of Coucy;
they said that they wanted to experience
the sort of strokes
that their lovers gave out for their sake.
Ladies from all over the place
organised it that each would
retain a household with her.
When they came to the meadows they got armed
then they mustered in front of Torcy.
Yolanda de Cailly went first on to the field;
Margaret d'Oisy was eager to joust with her;
Amice the hardy rides forward, seizing her reins.

c. 2 When Margaret saw Yolanda back off,
      She shouted 'Cambrai!' and grabbed the reins to drag her away;
      Let anyone who saw it launch at her and prevent it!
      Then Katherine with the eager face
      began to marshal the lines
      and to cry 'Move forward'.
      So let those who are watching for her sign go forward,
      pull at reins, give and evade swordstrokes
      and brandish their tall lances
          . . .
      cause iron to ring out
      and pull mail hoods out from under helmets
      and cause to break
          . . .
      with great panache!
      Bringing up the rear comes a great reinforcement,
      Isabel, who comes to maintain the fight;
      The lady seneschal also arrives
      and she will have no mercy on them at all.

c. 3 A squadron comes riding after her
      with Adeline riding and shouting ...
      for the lady seneschal.
          . . .
      Alice de Trie rides in front of Yolanda
      crying 'Aguillon!'.
      Very fine she looks, riding along the ranks.
      The queen rides before all on an iron gray steed
          . . .
      armed with a mace and wearing a silver hauberk;
      with no contradiction she carries it across the field;
      Jehane comes riding up behind her
      who has retained many a serjeant with her;
      Isabel rides out and encounters
      the brave Alice de Monceaux,
      and forces her to offer pledge for ransom;
      she is carried off with her
      riding on a roncin.

c. 4   The countess of Champagne soon appears
       riding on a Spanish dappled horse,
       and she and her people ride directly into the fight;
       everyone rides against her and mills around
       and the fight there is very fierce.
       More than a hundred attack her,
       and Alice reaches out to grab her,
       she and her company seize the countess's reins,
       Alice – she of the noble body –
       crying 'Montfort',
       and the countess dismounts now she is taken,
       and Yolanda is made a captive fairly,
       she who is not proud and scornful,
       as a German would be.
       Isabel – whom we all know – gallops on to the field,
       and attacks like a mad thing,
       crying over and over again her war cry,
       'Let's get them, Châtillon!'

c. 5   A company rides up in ambush
       and hems in Amice on every side,
       and her lance breaks on a shield;
       She cries 'Lille! Let's get their reins,
       they're in our power!'
       The countess of Clermont has been
       struck by a mace across her abdomen,
       right where her kidney is.
       Clemence attacks heedlessly with her club
         ...
       and cries 'Beausart!'.
       The whole company is routed and disperses in flight;
       and no one stays to fight
       when [Clemence] sees Ida of Boulogne, the distinguished;
       she rallies first on crossing a ditch,
       she takes the countess by the reins,
       and cries out 'God our help'.

c. 6   The fighting there is very intense
       Isabel of Marly rides up crying

'God our help!', and she gives and takes many cuts.
A company rides by on the other side of the river;
Gertrude, who cries 'Mello'
pursues it across the fords.
Agnes de Triecoc rides up, who has sustained
many cuts to her arms that day,
she has broken many lances, and seized many reins,
she has hit out at many, and many times attacked.
Beatrice cries out 'Poissy!'
There is no one

 ...

better than she,
and Joie d'Arsi approaches

 ...

Marion de Juilly and makes her turn and dismount,
then she jousts at her
and cries 'Saint Denis!'.

c. 7 All passed across the river, Alice de Rolleiz,
jaunty of body, rides up with her company;
Clemence de Bruai goes in front,
Cecilia de Compiègne rides directly behind
pushing forward
and attacks Isabel d'Ausnai
who has wandered into the middle of them;
The fair Alice falls on her with enthusiasm
who cries 'Garlandon!'

 ...

Agnes rides up crying 'Paris!';
Ada de Parcain sees them:
she cries 'Beaumont!',
and pursues them right into the middle of the town,
and she sees coming there Agnes of Cressonessart;
Isabel de Villegaignart also rides up.
The tournament breaks up
because it was now growing late.

c. 8 I have said and recounted a little,
and now I shall return to it;

they announced a tournament the next day.
You shall be told of the prowess of Yolanda.
When she had closed her helm
and urged forward her horse Morel,
she took her checkered shield,
hurling herself among the maidens in the meadows.
There were a hundred of them bearing lances;
she asked for no truce.
With no hesitation she rode to joust
right in amongst the other side.
far and wide and for a long time they have trumpeted
and serenaded what they witnessed.
She defeated and broke
all opposition on every side.
She set up her tent on the meadows outside Torcy;
She slept there, and gave away
whatever she had won.

Translated from text in A. Jeanroy, 'Notes sur le tournoiement des dames', *Romania*, 28 (1899), 240–44.

4

William Marshal Excels at his First Tournament between Ste-Jamme and Valennes in the Retinue of William, the Chamberlain of Tancarville (1166)

When day broke, the knights arrived.
They remained outside the front of their refuges (*recez*)
until such time as they were completely armed
at their leisure, as one would expect of them.
Then the companies rode forward
in tight and ordered formation.
And I can tell you that in front of the lists
this was no formal joust;
there was not a single word of argument spoken
except of winning or losing all.
The chamberlain remained at the back.
That day he had easily in his troop
forty knights or more,
and nobody had ever seen such finely equipped ones.
They rode with great skill
to the side of the tournament area.
Beyond, the king of Scotland
rode with a numerous company;
he had many finely equipped men with him,
and it would have been very hard to estimate their number.
Why should I spin out my tale at great length?
Sir Philip de Valognes
was armed so elegantly and so very finely,
and the handsomest knight of all of them;
he was also swifter than any bird.
For this many a knight observed him.
The Marshal observed him closely,
then immediately he left the ranks,

spurring on his horse Blancart;
he launched himself at great speed into their midst
and seized Philip's bridle.
Philip made every effort to defend himself,
but no effort was of any avail:
the Marshal by force dragged him towards himself
and took him away from the tournament.
Philip readily gave his pledge to the Marshal,
who so placed his trust in him
that, for that reason, he let him go.
And, after leaving Philip,
he rejoined the tournament.
Immediately he knocked down a knight
with a lance he had managed to pick up;
it was only a stump, but he did so well with it
that the knight pledged his word
to become his prisoner.
So now he had two very valuable prisoners,
and that without doing injury or harm to them.
He stretched out his hand to take a third.
and, as a result of his great effort and application,
he had him soon pledging his word to be his prisoner.
And, in the meantime, another knight came forward,
while he was getting him down from his horse,
and said: 'Since I was in on his capture,
I should also have a share in his horse.'
The Marshal replied: 'Willingly.
Since you wish to have your part,
turn up at the sharing out of the booty.'
So much he said, and regretted it afterwards,
but he never went back on his word.
My lords, in very truth, it is no lie
that God is wise and courtly:
he is swift to come to the help and assistance
of any man who puts his trust in him.
Only that day had the Marshal been
a poor man as regards possessions and horses,
and now he had four and a half,
fine mounts and handsome, thanks to God.

He also had hacks and palfreys,
fine pack-horses and harnesses.
The tournament disbanded
and the Chamberlain left
with the men in his company.
They paid the Marshal great honour
and treated him very courteously,
more so than they had done before.

History of William Marshal, ed. A. J. Holden and D. Crouch, trans. S. Gregory (3 vols, Anglo-Norman Text Society, Occasional Publications Series, 4–6, 2002–6), i, lines 1303–78.

5

Bertrand de Born Sings of How Count Raymond V of Toulouse Has Commissioned Him to Write a Poetical Summons to a Tournament (1181 x 1185)

This poem of Bertran's is generally dated to 1181 on the basis of a known campaign of King Alfonso II of Aragon in the south of France. The meeting advertised here is supposedly an episode in the warfare between Count Raymond and King Alfonso, who advanced into Toulouse and Aquitaine in June 1181, and the summons was supposedly more to defend Toulouse from siege than to attend a tournament. But the reference to a three-day meeting and the expectation of there being fighting between several Gascon counts hardly supports that interpretation ... It seems more likely to date from the period between 1181 and 1185 when Sancho, brother of the king, was regent of Provence and active in the Midi. The poem is in fact more likely to be an artfully composed summons to a tournament, dashed off by Bertran to be used by the count of Toulouse's heralds as they proclaimed it across Gascony and the Spanish marches. Many of the phrases are clearly designed to stir up the nobles of particular regions to come and compete. Although it doesn't publish the date, it gives the place of meeting, the manner of accommodation and the length of the tournament. It also seems to be giving a list of those princes and nobles who have already indicated that they intend to be present, so as to encourage others to attend what Count Raymond hoped to be an unmissable event, and a great parade of his own lordship and fame.

[1] The count has sent in haste by means of Ramon-Luc d'Esparron for me to compose for him the sort of song by which a thousand shields might be dented, by which helms, hauberks, mail and padded coats may be frustrated and broken.

[2] So I must do as he wishes, since he has communicated to me what

his reasons are. I can in no way refuse him this. But though it is advisable for me to obey, how the Gascons will take it out on me! But despite them, I must do my duty.

[3] The count will set up his gonfanon at Toulouse, towards Montaigut, on his meadows besides the quarter of Peyrou. When he has raised his tent we will settle ourselves around it and we will sleep there for three nights under the stars.

[4] The princes and the barons will be with us there, and the most celebrated fellow knights the world can offer. The men who are regarded as the most wealthy, the most brave and the most accomplished will join with us there.

[5] As soon as they will have arrived to engage in the tournament across the fields, the Catalans and the Aragonese will fall often and with little effort, for they won't be able to keep in their saddles, such frequent blows will we belabour them with there.

[6] It cannot fail to happen that lances will be raised towards the skies, and that samite, satin and sendal will be unfurled, and that the cords, the tents, the fastenings, the posts, the marquees and the pavilions will be erected.

[7] The king who lost Provence [*Alfonso II of Aragon*], the lord of Montpellier, Roger, the son of Bernard Aton, and the lord count Peter will fight together with the count of Foix, with Bernard and Sancho, the brother of the defeated king.

Let each man look to his arms, for he is awaited at Toulouse. I wish that the magnates would always be so moved against each other.

Translated from *Poésies complètes de Bertran de Born*, ed. A. Thomas (Toulouse, 1888), 4–6, with acknowledgement to the French translation in R. du Boysson, *Études sur Bertrand de Born* (repr. Geneva, 1973).

6

Lancelot, Although a Prisoner, Attends the Tournament of Pomeglai under Parole (*c.* 1220)

[41.1] So it was that Lancelot was a captive, as the story says, in the charge of the seneschal of Gorre, who was very fond of him and would let him do what he wanted, apart from leaving his castle. But so widespread was the news of the tournament that Lancelot got to know of it and he was deeply depressed that he could not be there. The seneschal was rarely to be found at home, but his wife was always there, a woman of great beauty and charm. Lancelot was under light guard and left his tower daily to dine with the lady, who was more taken with him than any other man because of the fascinating stories she had heard him tell.

[41.2] When the day of the tournament gathering (*assamblee*) was upon them, Lancelot was even more cast down and withdrawn than before. The lady observed how little he ate and drank and how ill he looked, so she asked him what was going on. He did not want to talk about it but she urged him to do so in the name of the thing he loved best. 'My lady', he said, 'since you have conjured me to tell you what it is that is bothering me, then be aware that I shall never eat or drink anything which does me good, as I am not going to be at that tournament gathering [*p. 96*] where I of all people should be; it is because of this I am unwell. So now you have heard of my troubles, it grieves me, but it was your insistence made me tell of it.' 'Lancelot', she replied, 'if it could be arranged that you were there, would you do me a great favour?' 'Yes, my lady', he said, 'whatever I have is yours'. 'If you give me a certain gift which I will ask of you, I will permit you to go there and provide you with arms and a good horse.'

[41.3] Lancelot was as pleased as it was possible to be, so he agreed to the terms. She continued: 'Do you know what it is that you have given me? It is your love.' At this Lancelot did not know what to say, for if he went back on his promise he knew he would not get to the tournament that he so wanted to attend. But if he bestowed his love on her, he would be lying to her, for she wanted all his affections, as had long been obvious. 'So what are you going to say to me?' she asked. 'My lady, may I never deny you anything that I have, for you have well earned it.' 'So do you give me your love?' she asked. 'My lady,' he said, 'I give you whatever I can give without reservation.'

[41.4] She saw that he was embarrassed, and thought that he was being tongue-tied from shyness, so she desired to know what he needed to equip himself until he got his own possessions back. She made ready horse and arms for him. When she knew the time had come for him to set off, she told him and he was delighted to hear it. In the morning once the sun was up she made him ready to go, and with her own hand she armed him. He swore to her on the thing he loved best that he would return as soon as he could get away from the gathering, and death alone would prevent him, and then he took an oath to that effect.

[41.5] So it was that he took his leave from her and rode to the tournament gathering, carrying the seneschal's arms and riding on his good [*p. 97*] horse. He took lodgings a good twenty-one miles from the site (*place*) in the most obscure location he could find, as he did not want to be recognised by anyone. The morning of the meeting came and the queen took her seat on a platform (*bretesche*) outside Pomeglai along with many other ladies and maidens. Many excellent jousts and great mêlées took place in various locations, and Bedivere, Dodinials the Savage, Guerrehes, Gaeries and Agravain his brother, Yvain the Adulterer, and Bors the Exile conducted themselves all too well.

[41.6] Lancelot positioned himself just below the platform and looked [on the queen] with tenderness. With him had come a squire (*vaslés*) from the place of his captivity, who carried his lance for him. The queen looked around at all those who were carrying on so well, but did not recognise her lover. Then Lancelot took his place in the ranks carrying a red shield with three silver bends. His line (*renc*) galloped in such a way that he came up against a knight called Herlions li rois, brother of the king of Northumberland, and quite an accomplished warrior; they exchanged some great strokes. Herlions broke his lance and Lancelot attacked him so fiercely that he threw him to the ground. Then the shout went up that Herloins had charged (*josté*) once too often that day. The people of Logres were very pleased and the other side was none too happy.

[41.7] Then Lancelot began to throw down knights and break lances. A knight rode against him [*p. 98*] called Godez of Beyond the Marches, who crashed into him with great force. Lancelot rode at him (*joste a lui*), he attacked him and threw him down in a heap, Godez and his horse together, and then began to do great deeds. He hurled down all that came against him, but jousted in such a way that he only needed the one lance. He raised it up, and then saw coming against him a knight who was the seneschal of King Claudas of the Desert Land, and they attacked each other. The seneschal splintered his lance and Lancelot struck at him in the throat and hurled him a spear length into the middle of the field. The seneschal was unconscious and the ground covered in his blood, and everyone shouted: 'He's dead! He's dead!'

[41.8] When Lancelot heard it he was deeply upset, he threw down his lance and declared that he would quit the field. He asked his squire (*escuier*) who it was that he had wounded and if he was dying. The squire told him that he was the seneschal of King Claudas and that he lay dead where he fell, for Lancelot had slit his throat. Lancelot said that God had avenged him and he wished to know no more about it. Then he drew his sword as a man who well knew how [*p. 99*], and he struck out heavily to right and left. He threw down horses and knights with his sword strokes and the blows of his fist. He pulled them off their horses by grabbing their mail hoods or the straps of their shields; he ripped helmets from their heads, he struck, pushed and thrust, and attacked with his limbs and his horse as one who is skilled in everything that the best of knights should do. He delighted the entire tournament (*assamblee*) and they wondered if this was Lancelot or not. Sir Gawain was more delighted than anybody else, and he went over to talk to the queen. But she had already worked it out, for she had seen Lancelot in action many times. She was ecstatic with joy, but thought to disguise her feelings before Gawain and the rest.

[41.9] Then she called over one of her ladies-in-waiting, for she dared

trust no one in case they found out her true feelings. The lady of Mal-
ohaut was mortally ill at home and the queen had no one with her with
whom she could share her feelings. She said to the girl: 'Go to that
knight over there and tell him that from now on he should perform as
badly as he has fought well up till now, and by these tokens that I tell
you, that he change his great joy to great misery'. So she [*p. 100*] went
up to the knight and told him, and he took the lance which his squire
was holding. So he hesitated to ride against another knight, and missed
his aim; the knight pressed in on him and knocked him over the crupper of his horse, and he was barely able to get up again.

[41.10] Then Lancelot rode back into the mêlée and whenever he had to
take a great blow he ducked down into the mane of his horse and pre-
tended that he was going to fall. From then on he avoided taking blows
from knights, and he held down his head and fled when he saw knights
coming to engage him; he behaved so that everybody jeered at him and
despised him. The squire who attended him was more embarrassed
about his master than if he had been naked. Lancelot carried on in this
way all day long, until he took himself off. Everybody who had reckoned
him a man of worth were shamefaced. When he came from the field to
his lodgings he dare not explain to his squire or anyone the reason for
his cowardly conduct.

[41.11] The next morning Lancelot got up and returned to the meeting,
not wearing his helmet. A young woman chased after him and recognised him (she was the girl who was with him in the church where he
had raised the tomb of Galahad, and so she knew him). When he had
put on his helmet, she went after him shouting: 'Now a mighty wonder
has happened!' and when they ran into hangers-on and braggarts she
began shouting all the louder. Lancelot started to overthrow knights
with such ease that everyone [*p. 101*] who saw him doing it was aston-
ished.

[41.12] For some while he continued performing with excellence until
the queen sent again by her lady-in-waiting to tell him to fight badly.
He began performing as poorly as he knew how, and the young woman
who had shouted out about him amongst the competitors was so mor-
tified that she dared not say another word, and he carried on doing
badly until midday. Then the queen sent to tell him to do his best and

defeat everyone there. From then onwards no one was talked about apart from him. When the evening came, he threw his shield into the middle of the mêlée and rode up to where it lay. By nightfall everyone knew that Lancelot had been at the tournament, and also they knew that he had fought poorly simply to fool them.

Translated from: *Lancelot: roman en prose du xiiie siècle*, ed. A. Micha (9 vols, Geneva, 1978–83), ii, 95–101.

7

Philip de Remy Pictures a Tournament
at Ressons-Gournay (1230 x 1240)

The following is an extract from the early thirteenth-century romance called La Manekine (the Little Lass) the long and involved story of the princess Joy, daughter of the king of Hungary. Joy is forced to flee Hungary after being threatened with sexual abuse by her father, and she travels incognita by sea (don't ask me how) from Hungary to Scotland, where the king falls in love with her, names her 'Manekine' and marries her. The king decides that for the sake of his reputation as a warrior he must travel to the Continent and join the tournament circuit. Despite Joy's grief, the young king departs from Berwick with his military household.

What follows is actually a lightly fictionalised account of life on the tournament circuit. It includes an account of a meeting of the great tournament held regularly between the villages of Ressons-sur-Matz and Gournay-sur-Aronde, some 15 kilometres north west of Compiègne. This tournament site had quite a history. A great tournament is recalled as being regularly held here as early as 1168, and the biography of Earl William Marshal of Pembroke noted further meetings between Ressons and Gournay in the early summer of 1176, late in November 1182 and on 15 January 1183. Its prominence as a site probably has much to do with the early patronage of Count Philip of Flanders, a generous patron of the twelfth-century tournament circuit. The site was on the borders of his counties of Montdidier and Clermont. The nature of the site was open moorland between two marshy valleys: a well-defined ground, with the two settlements at either end able to offer accommodation to the teams, and make a profit for the locals. Another known tournament site which is mentioned here is the site at Épernon, where William Marshal attended two tournaments in 1179.

The author of La Manekine was the French knight, Philippe de Remy, a prolific poet of the region of the Beauvaisis in northern France (to which, note, he gives a passing nod), who has left several works and who was also a man of affairs in the reign of King Louis IX of France. He was the father of the celebrated legal author and judge, Philippe de Beaumanoir. He almost certainly would have attended tournaments between Ressons and Gournay and at Epernay, and so his account (dating from the 1230s) reflects something of the reality of such an event.

They sailed through the night and as the morning broke they arrived directly at the Damme [the seaport of Bruges] without bad weather or any particular trouble. They arranged for their horses to be disembarked from their boat on the shore, which was accomplished smoothly. The king then entered the town, where lodgings were engaged for him. He had enquiries made about the present whereabouts of the count of Flanders so that he could meet him. He was told that the count was at Ghent where he was making his preparations to go to a tournament at Ressons-sur-Matz; the king was delighted to hear the news. The next day, ready to move on, he took the road to Ghent at first light. The count of Flanders had heard of the king of Scotland's arrival and hurried out to meet him, giving him greetings and a warm welcome.

The count said: 'My lord, I am delighted that you have chosen to come here. I and my people are entirely at your pleasure, whatever you have in mind to do.'

The king replied: 'Many thanks indeed'. And so they came to Ghent, talking as they went, and spent the night with the count. The king asked him about the tournament and where it would take place. The count told him: 'At Ressons'.

At this the king said: 'We will go there. We would ask one thing of you, that you will be willing to join my military household for the occasion.' The count happily consented.

The Scots spent a very comfortable night, and nothing was lacking to put them at their ease. Very early the next morning they took to the road. They came that night to Lille. They spent a good night in the town, which belonged to the count. The next day they again set off very early. They passed to the east of Artois and then entered Vermandois, taking the route through Roye [near Montdidier] and so they came to Ressons. The king dismounted in the town, and with him the Scots and the Flemings. People had begun to arrive and to arrange and occupy their lodgings, people from Boulogne, Artois, Brabant, Vermandois, Flanders, Normandy, Ponthieu, as well as Germans, Alsatians and Bavarians. All these folk took lodging at Ressons, and they fixed outside the windows many shields and banners of various types. On the other side [of the tournament ground] towards Gournay came people from Beauvais (I know it well), from Berry, Brittany, the Île de France, Poitou, Anjou and Champagne also. Such people dismounted at Gournay for the tournament.

So the day came on which the tournament was to happen. When it came, they went straight to hear mass, and then they armed themselves and mounted on their destriers. They rode out on to the field to tourney: a sight to alarm the faint-hearted.

The king of Scotland rode out first in the company of 1000 knights which he had retained with him. He had equipment so very fine that there never was seen its equal. His horse, which was large and tall, was covered with figured cloth of gold, the richest that ever had been. The king, who was handsome and well-built, was in appearance beyond compare, and as well armed as he could be. That day he carried no other device on his arms other than that they were of gold, and as well made as they were tough. He did this as a sign that he had achieved his heart's desire. His actual coat of arms was of three rampant lioncels [little lions] in black on a golden field. Those were what he should have carried, but he had omitted the lioncels and simply carried the golden field. The count of Flanders was with him, who was to serve him well that day.

When both sides had ridden out from Ressons and Gournay, and had entered the field, if you had been there that day you would have seen many a fine horse, shield and banner, of all sorts of fashion. Some black, some white, some gold, some silver and others again of red; they were painted in many colours. The bright sunlight made the colours very splendid. Music was to be heard on all sides, horns and drums, and at that moment the trumpets blared out and echoed across the field. In this way the two sides came out and quickly passed in review, in which it was established with whom each knight rode and to which household he was attached. Then each man took his place and each took the shield recognised as his, and placed his helmet on his head. The king showed his household what shield of his they should recognise, and one knight acted as his attendant. Then he had his helmet laced on which was not in the least rusty, for it was made of shining and bright gold, a pleasure just to look at.

When the king had his helmet laced on his head he rode to the front of his company. He knew much of love and arms, and he gripped his shield close to his side and took his heavy lance in his hand. He urged his horse and it surged forward, and he did not cease from spurring it on till he came up to the fighting. He approached a French knight who had good reason to regret that he did not run away from the king, for he rode at him so rapidly that he knocked the knight and his horse both on to the ground. The knight could not do other than fall, for both his saddle girths gave way and tipped him on the ground. The king had broken his lance, and now he drew his sword, which he put to good use that day. The combat was soon swirling about him. Over a score of knights tried to get to him, one made a grab for his arm, another his body. But he was so powerful and active and managed his horse so well that they could not bring him down. He was able to hold his attackers off until his company rode up. They jostled and shouted to get up with the king and fought off the attacks from either side. They exchanged such strokes that it seemed that he would be deafened. More than fifteen hundred lances flew into splinters. Many were knocked down as a result and plenty of horses were grabbed and captured, and many more mounts galloped across the field, their reins trailing on the ground. Some squires ran after them to capture them, others to recover them.

Now the tournament was fully engaged, where there were so many fine companies and well-mounted knights, and the other sort also, flat on the ground. One knight wins, and another loses, for the game sorts out who has the skill and who has not. Skirmishes are going on in over a score of places, and people are tumbling to the ground, and often they take sword blows on the head, and sometimes, if they are lucky, on the shields, if they have got them in the way. Each knight fights his combat and is not always happy with the blows he gets, for if he gets in one, three land on him. The king shows himself to be more than equal to anyone who has ridden to the tournament. He gives and takes many blows and strikes out to left and right. Anyone who takes him on is likely to end up flat on the ground. After that there is no point in their going to seek their horses, for they are no longer their concern. The king applied himself to the good fight, to attack and defend as well as he can, and devoted himself entirely to it. He put his whole heart into the fighting and is so wrapped up in the cut and thrust that he was the object of everyone's attention that day. One man said to another: 'Look at the marvels that man is accomplishing! It is hardly worth watching anyone else. He seems to be everywhere at once. Do you see how he takes and hands out blows? No one can long stand up to the sort of punishment he is handing out. He really must get recognition for such skill. He is the sort of man to lend money to, for he well knows how to reap rewards. See the shield slung at his shoulder! It's so little touched you'd think a dove could perch there and never get its wings clipped! There never was so fine a king who came from overseas to acquire a reputation and behaved so well. All knights must love him well, praise him and value him.'

All the knights in the various companies who had the space and time to do so watched the king. The rest fought and pushed, and damaged many a fine hauberk. A good few knights were sent somersaulting from their saddles that day, their helmets were crushed and faces bloodied. Some men did well out of it, others badly; some were forced to walk off the field, others rode; one lost and another won. There were many on the field who lost their horses and had afterwards to hand them over to those who had overcome them; they well regretted their losses. In many places were forges smoking to heat up the flames. For the swords there had been so hacked about that, had it been a wood, two thousand carpenters sawing could not have made such a din.

Such was the manner of that day and so it went on till night fell. But the night came and parted the combatants. Then they arranged it that there is another review, but very different from the first one: it was far more subdued. Most of the participants were worse for wear from the heavy blows they had taken. So they leave on foot or horseback and returned to their lodgings. The king came to Ressons and his friends with him, they rode right into the town. When he got there he was well enough, for he had been hit far less than he had struck out at others. He removed his armour quickly as did the count of Flanders, who had done very well that day although I did not mention it. If I had gone into what everyone had done, I could never get on with my story. So don't ask for any other information than that he had done well. The king issued an order that all might have dinner with him who wished it so; there was no knight left in Ressons who was not invited by him. They were supplied with plenty of food and wine. When the meal was over it was nearly morning; so they went off to their beds for the sleep that they all had need of. They slept till mid morning. Then they rose and dressed and returned together to the king's court. The king did not ignore them; he made much of them, showed them great affection and called them his friends and companions. He made up their losses to many of them and retained the best knights in his household, giving them many fine gifts. He could be so generous because he had the prize for the tournament; so he gave to each as befitted his merits. He spent a while making good the losses of either side; so you would find it difficult to find one national group which was willing to be less enthusiastic about him than another.

Before the king left Ressons, by the advice of those at Gournay, he undertook to go to another tournament in a fortnight's time at Épernon. On the king's part he made it generally known by the announcement of a herald around the town. As they know the news is official, everyone says that he wants to go to Épernon. They began to pack their clothes and lay their hauberks within ox hide wrappings; in this manner they readied themselves all to go to the tournament which had been announced by the king's order. The king travelled there with his household, which was made up of fair and noble people. He loved brave knights and was very generous to them with his possessions. At Épernon, where they had gone, they tourneyed at the exercise yards (*a la quisaine*) and the king won the prize there. In this way the king of Scotland acquired great reputation amongst the French, and worked hard to do well. It has turned out that everyone has good will towards him so far as they can; he is a man welcome everywhere he goes.

Translated from Philip de Remy, *La Manekine*, ed. H. Suchier (Société des anciens textes français, 1884), lines 2615–931.

8

The Verses of Henry de Laon on the Tournament (mid thirteenth century)

Nothing is known of Henry de Laon other than his verses, which exist in a corrupt fourteenth-century copy. His name tells us that he lived in the northern edge of the Capetian domain and in the tournament heartland. The detail and the particular complaints he gives tells us that he wrote in the years before the decline of the tournament brought on by Louis IX's prohibitions. Prohibitions were one problem that did not concern him. It seems also that his verses were copied by another poet, Baldwin de Condé, who was active in the second half of the thirteenth century. It is therefore probable that the poem was composed in the period between 1220 and 1250, a time when squires were changing their status within the tournament world, and when heralds were still mostly of little social consequence, as Henry assumes. Although the poem is called (from its rubric) the 'verses on heralds' it is in fact mostly about the tournament, and is highly critical of the state of the sport.

People who are reluctant to put themselves out	[p. 222]
can understand little and comprehend nothing,	
but people who wish to get on in life sensibly	
should press on with things and so learn the ropes.	
Because I am unable to support myself any longer,	5
I find I have to become a herald,	
for Idleness and Greed	
urge and press me so very much,	
telling me that it is ever so important	
to take up an undemanding profession	10
which involves little in the way of effort or pain.	
In my deliberations I find no	
better idea than to be a herald,	
so I require one of them	

to spend a day telling me   15
whatever a year in the profession of arms requires,
and avoid a lot of fatigue in consequence.
Absolute leisure is what I most value:
work puts me 'all out of sorts'
unless it is just talking;   20
that is where my gifts and talents lie,
that is what I am equipped for,
a job where one does no more than utter
words without sense or content.
It is fitting that as people nowadays do not maintain in any way 25
the proper principles of chivalry
or arms, as they were once supposed to be,
they do the very opposite of them.
Tournaments are like social gatherings.
People do not attend from any desire to excel   30
in achievement or in honour.
How I wish that the great lords,
who should be offering themselves in combat,
would leave the lawsuits and arbitrations
by which they keep everyone down.   35
No one wants to be tricked
and if overcome, should wish it done by prowess;
a man is given courage so as to earn fame.
If things carry on this way
the time will come when lawyers will be called on   40
to decide the direction of the sun and give signals
as they do in judicial combats.
Well do I know that true bravery
rejects this sort of nit-picking,
for men who really care for great accomplishments   45
like as much to be winners as losers;
they bear themselves with pride whatever happens.
Tournaments were not originally held   [p. 223]
as a way of capturing horses,
but so as to learn who was manly   50
in his conduct, and to do great deeds of arms,
because of which one would venture to trust such a man
to lead great companies of knights;

so that it would be known in truth and without doubt
that at need he would persist in the assault   55
and help and support his men
and perform great deeds;
and so that it would be known that he could wear a helmet -
which despite the heat and lack of air within
resists the belabouring and dents falling on it   -   60
as lightly as he would wear his cloth cap.
For the man who in such a situation is soaked
in his own blood and sweat,
this I call the high bath of honour.
Prowess, who loathes and despises   65
the magnate who disputes every point,*
requires her due payment and toll,
there, in that place where the mêlée is thickest,
showered with the blows of maces,
clubs and drawn swords,   70
in the combat and in the shock of battle,
whether from the flank or the rear,
whether on the hauberk or shoulder plate,
on flesh or on the ventaille.
Although such a magnate may want a fine reputation   75
he gets little honour or fame,
and so he loses what he is trying to achieve.
A magnate who wishes to triumph at that time
can neither know or demonstrate in advance
the resilience which he may be able to summon up   80
from deep within if he is brought to bay,
nor know how long he may last out
under the assault of arms,
nor how his noble heart and body may strive
to regain its breath and strength   85
under what it may have to endure

---

* *le grant seigneur qui trop bargaingne.* The translation here is that suggested by
Långfors and seems to echo lines 32–37, but it might be that the meaning of
bargaigner here is 'to joust' (the sense employed by *HWM*). In that case the
author is deploring magnates who are abandoning the grand tournament for
the joust.

until he has won what he set out to gain
and until he has the prize for it.
I am not of course saying that therefore
his own people and his team of knights   90
cannot properly fight alongside him
without committing a cheat on others.
But if such a magnate seeks to subvert others

 ...

or get the tournament judge to take himself off,   95
this is not chivalry in the least
so much as greed and pride;
in any case the horse on the winning side
cannot match in value
those of the losing side   100
for the winners lose three to every one that survives.
A long tour of the tournament fields
as we have often seen happen
brings many of our inexperienced knights
to ruin and poverty,   105
but there are as many of them who continue to attend
as there are those who still willingly join the circuit
not in any way perturbed about making a long tour
and the catastrophe awaiting them at the end,
and they go as happily as you please   110
at ease, full of fun and high spirits,
and so each of them looks for his own way
to lose a great deal of money.
My opinion, when I think about it,
is that you should go looking for honour with a solemn face.   115
There was a time when the great lords of the land,
who had paid their homage to Prowess,
men full of honour and high spirits,
gave fine dinners
lasting from sunset to sunrise   120
and truly valued knights,
at the very least those who were their relatives;
those lords knew when   [p. 224]
a poor young knight of talent
came to their doors,   125

but now their shields are taken
and hung next to their banners.
The behaviour of barons today is different,
and you will often see them hestitate
when the cry goes up to lace on their harness;   130
and so the profession of arms falls into decadence.
If the great lords and knights
once were prosperous and powerful;
now they have little ability to get out and about
so poor and indebted are they,   135
but yet they have as great inheritances of land
as their ancestors once did.
I do not know how it happened
that they became so miserly
and began to pursue unfair means   140
in the profession of arms and on the tournament circuit.
Nowadays the lords surround themselves
with their squires
so densely that a poor knight
cannot get anywhere near them,   145
before he can get in two blows
the squires descend on him and he cannot do other than lose,
for now they go for him
and soon they have the knight down on the ground
and often enough he has not even time   150
to lace up his helm before he finds himself flat on his back.
Squires are keen to have the honour
and all the rewards
and want the prize and gifts
and demand all the horses captured.   155
It really seems to me a terrible thing
when squires now are better mounted and equipped
than their masters,
at great expense and luxury.
How a poor man can survive   160
at a tournament, I cannot see for the life of me;
a man who is unable to afford a bodyguard
will not last long on the circuit.
As a result they will very soon damage

the tournament, if it cannot be set up   165
in another way or on another footing,
for I see no man so rich
who can afford the cost of it for very long,
the price of horses being what it is.
But what may well plague a tourneyer more   170
is that he cannot find enough cash,
he has to buy at high prices with no chance of credit:
everyone cheats and impoverishes them,
they are so hounded about that it is a miracle
any people want to live by their arms.   175
One says he is a jester, another that he is a drinking companion,
a third that he is a musician,
but when they get inside the hall
none of them can do or say anything.
Something else that angers me very much   180
is that knights travel around surrounded
by three or four heralds
to tell them what it is that is going on,
and a herald is so expensive
that there is no way the knight can pay for   185
the food and drink he consumes.
So the knight spends all he has
and gets little honour from it.
According to what I gather,
there is hardly any point defending   [p. 225]   190
tournaments, for anyone involved in them knows
they have put themselves beyond any help
and there is no value in their continuing as they are:
but for this let no one person be blamed.

Translated from text in A. Långfors, 'Le dit des hérauts par Henri de Laon', Romania, xliii (1914), 222–25.

9

Matthew Paris on the Death of Gilbert Marshal, Earl of Pembroke, at a Tournament near Hertford (Thursday 27 June 1241)

Gilbert, the earl Marshal, along with a number of other noblemen, fixed a tournament, as military men do, the sort commonly called 'pot luck' (although it turned out anything but lucky) to be held a bowshot from Hertford, for the purpose of training and keeping up their strength. The earl was eager to earn the admiration of his fellow knights at Hertford by the manful and energetic pursuit of military skills, so that everyone would be deservedly united in admiration for the undaunted prowess of himself, a man who was lacking in physical stamina compared to the rest. Earl Gilbert was all the more eager to earn this praise because his first vocation was as a clergyman, and common gossip had it that he was inexperienced and useless as a knight.

The earl mounted up on a very fine horse, an Italian destrier, which he had not ridden before, equipped with a very becoming set of arms, surrounded by a crowd of his knights, who were very soon scattered about and dispersed, chasing eagerly after ransoms. At one point the earl was struggling to rein in his horse from galloping off, and at another was spurring it on ferociously to its full speed, and when he tugged frantically and suddenly back on the reins, both of them snapped off right where the chains connected them to the bit. Now running wild, with head high, the horse managed to catch its rider with a heavy blow on the chest. Quite a few people alleged with some appearance of truth that the reins had been treacherously cut through by some personal enemy of the earl, so that he should be killed when he was carried away or kicked by his high-mettled horse, or at least be taken captive and be at the mercy of his enemies.

The earl had eaten too much, and was blinded by heat, dust and sweat, with the heavy helmet pressing hard on his head. Neither he nor anyone else could restrain the horse. Carried off by a horse running wild, the earl began to sway in the saddle and after a little while fell in a swoon from the animal, and, still caught by one of the stirrups, was dragged for some while across the field; so his body was shattered, with broken limbs and gashes. As a result, the earl died wretchedly on 27 June, as the evening was drawing on, in Hertford Priory, in distressing agony and surrounded by sobbing onlookers. Gasping out his final breath, just after taking his last communion for his soul's salvation, he died in the priory church.

When his body was disembowelled they found his liver was crushed and blackened from the impact of the blows the earl had taken. His entrails were buried in the priory church where he had died, in front of the altar of the blessed Virgin. The next day his body was taken to London, escorted by his younger brother and all his household, for burial next to his father and elder brother. A knight of the earl's household also died in the same tournament, one Robert de Saye, whose entrails were buried along with the earl's. On that day there were many knights and squires injured, their limbs broken and seriously wounded, because the grudges of many of the participants turned a tournament into a battle.

Translated from Matthew Paris, *Chronica Majora*, ed. H. R. Luard (7 vols, Rolls Series, 1884–87), iv, 135–36.

10

Matthew Paris on an Accidental Death at a Round Table Held over Several Days near Walden Abbey, Essex (September 1252)

In that same year some knights, in order to put their skill and hardiness to the test by military exercises, decided that they would test their strength not in the hastilude commonly called a tournament, but rather in that knightly game called a 'round table'. So they gathered on the octave of the Nativity of the Blessed Virgin in formidable numbers near the abbey of Walden: northerners, southerners and not a few knights from overseas. On that day and the next, according to the manner in which this sort of military game is organised, the English knights jousted energetically but in high good humour, so that all the foreigners present there were filled with admiration.

On the Wednesday,* two particularly admired knights, namely Ernaut de Montigny and Roger of Leyburne, fully armed according to the manner of knights and mounted on very fine destriers, rode each other down with lances. Roger, targetting his lance – of which the point was not blunted as it ought to have been – under Ernaut's helm, sliced through his throat, windpipe and arteries, for he was unarmoured in that area and lacking a collar piece. So, the mortally wounded man falling headlong to the ground, Roger was deeply upset, as it seemed. Ernaut died on the spot. Because the dead man left no one equal or even close to him in accomplishment in England, an unheard of wailing and mourning was raised among the knights gathered there. Those who had arrived at Walden full of happiness were suddenly scattered in sadness and grief.

The body was buried with a great many tears and with due propriety in the nearby abbey, while many nobles were still at Walden and preparing to depart. No knight grieved so much for the dead man as the one who had brought about his death, namely Roger, who promptly announced that he would go on crusade for the salvation of his soul.

Since it was accepted that he had mortally wounded Ernaut unwittingly and unintentionally he was not blamed for, or accused of the death. There were many English nobles present at that knightly gathering, however, and particularly the earl of Gloucester, who immediately after the blow to Ernaut pressed for the extraction of the fragment of the lance from the throat of the wounded man, as the iron and splintered wood remained protruding from the wound. When it was taken out and inspected by the knights it was found to have a very sharp point in the fashion of a dagger, being as broad as a knife, when it ought to have been and was expected to be blunt, shaped rather like a short plough blade or 'vomerulus', called in French a 'soket'. For this reason Roger, who had acted so innocent, became a suspect that he had treacherously carried out a vile murder, particularly since Ernaut had broken Roger's leg in an earlier tournament.

Translated from Matthew Paris, *Chronica Majora*, ed. H. R. Luard (7 vols, Rolls Series, 1884–87), v, 318–19.

---

* 'Quarta die sequenti' probably referring not to the fourth day after the Monday, but to Wednesday, which was the 'fourth day' of the week.

11

Sarrazin, a Herald, Attacks King Philip III of France's Prohibition of Tournaments (1278)

This passage is part of the introduction to Sarrazin's long poem on the organised jousting held at Hem-sur-Somme in September 1278. It cannot have been written long after the Hem meeting, because King Philip temporarily lifted his ban early in 1279. We know little of Sarrazin other than that he was evidently a herald commissioned by the organisers of the festivities to immortalise their efforts. Sarrazin did them proud, but he took the opportunity in his introduction to lay out the grievances of the aristocracy and people such as himself on the prohibition of tourneying by King Philip III. The arguments are surprisingly cogent and wide-ranging, and would seem to be more than the individual contribution of Sarrazin. It may be that there is the text or agenda of some sort of noble petition lying behind his work.

It is for me to weigh into those men who give the king the sort of advice through which his royal decrees undermine progress and Prowess is exiled from the realm. My lord Leisure rejoices in every part of France and does what he likes: he hunts with his dogs and hawks and after that he drinks, he eats and falls asleep. Idleness makes herself at home and is seen with all the best people. Idleness is the most good natured lady that ever was born, for which you need only observe Lord Leisure; for she is quite at his disposal and lies late in bed with him every morning, hindering any request made to him. She it is who is all too good at excuses, and she it is who always puts herself first. It seems to me that in France Generosity, Prowess and Courtliness have all of them been subdued by her and her daughter Shame, a fact that ought to be causing the king and all his good friends anxiety.

If you listen, please, to me, you may not be misled further about the truth of all this. It used to be that the whole world came to tourney in France. I see the French now dismayed that they have lost that happy predominance, and my God, how much they had need of it! How many people gained their reputation because of it! But the man of prowess has gone abroad. Do we not know that he has gone away to the tourney fields where he is cut off from his old friends, whom once he used to respect? There was a time when King Philip came to Compiègne or Creil-sur-Oise, and many knights in white and red did deeds of arms in his presence. But never have I heard it said by anyone that the king of France entered into the marches.* No king of France has ever participated in a tournament from the time when Noah entered the ark, and no one knows if a king ever did more than come to one, and I have never heard talk of it. I don't believe it has ever happened, and I don't believe it ever will.

Because something of the sort may yet happen however, I, the writer of this tale, tell you that are yet to be born, that this is the year of the incarnation 1278. It is no more than that by a day or night, than the date I have told you. The particular king I am telling you about is the son of the good King Louis, and whether he is right or wrong, he has banned the tournament. This has deeply distressed many people. First there is the professional entertainer who once earned money there daily, and then there is the herald, the harness-maker, the farrier and the saddler. Even those who open their houses for lodgings continually go around cursing the king who has forbidden the tournament. 'Forbid the tournament and you forbid everything that goes with it!' say the retailers of fine wines and the sellers of spices, partridges and plovers. Everybody whose living depends on the tournament says: 'Amen, so may God grant it!' Many poor fellows got their wages there who are now living in poverty, men who would be prosperous and happy if tourneying was going on as it should do.

Some people have nothing to say about it, who ought to say much. What sort of people are these? They are the retained knights (*baceler*). They should by no means keep their heads down for such men lose more by the ban than anyone, an argument which is no fantasy; it is gospel truth. These knights and their men nowadays hang around towns looking for trouble and fights, men who would not be there at all if they had money and other rewards to earn; that is what it is to be on the tournament circuit, so the ban is a bad bargain for them. These knights

---

* *marce*, here seems to signify 'march': perhaps meaning the northern counties of France beyond the royal demesne where tourneying was still prevalent.

ought to be earning honourable rewards for themselves and putting those bodies at risk that are not now valued at a halfpenny. What must happen for them to speak out?

Peasants are becoming knights and knights are becoming less in status than minstrels. So I say loud and clear to everyone that knights should be valued for their deeds of arms, and a man should make his name before he takes his place amongst them. But everything is turned on its head because of this ban. Men are ever so full of their deeds at the opening events and full of their bravery during the first day's jousting. But if everyone is a beginner they can all play at being seasoned knights. But I will say what I think about them: no one can assert his worth just by talking. A knight does not make himself famous by prattling on so much that he is tiresome, just like some gales blow themselves out with little rain. A knight who has little talent, I would remind you, cannot hide it when he rides his jousts.

My fair lords, please note this, may God grant that all noble men live so well and in such a state that he does not find fault with any of them! And may God grant also that the king realise how his kingdom has fallen so low that knights now cross into the Empire to tourney and France is spurned. This is such a matter for grief. King of France, you should be very much concerned that money from Artois, England and Cologne in the Rhineland ought to be spent in France in those tournaments you have banned.

Translated from Sarrazin, *Roman de Ham*, in *Histoire des ducs de Normandie et des rois d'Angleterre*, ed. F. Michel (Paris, 1840), 215–21.

12

The 'Statute of Arms' of King Edward I of England
(1292)

It is ordained and confirmed by statute at the petition of the bannerets of England that from henceforth no tourneyer, however wealthy he may be, may take as escort more than three squires to serve him, and the squire will carry the arms of the lord he will be serving on the day as a device.

No knight or squire attending a tournament shall carry a pointed sword, nor a pointed knife, nor mace, nor sword with sharpened edge during the event. Those who carry the banners may be armed with a mail corselet, leggings, shoulder plates and helmet, but nothing else.

If it happens that any earl or baron or other knight act against this statute, that offending knight should, for all his status, lose his horse and arms, and be detained at the pleasure of my lord the king's brother [Earl Edmund of Lancaster], [Gilbert de Clare] earl of Gloucester and [Henry de Lacy] earl of Lincoln. If any squire should do anything in breach of the statute on any particular, then he is to lose horse and arms, and may spend up to three years in the king's prison.

If any landed knight offend, other than the knights in the service of their lords, then he may reclaim his horse but otherwise be subject to the same penalties as the aforesaid squires.

No one except the great lords, that is earls and barons, may be armed with more than knee-pieces, leg armour, shoulder plates and helmet. No one can carry pointed swords and knives, mace or broadsword, and if anyone is equipped in breach of this statute, then he will lose the horse on which he rides and may be in prison for as long as a year.

Those who come to watch the tourneying should be completely unarmed, and carry no pointed knives, sword, mace or club, on pain of the same forfeitures as applies to the aforesaid squires. No attendant or footman should carry sword, knife, club or lance, and if any are found on them the penalty is a year in prison.

Furthermore, if great lords hold dinners then they should admit no squires other than those who normally carve before their lords.

No king of arms or minstrels may carry concealed weapons on them other than their blunted swords. The kings of arms should wear only their armorial tabards, etc.

Translated from an early seventeenth-century copy British Library, MS Harley 69, fo. 17r.

13

Jean de Condé, a Noble Poet of Hainault, Writes on the Tournament and Joust as a Proving Ground (*c.* 1317 x 1337)

The date of this poem can only be assigned on the basis of Jean's known period of attachment to the court of Hainault, where he was body squire to the count. It deals with all three 'matters of arms', joust, tournament and war. The translation given here deals only with the jousting and tourneying section.

> The veterans who participate in feats of arms
> insist that youngsters go jousting,
> firstly so as to learn to manage their horses 35
> restraining them and urging them on;
> secondly so as to toughen up their bodies in respect of arms
> and know how to strike out with a sword
> and grow more used to wearing armour
> so that they lose their timidity 40
> and can take a great blow well.
> No one should undertake the joust lightly,
> for by entering into it
> he places both his horse and his own life at risk;
> the strain of it is grim, 45
> but, if he wishes to pursue it, a man may do many great things.
> The tournament, as is maintained in all truth,
> is more of a finishing school
> for the young folk in how to fight well
> and throw down their opponents, 50
> so that they know how to take care of themselves
> during the event and to perform well in the grand charge;
> to suffer the hardship and the labour of it all;
> to carry their armour with stoicism;

to get themselves known and to know others.   55
and to increase their fitness and their fame.
A new knight who enters into a tournament
and lines up with the others with any confidence
has to have a resolute spirit and disposition,
he has to brace himself in all his limbs   60
whether to exchange sword blows
or suffer attack from all sides,
so that if he is battered about in this way
he is still clinging to his horse
so strongly that no one can haul him off it,   65
and he charges down his opponents
so powerfully that he makes them all veer away;
and thus he makes his appearance an object of fear
to all who see him coming
and whoever they are, they keep out of his way.   70
He places himself there where the line of the charge is deepest
as firm as any tower,
like a veritable Gawain or Perceval,
amongst the steaming horses
and the dust as it climbs in the air,   75
in the thunder of drums
and the blaze of trumpets,
of attackers and defenders,
in the clatter of sword strokes,
where their ventailles are slashed,   80
where their coats of arms ripped;
there where the press of men is pushed apart
by the power of the strongest,
where the heart of the young knight ever beats high.

Translated from text in *Li dis des .iii. mestiers d'armes*, in *Dits et contes de Baudouin de Condé et de son fils Jean de Condé*, ed. A. Scheler (3 vols, Brussels, 1866–67), ii, 72–74.

Notes

Notes to Acknowledgements

1. M. Vale, *The Princely Court: Medieval Courts and Culture in North West Europe, 1270–1380* (Oxford, 2001), 184.

Notes to Chapter 1: Beginnings and Sources

1. *Li dis des .iii. mestiers d'armes* in, *Dits et contes de Baudouin de Condé et de son fils Jean de Condé*, ed. A. Scheler (3 vols, Brussels, 1866–67), ii, 71–72.
2. *Passio Karoli comitis auctore Galberto*, ed. G. H. Pertz, in, *MGH Scriptores*, xii (Hanover, 1856), 564. See Keen, 84, Bumke, 248.
3. As noted by J. B. Ross, *The Murder of Charles the Good* (Toronto, 1982), 92.
4. *Liber monasterii de Hyda*, ed. E. Edwards (Rolls Series, 1866), 315.
5. *Actes des comtes de Flandre, 1071–1128*, ed. F. Vercauteren (Brussels, 1938), 249.
6. 'ad faciendum hastiludia, torneamenta aut consimilia ...', *Charta pacis Valencenensis*, in, *MGH Scriptores*, xxi, 608. The circumstances around the count's establishment of the Peace in Valenciennes are described in GM, 78–79.
7. Parisse, 182. By the later twelfth century, *hastiludium* and *torneamentum* can feature as synonyms, as for instance, MP ii, 614–15; v, 83. Barker, 138–39, takes 'hastilude' to be a generic term during the period from 1100 to 1400, to which the more precise 'tournament' was contrasted.
8. *Liber de restauratione ecclesie sancti Martini Torniacensis*, in, *MGH Scriptores*, xii, 282, translated as, *The Restoration of the Monastery of Saint Martin of Tournai*, trans. L. H. Nelson (Washington, DC, 1996), 34, see Bumke, 247–48. Cardinal James de Vitry used the words *torneamentum*, *ludus* and *exercitium* all to designate a tournament, *The Exempla of Jacques de Vitry*, ed. T. F. Crane (New York, 1890), no. 141.
9. *The Song of Roland*, ed. F. Whitehead (2nd edn, Oxford, 1946), lines 110–14.
10. Nithard, *Histoire des fils de Louis le Pieux*, ed. and trans. P. Lauer (Paris,

1926), 110–12. See Parisse, 179; J. Nelson, 'Ninth-century Knighthood: The Evidence of Nithard', in, *Studies in Medieval History Presented to R. Allen Brown*, ed. C. Harper-Bill, C. Holdsworth and J. L. Nelson (Woodbridge, 1989), 260.

11. Orderic Vitalis, *The Ecclesiastical History*, ed. M. Chibnall (6 vols, Oxford, 1969–80) vi, 80, 182.

12. *The Chronicle of John of Worcester*, iii, *The Annals from 1067 to 1140*, ed. P McGurk (Oxford, 1998), 266; *HWM* i, lines 174–80.

13. Wace, *Le Roman de Rou*, ed. A. J. Holden (3 vols, Société des anciens textes français, 1970–73), ii, pt 3, lines 10957–11060.

14. Suger, *Vita Ludovici Grossi regis*, ed. and trans. H. Waquet (Paris, 1964), 104–10, discussed in Flori, *Chevaliers*, 133. English translation, *The Deeds of Louis the Fat*, trans. R. C. Cusimano and J. Moorhead (Washington, DC, 1992), 72–74.

15. For some observations on this see, G. Koziol, 'The Making of Peace in Eleventh-century Flanders', in *The Peace of God: Social Violence and Religious Response in France around the Year 1000*, ed. T. Head and R. Landes (Ithaca NY, 1992), 239–58.

16. Ibid., 333; C. Héfelé and H. Leclerq, *Histoire des Conciles*, iv, pt 2 (Paris, 1911), 1409.

17. The classic statement of this view is by G. Duby, 'Youth in Aristocratic Society: Northwestern France in the Twelfth Century', in, *The Chivalrous Society*, trans. C. Postan (London, 1977), 112–22.

18. For Robert Curthose's 'youth', D. Crouch, *The Normans: The History of a Dynasty* (London, 2002), 207–12.

19. E. H. McNeal, 'Fulk of Neuilly and the Tournament of Écry', *Speculum*, 28 (1953), 371–75.

20. J. Gillingham, 'Conquering the Barbarians: War and Chivalry in Twelfth-Century Britain', *Haskins Society Journal*, 4 (1992), 76.

21. Keen, 88; J. Flori, 'Encore l'usage de la lance: la technique du combat chevaleresque vers 1100', *Cahiers de civilisation médiévale*, 31 (1988), 213–40.

22. *Chronicon Turonensis*, in *RHF*, xi, 31; an observation considered with scepticism in, Barker, 5 and with neutrality in Parisse, 176 and n. The reference is given some credit in Flori, *Chevaliers*, 133–4. My view is that if the tournament had a region of origin it was not in the Angevin lands, for which see above.

23. Lambert of Ardres, *The History of the Counts of Guines and the Lords of Ardres*, trans. L. Shopkow (Philadelphia, 2001), 66.

24. Barker, 5.

25. For the origins of heraldry, M. Pastoureau, 'L'origine des armoiries: un problème en voie de solution?', in *Genealogica & Heraldica*, ed. S. T. Achen (Copenhagen, 1982), 246–51; for its identifying purposes, A. Ailes, 'The

Knight, Heraldry and Armour: The Role of Recognition and the Origins of Heraldry', in *Medieval Knighthood: Papers from the Fifth Strawberry Hill Conference*, ed. C. Harper-Bill and R. Harvey (Woodbridge, 1992), 1–21.

26. *HWM* i, lines 1207–12.

27. Bertran, 3–6. The tournament in the Midi is underplayed in L. Macé, 'La culture chevaleresque méridionale au XIIe siècle: une idéologie sans tournoi', in *L'homme du Midi*, ed. C. Desplat (Paris, 2003), 173–84.

28. *Les conciles œcumeniques: les decrets*, ii pt 1, *Nicée à Latran V*, ed. A. Duval and others (Paris, 1994), 439.

29. Otto of Freising, *Gesta Frederici*, in, *MGH Scriptores* xx, 158. See the comments of Bumke, 79–80, and on the translation of *tirocinium*, Flori, *Chevaliers*, 134.

30. *Chronicon montis Sereni*, in, *MGH Scriptores*, xxiii, 155; Bumke, 250.

31. *HWM*, i, line 6021.

32. *Ex gestis sanctorum Villariensium*, in, *MGH Scriptores*, xxv, 220.

33. *HWM* i, lines 1518–19, 6588–98, which says he went to Cologne on pilgrimage; for *Noauz, Charette*, lines 5502–5.

34. Bertran, 162–63.

35. For some reflections on the history and definition of sport, modern or premodern, R. Holt, *Sport and the British: A Modern History* (Oxford, 1989), esp. 28–29; A. Guttman, 'The Development of Modern Sports' in, *Handbook of Sports Studies*, ed. J. Coakley and E. Dunning (London, 2000), 248–59.

36. On the suitability of the term 'team sport' (*sport d'équipe*) to describe the tournament, see also Flori, *Chevaliers*, 138–39.

37. Baldwin, 11–21.

38. Neither of these romances are closely datable, but the details and personages described justify a date sometime between 1260 and 1290 for both.

Notes to Chapter 2: Sponsorship

1. The author of the Marshal biography comes out in the 1220s with this very explanation of the way that the tournament spread, commenting on the impact of the Young King Henry's generosity in the 1170s: 'Seeking to vie with the Young King, those powerful nobles took care to retain the services of worthy knights, maintaining and advancing them', *HWM*, i, 2663–66.

2. *militares nundinae*, see *Symeonis Historia Regum Continuata per Johannem Hagustaldensem*, in, *Historia Regum*, ed. T. Arnold, ii (Rolls Series, 1885), 312. The papal prohibition against tourneying in 1130 had also called the events *nundinae* or *feriae* (for more on this choice of name, see p. 62).

3. British Library, Cotton charter xxii 3. This contract may date to as early as 1124 and cannot be later than 1139, with the outbreak of civil war in England. The document as we have it is a later copy and resealing, the handwriting

indicating it was made in the third quarter of the twelfth century. The copy was probably made when Turkill's son renewed the arrangement with Osbert's successor at Kingsbury, Peter of Bracebridge, a document which survives only in copy form.

4. *The Letters of St Bernard of Clairvaux*, trans. B. Scott James (repr. Stroud, 1998), 476–77.

5. *Chronica Rogeri de Hoveden*, ed. W. Stubbs (4 vols, Rolls Series, 1868–71), ii, 4–5n.

6. For William Marshal's early career, Crouch, *Marshal*, 24–39.

7. *HWM*, i, lines 1935–90.

8. For the thirty-six genuine and suspect acts attributed to Young King Henry, R. J. Smith, 'Henry II's heir: the *Acta* and Seal of Henry the Young King, 1170–83', *English Historical Review*, 116 (2001), 297–326, for his long-term household after 1174, see ibid. pp. 300–1.

9. *Chronica Rogeri de Hoveden* ii, 68.

10. *HWM* i, lines 2412–17.

11. Bertran, 18.

12. Bertran, 25.

13. Niger, 114.

14. For this question, S. Painter, *William Marshal* (Baltimore, 1933), 49 and n; Crouch, *Marshal*, 52 and n. For the location of the fee in Flanders, National Archives (formerly Public Record Office), KB26/146, m. 9.

15. *HWM*, i, lines 4750–85, 5073–95.

16. For Young Henry's death, Crouch, *Marshal*, 52–55. Ralph Niger, his former chaplain, commented that the Young Henry's troubles were a visitation not so much on him, his mother or his men, but on Henry II for his part in the death of Becket, Niger, 7.

17. For verdicts on the significance of Henry's death, *HWM*, i, lines 5060–72; Bertran, 28–30; Gervase of Tilbury, *Otia Imperialia*, ed. and trans. S. E. Banks and J. W. Binns (Oxford, 2002), 486.

18. The theologian Ralph Niger, attached at some time to his household, called Young Henry 'the most beautiful of the men of our time', in the prologue to the manuscript of his *Liber Regum*, see Niger, 7.

19. Ailred of Rievaulx, *Genealogia regum Anglorum* in, *PL*, 195, col. 715.

20. Seven years after Young Henry's death, William Marshal founded an Augustinian priory and instituted there prayers for the souls of all the three kings of England he had served; of the three the Young Henry was the one he called *dominus meus*, 'my lord', Crouch, *Marshal*, 73 and n.

21. *Cartulaire de l'abbaye de Notre-Dame d'Ourscamp*, ed. M. Peigné-Delacourt (Amiens, 1865), 150.

22. *Couci*, lines 932–3 refers to Hainault 'where knights were exceedingly accomplished'.

23. GM, 95.

24. *HWM*, i, lines 3332–52.

25. GM, 97–98.

26. GM, 101–2.

27. GM, 107–9.

28. GM, 156.

29. *HWM*, i, lines 1201–14; GM, 97–8.

30. *The Exempla of Jacques de Vitry*, ed. T. F. Crane (New York, 1890), 62–64.

31. C. Bullock-Davies, *Menestrellorum Multitudo: Minstrels at a Royal Feast* (Cardiff, 1978), 160

32. Bertran, 4–6, see Appendix 5. For the origins of the herald, A. R. Wagner, *Heralds and Heraldry in the Middle Ages* (Oxford, 1939) 46–48, App. B. Written summonses to tournaments may well have circulated in the twelfth century, for in 1203 Count Hugh of St Pol wrote an invitation to Duke Henry of Brabant to join the coming Fourth Crusade in apparent imitation of a form of invitation to a tournament, see *Annales Colonienses maximi* in, *MGH Scriptores*, xvii, 812–14.

33. *HWM*, i, lines 3427–32.

34. *Couci*, lines 2100–4.

35. *Patent Rolls, 1216–25*, 174, 257.

36. *Patent Rolls, 1225–32*, 118, 125–26, 142, the fact that the tournament met at Chepstow can be deduced from the tournament-related death of Hugh de Mortemer soon after the time of the meeting, Denholm-Young, 102n, see *Fundationis et fundatorum de Wiggemora historia*, in, *Monasticon Anglicanum*, ed. J. Caley and others (6 vols in 8, London, 1817–30), vi, pt 1, 350.

37. *Manekine*, lines 2909–11.

38. *HWM*, i, lines 1201–14, 2875–79. The Pomeglai tournament was another literary tournament announced fifteen days in advance, *Lancelot* ii, 95.

39. *Close Rolls, 1227–31*, 113.

40. N. Elias and E. Dunning, 'Folk Football in Medieval and Early Modern Britain', in *Quest for Excitement: Sport and Leisure in the Civilizing Process*, ed. N. Elias and E. Dunning (Oxford, 1986), 181.

41. *Milun*, lines 382–4, in *Les Lais de Marie de France*, ed. J. Rychner (Classiques français du moyen âge, 93, 1983), 138.

42. *HWM*, i, lines 3409–24.

43. *Manekine*, lines 4007–12, '. . . encor est la coustume tex'.

44. MP, v, 54–55.

45. E. van den Neste, *Tournois, joutes, pas d'armes dans la villes de Flandre à la fin du moyen âge, 1300–1486* (Paris, 1996), 62–63, 362, 364.

46. Barker, 76.

47. Albert de Trois-Fontaines, *Chronicon*, in *RHF*, xxi, 629; Philip Mousket, *Chronique rimée*, in *RHF* xxii, 74.

48. *Lancelot*, ii, 356; *Sone*, lines 8900–4, 9828–33; and see Parisse, 200.

49. *HWM*, i, lines 3041–49; Roger of Wendover, *Chronica sive Flores Histori-arum*, ed. H. G. Hewlett (3 vols, Rolls Series, 1886–9), ii, 138; *Gui*, i, lines 763–74.

50. *HWM*, i, lines 4443–785.

51. de Dornon, 61–114: despite the author's attribution of the date, the appearance of Charles, prince of Salerno, in the list firmly dates it to the Compiègne tournament of 1279, see L. Carolus-Barré, 'Les grand tournois de Compiègne et de Senlis en l'honneur de Charles, prince de Salerne (mai 1279)', *Bullétin de la société nationale des antiquaires de France* (1978/9), 87–100.

52. C. E. Long, 'Tournament at Stepney, 2 Edward II', in *Collectanea Topographica et Genealogica*, iv (London, 1837), 61–72, corrected as to attribution by A. Tomkinson, 'Retinues at the Tournament of Dunstable, 1309', *English Historical Review*, 74 (1959), 70–71.

Notes to Chapter 3: The Site

1. D. Crouch, *The Beaumont Twins: The Roots and Branches of Power in the Twelfth Century* (Cambridge, 1986), esp. 76–77.

2. William fitz Stephen, 'A Description of the Most Noble City of London', trans. H. E. Butler, in F. M. Stenton, *Norman London: An Essay* (London, 1934), 28; Gerald of Wales, *Itinerarium Kambriae*, in *Opera*, vi, ed. J. F. Dimock (Rolls Series, 1868), 121; *De miraculis sanctae Frideswidae*, in *Acta Sanctorum (October 8)*, 570.

3. Laon, 224; *HWM*, i, lines 4971–76.

4. British Library, Cotton charter xxii 3. For translation and commentary, see Documentary Appendix, no. 1. Barker, 7, dates the charter to the reign of Henry I, but it could date to the early part of Stephen's reign, see P. R. Coss, *Lordship, Knighthood and Locality: A Study in English Society, c. 1180-c. 1280* (Cambridge, 1999), 281n. The outbreak of the civil war in 1139 probably curtailed English involvement in the continental circuit, and is a likely terminal point for dating the Arden charter.

5. For the origin of the Ardens, A. Williams, 'A Vice-Comital Family in Pre-Conquest Warwickshire', *Anglo-Norman Studies*, 11 (1989), 327–43. For Osbert's connection to Earl David, *Early Scottish Charters*, ed. A. C. Lawrie (Glasgow, 1905), 47, 108, and see *Regesta Regum Scottorum*, i, *The Acts of Malcolm IV*, ed. G. W. S. Barrow (Edinburgh, 1960), 158.

6. *Forma pacis servandae a torneatoribus*, in, T. Rymer, *Foedera, Litterae et Acta Publica*, ed. A. Clarke and F. Holbrooke (7 vols, London, 1816–69), i, pt 1, 65; MP, v, 318. Philip de Remy intriguingly suggests that in the early thirteenth century young Frenchmen might travel to England as language

tutors and find places in noble households, *Jehan et Blonde*, ed. S. Lécuyer (Classiques français du moyen âge, 1984), lines 127–36, 391–95. *Couci*, lines 6838–45, depicts a proclamation of a tournament in England circulating in Vermandois in King Richard's reign, enticing many French knights to cross the Channel.

7. For Scottish knights abroad, *HWM*, i, lines 1319–22 (1166); de Dornon, 84, 89–90 (1279).

8. *Gui*, i, lines 1128–74: 'there was not a field as far as Spain on which he was not seen tourneying, and he raised himself above all men in reputation' (lines 1172–4). See also, Keen, 89. For the earlier dating of *Gui*, see D. Crouch, 'The Romance of Gui de Warewic and the Earls of Warwick', *Midland History* xxi (1996), 20.

9. MP, v, 319, 367 (MP, v, 96 implies that Earl Richard crossed to tourney in France in 1250); *Annales de Theokesberia*, in *Annales Monastici*, ed. H. R. Luard (5 vols, Rolls Series, 1864–9), i, 143, 151. See Barker, 118, for this and the argument that Richard was patron at Walden.

10. *Historia monasterii Viconiensis* in, *MGH Scriptores*, xxiv, 299.

11. *The Exempla of Jacques de Vitry*, ed. T. F. Crane (New York, 1890), 30–31.

12. *HWM* i, lines 6677–6860.

13. Andrew the Chaplain, *Tractatus de amore*, ed. and trans. P. G. Walsh (London, 1982), 86; Joinville, 252.

14. *Curia Regis Rolls*, vi, 23–24.

15. *Forma pacis servandae a torneatoribus*, 65.

16. *The Chronicle of Jocelin of Brakelond*, ed. H. E. Butler (London, 1949), 55.

17. L. Carolus-Barré, 'Les grand tournois de Compiègne et de Senlis en l'honneur de Charles, prince de Salerne (mai 1279)', *Bullétin de la société nationale des antiquaires de France* (1978/9), 87–100.

18. *Manekine*, lines 2623–90.

19. MP, v, 97.

20. Thomas of Kent, *Le Roman de Toute Chevalerie*, ed. B. Foster (2 vols, Anglo-Norman Text Society, 1976–7), i, lines 670–73.

21. British Library, Cotton Charter xxii 3.

22. For the evolution of the term 'squire' throughout the twelfth and thirteenth century, see D. Crouch, *The Image of Aristocracy in Britain, 1000–1300* (London, 1992), 164–71; M. Bennett, 'The Status of the Squire: the Northern Evidence', in *The Ideals and Practice of Medieval Knighthood*, i, ed. C. Harper-Bill and R. Harvey (Woodbridge, 1986), 1–11.

23. *HWM*, i, lines 767–68.

24. *Gui*, i, lines 6192–98; *Lancelot do Lac*, i, 542; *Jehan et Blonde*, lines 4023–26.

25. National Archives (formerly Public Record Office), E164/1 (Breviate of Domesday), p. 478.

26. Stephen de Fougères, *Livre des manières*, ed. R. A. Lodge (Geneva, 1979), lines 485–86.

27. Liechtenstein, 99–102, 117, 118.

28. Laon, 224.

29. *Chauvency*, lines 3186–94.

30. *Statuta Armorum*, British Library, MS Harley 69, fo. 17r.

31. *Private Indentures for Life Service in Peace and War, 1297–1496*, ed. M. Jones and S. Walker, in, Camden Miscellany, xxxii (Camden Society, fifth series, 3, 1994), no. 7.

32. *Ham*, 216, for which see Parisse, 191n.

33. For tournament sites on political borders, G. Duby, *La Dimanche de Bouvines* (Paris, 1973). Duby regarded this as symptomatic of the *marginalité* of the early tourneyers in society.

34. *Liber Luciani de laude Cestrie*, ed. M. V. Taylor (Lancashire and Cheshire Record Society, lxiv, 1912), 61–62.

35. For the topography and history of the towns, A. Gnat, 'Les principaux bâtiments religieux, civils et militaires de Gournay-sur-Aronde: essai sur la localisation du bâti ancien', *Annales historiques compiègnoises*, 79/80 (2000), 38–48; idem, 'Évolution et structuration de l'habitat dans le terroir de Ressons-sur-Matz au moyen âge', *Bullétin de la société historique de Compiègne*, xxxviii (2002), 227–51.

36. Large sites are characteristic of the tournament grounds depicted in the Prose Lancelot: that of Chastel de Molin was a grassy plain (*praerie*) surrounded by hills, three miles by six in length, *Lancelot*, ii, 358.

37. *Historia Gaufredi ducis Normannorum*, in *Chroniques des comtes d'Anjou et des seigneurs d'Amboise*, ed. L. Halphen and R. Poupardin (Paris, 1913), 182.

38. Fictional tournaments also were staged on a variety of terrains: sometimes arable fields, sometime meadows, sometimes a featureless plain, Parisse, 191.

39. Four English urban sites are mentioned as supporting tournament fields before the 1154 ban. The charter of Osbert of Arden to Thurkill Fundu talks of him frequenting meetings at Northampton and London in the 1120s or 1130s, and a contemporary chronicle talks of a meeting sponsored by the earls of York and Richmond at York in 1142, British Library, Cotton Charter xxii, 3; *Symeonis Historia Regum Continuata per Johannem Hagustaldensem*, in, *Historia Regum*, ed. T. Arnold, ii (Rolls Series, 1885), 312. The monastic chronicle of Wigmore abbey refers to the death of Hugh, the younger son of Hugh de Mortemer (who died in 1135), in a tournament at Worcester which must date to before 1154, *Fundationis et fundatorum de Wiggemora historia*, in *Monasticon Anglicanum*, ed. J. Caley and others (6 vols in 8, London, 1817–30) vi, pt 1, 349.

40. For the Anglo-Scottish border tournaments, MP, iv, 200.

41. *Ham,* 217, lists most of these trades as being affected financially by King Philip III's prohibition of the tournament in France.

42. *Foedera, Litterae et Acta Publica,* i pt 1, 162; *Calendar of Patent Rolls, 1232–47,* 17, 20, 266, 424.

43. *Ordonnances des roys de France de la troisième race,* ed. M. de Laurierie, i, (Paris, 1723), 421–22, 434.

44. See *Victoria County Histories of England: East Riding,* iii, 120–6 for Langwith's tenurial history, and for its state in 1270, *Yorkshire Inquisitions,* ed. W. Brown (4 vols, Yorkshire Archaeological Society, record series, 1892–1906), i, 111–12. Langwith in 1142 was a possession of the earl of Richmond, the same man who sponsored a tournament at York in that year, which makes it tempting to give Langwith a twelfth-century origin as a tournament site. By the time it was mentioned as a tournament site in 1244 it had been taken into the royal forest, *Calendar of Patent Rolls, 1232–47,* 424.

45. *Foedera, Conventiones, Litterae et Acta Publica,* i, pt 1, 65. The fact that Salisbury was chosen may reflect the prominence of Earl William fitz Patrick of Salisbury as one of the three earls who offered sureties for the tournament licensing in 1194.

46. *Patent Rolls, 1216–25,* 174.

47. For Staines, *Patent Rolls, 1216–25,* 198 (1219), and the letter of Robert fitz Walter (1215) which refers to a tournament planned near London on the heath between Staines and Hounslow, Roger of Wendover, *Chronica sive Flores Historiarum,* ed. H. G. Hewlett (3 vols, Rolls Series, 1886–89), ii, 137–38.

48. *The Exempla of Jacques de Vitry,* 63–64; Méry, lines 368–78.

49. GM, 108–9.

50. For *fautores, Annales de Dunstaplia,* in, *Annales Monastici* iii, 60. For the other references, *Lancelot,* ii, 100.

51. *HWM,* i, line 4347.

52. *Sone,* lines 1349–50.

53. See the descriptions in *Chauvency,* 27.

54. *Lancelot,* ii, 98.

55. *HWM,* i, lines 3438–74, quotation from lines 3466–7.

Notes to Chapter 4: The Gathering and Vespers

1. Joinville, 126; *Couci,* lines 3332–35.

2. Born, 4–6.

3. *Patent Rolls, 1216–32,* 464; *Close Rolls, 1231–34,* 131; *Calendar of Patent Rolls, 1232–47,* 67.

4. Bumke, 261.

5. MP, v, 318–19.

6. *Chauvency*, pp. xix-lii.

7. For the predominance of Monday, S. Painter, 'Monday as a Date for Tournaments in England', in *Feudalism and Liberty: Articles and Addresses of Sidney Painter*, ed. F. A. Cazel (Baltimore, 1961), 105–6, originally printed in *Modern Language Notes*, xlviii (1933), 82–83, this is a pioneering analysis, but although Painter justified his main conclusion I found his dating to be occasionally inaccurate, especially in the location of weekdays. See also for the Empire, Bumke, 252.

8. Lambert de Wattrelos, *Annales Cameracenses*, in *MGH Scriptores*, xvi, 154.

9. *HWM*, i, lines 3681–83.

10. See on Sunday travel, Peter of Blois, *Epistolae*, in *PL*, 207, col. 43.

11. *Couci*, lines 897–900, 926–28.

12. E. van den Neste, *Tournois, joutes, pas d'armes dans la villes de Flandre à la fin du moyen âge, 1300–1486* (Paris, 1996), 364.

13. For the English royal crown-wearings, M. Biddle, 'Seasonal Festivals and Residence: Winchester, Westminster and Gloucester in the Tenth to Twelfth Centuries', *Anglo-Norman Studies* viii, ed. R. A. Brown (Woodbridge, 1985), 51–63. For the length of the Anglo-Norman ceremonial courts, *Herefordshire Domesday, c. 1160–70*, ed. V. H. Galbraith and J. Tait (Pipe Roll Society, new series, xxv, 1947–8), 76.

14. Geoffrey of Monmouth, *Historia Regum Britanniae*, i, Bern, Burgerbibliothek MS 568, ed. N. Wright (Cambridge, 1984), 112.

15. GM, 151–52.

16. *HWM*, i, lines 5974–76.

17. As an example of this, when Count Fulk IV of Anjou was besieging Château-du-Loir in Maine in the 1080s, he was following the hours of the Passion of Christ, and observed that the castle fell on the very hour Christ gave up the ghost, *Cartulaire du chapitre de Saint-Laud d'Angers*, ed. A. Planchenault (Angers, 1903), 97–98.

18. *Lancelot*, ii, 96, 360.

19. GM, 97, 116–17; d'Oisy, 240.

20. Gerbert, lines 5854–62

21. Méry, lines 294–312, 359–65, 368–78.

22. William of Malmesbury, *Historia Novella*, trans. K. R. Potter and ed. E. J. King (Oxford, 1999), 26–7.

23. MP, v, 267.

24. MP, iv, 481.

25. Born, 4–5; *Charette*, lines 5521–23.

26. Generally on tents see, Bumke, 126–28. For the cutting of flowers for tent floors, *HWM*, i, lines 596–600; *Manekine*, lines 2272–74. For tapestries and carpets in luxurious twelfth-century tents, see *Le Roman de Thèbes*, ed. F. Mora-Lebrun (Paris, 1995), lines 3225–76, 4300–91.

27. Méry, lines 340–42; Renart, lines 2160–68. Lancelot fixed his shield over the door of his lodgings before the tournament at Noauz, *Charette*, lines 5526–27; see also *Cligés*, lines 4664–72, but since here the hero wore different colours on each day of the prolonged fictional tournament between Oxford and Wallingford, heraldic identification was clearly not on his mind. For the social importance of the banner in the late twelfth century, D. Crouch, *The Image of Aristocracy in Britain, 1000–1300* (London, 1992), 114–16.

28. HWM i, lines 4361–430; *Curia Regis Rolls* i, 50.

29. *Charette*, lines 5535–60.

30. See generally, A. R. Wagner, *Heralds and Heraldry in the Middle Ages* (Oxford, 1939), 25ff. and appendix B, and comments in Parisse, 194.

31. Laon, 222, 224.

32. Bertran, 51. If this early Angevin 'king of arms' had the sole task of managing the tournament, it is odd to find one in the employment of Henry II, who was no fan of the amusement; however it is worth noting the remark of Ralph de Diceto that Henry II in 1180 employed men whose duty was to identify and announce visitors to his presence (*voce praeconia*) and to award them their appropriate titles, which might be a task for such an officer, *Ymagines Historiarum* in, *Opera Historica*, ed. W. Stubbs (2 vols, Rolls Series, 1876), ii, 3.

33. C. Bullock-Davies, *Menestrellorum Multitudo: Minstrels at a Royal Feast* (Cardiff, 1978), 78, 160.

34. For *Corbiois* as the designation for the men of southern Picardy, *Couci*, lines 884–85. For Jakemes's *roi des hiraus*, ibid., line 2002.

35. *HWM*, i, lines 6193–6236.

36. *Couci*, lines 6942–75.

37. *Lancelot*, ii, 180–1.

38. Renart, lines 1996–2005, 2062–73, 2076–141, 2336–45; *Chevalier de la Charette*, ll. 5561–74: 'Or est venuz qui l'aunera', translation, *Arthurian Romances*, trans. D. D. R. Owen (London, 1987), 259.

39. Liechtenstein, 166.

40. *Charette*, lines 5561–74: 'Or est venuz qui l'aunera', translation, *Arthurian Romances*, trans. D. D. R. Owen (London, 1987), 259; *Lancelot*, ii, 100.

41. Méry, lines 386–8. The holding of the stirrup when a man dismounted was a public acknowledgement of his celebrity and power, see *HWM*, i, lines 4091–2.

42. Méry, lines 379–418.

43. *Couci*, lines 976–1021: for the refrain, 'Tout nostre gent sont li plus joli dou tournoiement' (lines 989–91).

44. *HWM* i, lines 4329–38.

45. *HWM*, i, lines 2600–4. This story compares with one told by Walter Map

c. 1181, of a mysterious knight who boasted on the eve of a tournament at Louvain that he would overthrow the entire field the next day, Walter Map, *De Nugis Curialium*, ed. and trans. M. R. James (revised edn, Oxford, 1983), 164.

46. Lambert of Ardres, *The History of the Counts of Guines and Lords of Ardres*, trans. L. Shopkow (Philadelphia, 2001), 156.

47. See generally, Barker, 140–41; Bumke, 244–45

48. Renart, lines 2218–22.

49. *HWM*, i, lines 3213–14.

50. *HWM*, i, lines 3255–59.

51. *HWM* i, lines 2502–3, 3213–24, 3491–516

52. *HWM* i, lines 3707–22.

53. Alexander Neckam, *De Naturis Rerum Libri Duo*, ed. T. Wright (Rolls Series, London, 1863), 312.

Notes to Chapter 5: The Commencement

1. Méry, lines 498–509; *Couci*, lines 1050–62.

2. Walter Map, *De Nugis Curialium*, ed. and trans. M. R. James (revised edn, Oxford, 1983), 58–60.

3. Gerbert, lines 5864–80; Renart, lines 2441–45, for parallels see also *Couci*, lines 1051–53, 1500–3.

4. Gerbert, lines 5868–74 For the later belief that witness to the elevation preserved one from sudden death, see E. Duffy, *The Stripping of the Altars: Traditional Religion in England, 1400–1580* (London, 1992), 100.

5. Liechtenstein, 166.

6. *Visitatio Odonis Rigaudi archiepiscopi Rothomagensis*, in, *RHF*, xxi, 591.

7. *Lancelot* iv, 191: 'distrent a Lancelot qu'il manjast . i. poi pour aler plus seurement'.

8. A suggestion I owe to Antoinette Pearce.

9. Liechtenstein, 166.

10. Bumke, 252; A. Tomkinson, 'Retinues at the Tournament of Dunstable, 1309', *English Historical Review*, 74 (1959), 85–6.

11. GM, 97; John of Marmoutier, *Historia Gaufredi ducis Normannorum*, in *Chroniques des comtes d'Anjou et des seigneurs d'Amboise*, ed. L. Halphen and R. Poupardin (Paris, 1913), 182.

12. *HWM*, i, lines 3447–54, 3549–57.

13. *Lancelot*, ii, 184.

14. *Lancelot*, iv, 190, 385.

15. *HWM*, i, lines 3441–52.

16. *Chauvency*, lines 3075–109.

17. *Manekine*, lines 2727–37; Renart, lines 2449–80; *Chauvency*, lines 3126–33.

Méry, line 575ff, uses this part of the tournament as a narrative device to introduce a parade of infernal demons and vices coming out of Despair after the Antichrist, and a contrasting parade of virtues, angels and model Christian knights leaving Hope, to join battle on the field between.

18. 'Munjoie' was the recognised warcry of the French as early as c. 1100, *La Chanson de Roland*, ed. F. Whitehead (2nd edn, Oxford, 1947), line 1181.

19. 'Dex aïe' was being described c. 1160 as the ancestral warcry of the Normans in Wace, *Le Roman de Rou*, ed. A. J. Holden (3 vols, Société des anciens textes français, 1970–73) i, pt 2, line 3925; i, pt 3, lines 1607–8. The Young King Henry used it (*HWM*, i, line 2750) as did his father, see Bertran, 21. It was also associated in the 1180s with his cousins, the counts of Boulogne descended from King Stephen of England, d'Oisy, line 140.

20. For the presumptuous Marshal warcry, *HWM*, i, lines 5226, 5862, 6226. It was still being used by his son, Earl Richard Marshal, in the 1230s, see M. L. Colker, 'The "Margam Chronicle" in a Dublin Manuscript', *Haskins Society Journal*, 4 (1992), 137. For comments, D. Crouch, *William Marshal: Knighthood, War and Chivalry, 1147–1219* (London, 2002), 48 and n.

21. Many warcries of the 1180s are recorded in the *Tournoi des Dames*, see d'Oisy, lines 30, 95, 142, 153. For the Lotharingian 'Metz!', *Garin le Loherenc*, ed. A. Iker-Gittleman (3 vols, Classiques français du moyen âge, 1996–97), i, line 682.

22. For the Breton 'St Malo!', *La Chanson d'Aspremont*, ed. L. Brandin (2 vols, Classiques français du moyen âge, 1923–24), ii, lines 9708–9. For the Anglo-Welsh 'St David!', *The Deeds of the Normans in Ireland*, ed. and trans. E. Mullally (Dublin, 2002), lines 745, 753.

23. d'Oisy, line 108.

24. *Lancelot*, iv, 386: 'por ce qu'il fussent conneu des autres'.

25. For banners generally, *Image of Aristocracy*, 180–90.

26. For banner cases, *Lancelot do Lac*, i, 550.

27. Beelzebub carried the gonfanon of the Antichrist alongside his lord in the review before the tournament between Hope and Despair, Méry, lines 566–69.

28. *De Nugis Curialium*, 164.

29. For the Lagny list see *HWM*, i, lines 4481–4796.

30. de Dornon, 61–114. For the tournaments in honour of Prince Charles of Salerno, L. Carolus-Barré, 'Les grands tournois de Compiègne et de Senlis en l'honneur de Charles, prince de Salerne (mai 1279)', *Bulletin de la société nationale des antiquaires de France* (1978/9), 87–100

31. Bumke, 252.

32. For the text of the Dunstable list, C. E. Long. 'Tournament at Stepney, 2 Edw. II', in, *Collectanea Topographica et Genealogica*, iv (London, 1837),

61–72, but see the analysis in A. Tomkinson, 'Retinues at the Tournament of Dunstable, 1309', *English Historical Review*, lxxiv (1959), 70–89.

33. *Garin le Loherenc*, i, lines 1453–5.

34. *Lancelot* i, 92.

35. *Lancelot* i, 90–2.

36. MP v, 318–19.

37. S. Lysons, 'Copy of a Roll of Purchases Made for the Tournament of Windsor Park in the Sixth Year of King Edward the First', *Archaeologia*, 1st series, xvii (1814), 302–3.

38. *HWM*, i, lines 1303–10, 2497–501, 3240–41, 3453–55; Méry, lines 528–29. Philip de Navarre refers to the *barre* and *lices* which surround Paradise, which indicates a gate and substantial wall, *Les Quatre Âges de l'Homme*, ed. M. de Fréville (Société des anciens textes français, 1888), c. 116, p. 64. For their nature see Parisse, 191, although the example he cites in *Le Conte de Graal* to support his contention is ambiguous. The tendency of literary scholars to translate *chastel* as 'castle' often obscures the nature of these team-bases. The twelfth-century Latin *castellum* or *castrum* signified any walled enclosure, and was frequently applied to towns.

39. *Actes du Parlement de Paris*, ed. M. E. Boutaric, i, *1254–99* (Paris, 1863), 19.

40. E. van den Neste, *Tournois, joutes, pas d'armes dans la villes de Flandre à la fin du moyen âge, 1300–1486* (Paris, 1996), 74, 81. When we get glimpses of the layout of the great thirteenth-century jousts, they were held in enclosures marked out by lists on the edges of just such ditches.

41. *Cligés*, lines, 1883, 2113, 4583. See also, Bumke, 254; Parisse, 195.

42. *The Exempla of Jacques de Vitry*, ed. T. F. Crane (New York, 1920), 62–64. The sleeve given to Reginald the castellan to carry at his tournaments and jousts by the lady of La Fayel is a major part of the plot of the *Castelain de Couci*.

43. *Charrete*, lines 5580–83.

44. van den Neste, *Tournois, joutes, pas d'armes dans la villes de Flandre*, 71–72, 74, 79–80.

45. At Chastel de la Marche there was one elevated *loges* with windows 'where the ladies and the maidens might go to watch the tournament', *Lancelot* ii, 183; iv, 391.

46. *Lancelot* iv, 189.

47. *Lancelot*, ii, 97, 'et Lancelos s'areste sos la bretesche et regarde molt dolcement, et avec lui venoit .i. vaslès …'; ibid., iv, 189, 'Celui jour firent li dui roi loges drecier en mi les prez …'; ibid., v, 225, 'En mi les prez avoit loges drecues ou les dames et les damoiseles estoient por resgarder le tornoiement'. *Couci*, lines 1390–93, 'Desous as piés des escaffaus, oïssiés crier ces hiraus et haut dire a ces damoisielles, et as dames et as pucielles'.

48. *Lancelot,* ii, 97–98.

49. *Sone,* lines 13237–41, see on this, Parisse, 192n.

50. *Chauvency,* lines 3134–36. *Couci,* line 1074, also calls them *hourdeys,* or 'shelters'.

51. *Lancelot,* iv, 190, 191–92.

52. *Couci,* lines 3252–75,

53. *Lancelot,* iv, 191.

54. *HWM,* i, lines 1210, 4987.

55. *Histoire des rois de France,* in, *RHF* xxiv, 769.

56. d'Oisy, lines 14–15; *Gui,* i, lines 808–32; Renart, lines 5969–70

57. *HWM,* i, lines 1309–10, 2502–3, 3455–520

58. *Lancelot,* ii, 359.

59. *HWM,* i, line 2728

60. See the custumaries printed in, *Chartes de coutume en Picardie (xie-xiiie siè-cle),* ed. R. Fossier (Paris, 1974), nos 135, 140–41.

61. GM, 101–2.

62. GM, 97–98.

63. *HWM,* i, lines 2820–31.

64. Laon, 223.

Notes to Chapter 6: The Grand Tournament

1. So the tournament in which young Amadas distinguished himself began in mid-morning, at the canonical hour of 'tierce', *Amadas et Ydoine: roman du xiiie siècle,* ed. J. R. Reinhard (Classiques français du moyen âge, 1998), lines 4248–49.

2. *Chauvency,* line 3669.

3. Laon, 223; *Couci,* lines 3271–73.

4. *Chauvency,* line 3641.

5. *Lancelot,* ii, 97.

6. For the marshalling into extended lines, *Chauvency,* lines 3555–75.

7. *HWM,* i, lines 2797–816.

8. *Chronica Rogeri de Houedene,* ed. W. Stubbs (4 vols, Rolls Series, 1868–71), i, 309: 'in conflictu militari pedibus equinis contritus'. The fullest description is in *Gesta Henrici Secundi,* ed. W. Stubbs (2 vols, Rolls Series, 1867), i, 350

9. GM, 97–98. For the whole episode, C. Gaier, 'A la recherche d'une escrime décisive de la lance chevaleresque: le "coup de fautre" selon Gislebert de Mons (1168)', in, *Femmes, Mariages-Lignages, xiie-xive siècle. Mélanges offerts à Georges Duby,* ed. J. Dufournet and others (Brussels, 1992), 177–96, especially 192–95. Another reference to a knight resting his spear on a 'fautre' comes in 1278, *Ham,* 279, and in 1280 to 'foudre' and 'fautre',

Chauvency, 17, 27. In one desperate joust described by Jakemes, both knights placed their lances *sour fautre*, *Couci*, line 1241.

10. *Historia Gaufredi ducis Normannorum*, 182.

11. *Li dis des . iii. mestiers d'armes*, in *Dits et contes de Baudouin de Condé et de son fils Jean de Condé*, ed. A. Scheler (3 vols, Brussels, 1866–67), ii, 74.

12. *Lancelot*, ii, 100, 'et il prent une lance que ses escuiers tenoit'. This is the sequence of events presented at the tournament of Chastel de la Marche: first the opening charge, then additional attacks with lances and when those were done, the knights resorted to swords, *Lancelot*, ii, 184–85.

13. *Lancelot*, iv, 360, where Lancelot rode around the field looking for the 'greater *presses*' into which to throw himself.

14. *HWM*, i, lines 3926–4056.

15. *Couci*, lines 3292–97.

16. Liechtenstein, 144, 155.

17. See the description of the charge at Pleurs, *HWM*, i, lines 2941–51. For the lances, Liechtenstein, 175.

18. The best instance is Marshal's capture of Simon de Neauphle in the streets of Anet, *HWM*, i, lines 2840–56.

19. d'Oisy, lines 115–16.

20. *The Chronicle of Walter of Guisborough*, ed. H. Rothwell (Camden Society, third series, lxxxix, 1957) 211.

21. d'Oisy, lines 28–29; *Lancelot*, ii, 98–99, 181: 'si li abat la ventaille tant que la teste remaint tote nue'.

22. *Lancelot*, v, 231.

23. *Manekine*, lines 2737–79.

24. MP, iv, 135–6.

25. *Charette*, lines 5949–51.

26. d'Oisy, lines 82–98.

27. *HWM* i, lines 3780–92.

28. British Library, MS Harley 69, fo. 17r.

29. *HWM* i, lines 2541–62.

30. MP, iv, 135–6.

31. *Lancelot*, ii, 361.

32. *Lancelot*, iv, 357.

33. *Couci*, lines 1302–6.

34. *Lancelot*, iv, 361–62.

35. *Lancelot*, iv, 387.

36. *Lancelot*, i, 384.

37. Laon, 223, and see Keen, 88–89.

38. As with the Marshal's capture of Philip de Valognes in 1166, *HWM*, i, lines 1337–43

39. *HWM*, i, lines 4871–77, 5019–21.

40. *HWM*, i, lines 1351–62, 1423–57.

41. *HWM*, i, lines 1354–62, 3367–69.

42. *HWM*, i, lines 3995–4036.

43. *Jehan et Blonde*, ed. S. Lécuyer (Classiques français du moyen âge, 1984), lines 59–64.

44. *HWM*, i, lines 3417–21.

45. *Historia monasterii Viconiensis*, in *MGH Scriptores*, xxiv, 299.

46. GM, 95.

47. *Lancelot*, ii, 97.

48. *Chauvency*, 32.

49. MP, v, 318–19. Another such anecdote, with a happier outcome, was the encounter between Ulrich von Liechtenstein and Ruprecht von Purstendorf at Feldsberg, in which Ulrich's lance pierced Ruprecht's ventaille and hurled him to the ground, with blood spraying from a throat wound on to the grass. Ulrich too proposed leaving the field in remorse, but in this case Ruprecht's injury was not mortal, Liechtenstein, 156.

50. MP, iv, 135–36.

51. Philip Mousket, *Chronique rimée*, in *RHF*, xxi, 74; *Chronicle of Albert de Trois-Fontaines* in, *RHF*, xxi 629; *Annales sancti Pantaleonis Coloniensis*, in *MGH Scriptores*, xxii, 586.

52. *Annales de Dunstaplia*, in *Annales Monastici*, iii, 45.

53. *Gesta abbatum Horti sanctae Mariae*, in *MGH Scriptores*, xxiii, 595; *Balduini Ninovensis Chronicon*, in *MGH Scriptores*, xxv, 543; *The Chronicle of Bury St Edmunds, 1212–1301*, ed. A. Gransden (London, 1964), 87

54. *Annales Colmarenses majores*, in *MGH Scriptores*, xvii, 204.

55. *Anonymous Chronicle of the Kings of France*, in *RHF*, xxi, 134.

56. *Lancelot*, i, 92–93.

57. Liechtenstein, 84–93, 129.

58. *Ex gestis sanctorum Villariensium*, in *MGH Scriptores*, xxv, 220; MP, v, 319.

59. *Lancelot*, ii, 127.

60. Laon, 223.

61. Laon, 223.

62. *Records of the Wardrobe and Household, 1285–6*, ed. B. F. and C. R. Byerley (London, 1977), 63, 244; Barker, 174.

63. A. Hyland, *The Horse in the Middle Ages* (Stroud, 1999), 110–11; *Account of the Expenses of John of Brabant, 1292–3*, ed. J. Burtt (Camden Society, old series, ii, 1853), 5.

64. 'Li tournois departi pour ce que trop fu tart', d'Oisy, lines 188–9. As also at Korneuburg, Leichtenstein, 175.

65. *Manekine*, lines 2780–84.

66. Méry, lines 2978–90.

67. *Lancelot do Lac*, i, 306; *Lancelot*, ii, 124–26.

68. *Lancelot*, ii, 364; iv, 363–64.
69. MP, v, 265.

Notes to Chapter 7: The Après-Tournoi

1. Méry, lines 2991–3035, gives an allegorical adaptation of the endeavours of physicians after the day was over.
2. *Lancelot*, iv, 391.
3. *HWM*, i, lines 3016–40.
4. *HWM*, i, lines 3301–66.
5. *HWM*, i, lines 4076–284. Half the value of the other horse was recovered from the anonymous second knight by the mediation of another, unnamed magnate.
6. *Lancelot*, ii, 129–30.
7. *HWM*, i, lines 3041–144, 5589–610.
8. *Lancelot*, ii, 186–87.
9. *Couci*, lines 1988–94.
10. Gerbert, lines 6032–36, 6062. For Guy's prize, awarded by judgement of Duke Reiner with the acclamation of all around, *Gui*, i, lines 907–20.
11. *Lancelot*, ii, 185–86; iv, 358.
12. *HWM*, i, lines 3041–48.
13. *Couci*, lines 2002–64.
14. Bertran, 26.
15. Laon, 223, 224.
16. *Lancelot*, ii, 130, 187.
17. *Sone*, lines 10253–86; *Couci*, lines 1816–35.
18. *Couci*, lines 1865–89.
19. Renart, lines 2892–907.
20. Note his knowing aside 'che savon' ('don't we just know her') when imagining the exploits of Isabel de Châtillon, d'Oisy, line 104.

Notes to Chapter 8: The Rise of the Joust

1. Bumke, 259–60, proposed a different model, where the tournament developed out of the bohort, which he saw as the older form of the hastilude.
2. Galbert of Bruges, *The Murder of Charles the Good*, trans. C. B. Ross (repr. Toronto, 1982), 227–29.
3. *The Description of London*, trans. H. E. Butler, in F. M. Stenton, *Norman London: An Essay* (London, 1934), 30–31.
4. *Girart de Rousillon: Chanson de Geste*, ed. W. M. Hackett (3 vols, Société des anciens textes français, 1953–55), i, lines 36–44.
5. *Raoul de Cambrai*, ed. W. Kibler and trans. S. Kay (Paris, 1996), lines 425–44.

A romance of around 1200 begins with an episode at a quintain, described as made of two stakes on which were hung two shields and a hauberk. The young hero, only recently knighted, demonstrates his skill and potential by striking such a blow that he pierced the shields, ripped the hauberk and toppled the entire structure, *Elie de Saint-Gille: Chanson de geste*, ed. G. Raynaud (Société des anciens textes français, 1879), lines 69–74, 133–36.

6. *Lancelot do Lac*, i, 135.

7. Gerald of Wales, *De rebus a se gestis*, in *Giraldi Cambrensis Opera*, ed. J. S. Brewer, J. F. Dimock and G. F. Warner (8 vols, Rolls Series, 1861–91), i, 50.

8. MP, v, 367.

9. *Le Roman de Thèbes*, ed. F. Roma-Lebrun (Paris, 1995), lines 4626–27; *Raoul de Cambrai*, line 7435. Barker, 148–49, was the first attempt to define the bohort, a pioneering study expanded in, Barber and Barker, 164–65, but see also Bumke, 258–60.

10. Wace, *Roman de Brut*, ed. I. Arnold (2 vols, Société des anciens textes français, 1938–40), i, lines 4356–57; Bumke, 258.

11. L. Dailliez, *La règle des Templiers* (Nice, 1977), 158, 252.

12. *Calendar of Patent Rolls, 1232–47*, 84.

13. *Gesta Henrici Secundi*, ed. W. Stubbs (2 vols, Rolls Series, 1867), ii, 155.

14. Philip de Novara, *Mémoires, 1218–43*, ed. C. Kohler (Classiques français du moyen âge, 1913), 3.

15. *Lancelot*, i, 90–2.

16. Barber and Barker, 165.

17. *Visitatio Odonis Rigaudi archiepiscopi Rothomagensis*, in *RHF* xxi, 591.

18. Walter of Arras, *Eracle*, ed. G. Raynaud de Lage (Classiques français de moyen âge, 1976), lines 2891–99; *Garin le Loherenc*, ed. A. Iker-Gittleman (3 vols, Classiques français de moyen âge, 1996–97), i, lines 1059–67; ii, lines 11436–11548.

19. John of Marmoutier, *Historia Gaufredi ducis Normannorum*, in *Chroniques des comtes d'Anjou et des seigneurs d'Amboise*, ed. L. Halphen and R. Poupardin (Paris, 1913), 179–80.

20. GM, 155–56; Bumke, 258.

21. *HWM*, i, lines 4304–7.

22. Liechtenstein, 96–156.

23. This arrangement seems to be implied by the Prose Lancelot's account of the second tournament at Camelot, *Lancelot*, iv, 354. It is also implied by the evidence of two-day events being advertised in England in the 1220s and 1230s, see above p. 57.

24. See generally R. H. Cline, 'The Influence of Romances on the Tournaments of the Middle Ages', *Speculum*, 20 (1945), 204–11; Denholm-Young, 107–8; Barker, 75–95; Bumke, 262–64.

25. *Lancelot do Lac*, i, 138. See further Keen, 190.

26. The Prose Lancelot in fact contains a reference to a table being used in connection with a tournament. The winner of King Brangoire's tournament at Chastel de la Marche was awarded the top place at a table for the twelve best knights. Although the table was not round, its use in deciding the elite in a tourneying event is suggestive and perhaps earlier than the first known jousting Round Table, *Lancelot*, ii, 176.

27. *Mémoires, 1218–1243*, 7.

28. *Foedera*, i, pt 1, 205; *RHF*, xxi, 615.

29. Denholm-Young, 108 and n., points out that there was no Arthurian element in the actual fighting, he suggests that the social preliminaries may have had some literary resonances, but there is no evidence of this other than the name.

30. MP, v, 318–19; *Annales de Wigornia*, in, *Annales Monastici*, ed. H. R. Luard (5 vols, Rolls Series, 1864–9), iv, 444.

31. Bumke, 263.

32. *Sone*, lines 619–25, 1163–98. For the rules see Parisse, 195–96, who makes the point that the way the event was organised did not allow for there to be a tidy elimination down to two final opponents; ultimately a winner had to be selected by the patron from the surviving group of knights.

33. Some evidence that the sort of Round Table described in *Sone* was known in England is a general royal prohibition of 'jousting at a pavilion (*papilionem*)', along with other sorts of joust, issued in 1255, Denholm-Young, 109n.

34. *Sone*, 1325–2130.

35. *Sone*, lines 9781–98, 9828–36, 9875–84, 10136–86, 10217–20, 10843–54

36. *HWM*, i, lines 4297–4307.

37. Denholm-Young, 109–10.

38. *Li dis des . iii. mestiers d'armes*, in *Dits et contes de Baudouin de Condé et de son fils Jean de Condé*, ed. A. Scheler (3 vols, Brussels, 1866–67), ii, 71–72.

39. J. Vale, 'The Late Thirteenth-Century Precedent: Chauvency, Le Hem and Edward I', in, *Edward III and Chivalry: Chivalric Society and its Context, 1270–1350* (Woodbridge, 1983), 12–13, suggests that Sarrazin hoped for a tournament to close the event, despite the royal prohibition he bemoaned in his introduction.

40. *Ham*, 216–19.

41. *Ham*, 225–26; and see comments in Vale, 'Chauvency, Le Hem and Edward I', 15–16, although it has to be said that Sarrazin's flattery only implies approval of Edward, not an acknowledgement of English tourneying superiority, as Vale suggests.

42. *Ham*, 311.

43. *Couci*, lines 1236–40.

44. *Ham*, 269–71.

45. *Ham*, 357, where the count of Artois was reckoned as 'de ciaus dedens' because he was in Guinevere's court, and where knights of the court were jousting with the rest. *Ham*, 373, refers to each pair of jousters as 'cil dehors et cil dedens'. See for this Vale, 'Chauvency, Le Hem and Edward I', 13.

46. Parisse, 197, who points out that six pairs of knights launching themselves simultaneously down parallel runs would have the effect of a miniature tournament *estor*, and amounted in effect to thumbing the nose at authority. *Ham*, 307, says the *rens* were 'a stone's throw' from Guinevere's box. 'More than six' were opened as vespers approached on the second day, *Ham*, 373.

47. *Ham*, 276, 279.

48. *Ham*, 361–62.

49. *Ham*, 287, 296, 348. See the informative distribution map of participants' origins in J. Vale, *Edward III and Chivalry*, appendix 5.

50. The date of this tournament is frequently confused, see Parisse, 190n (who suggests 1284). It is usually dated to 1285 because that is the date Jacques Bretel mentions in his introduction that he began his book (*Chauvency*, 1–2). But the firmest indication of the date in the narrative is that Bretel says the first day of the tournament was a Monday, the day after the feast of St Remy (*Chauvency*, 14). Since the feast of Remy was on 13 January, that rules out 1285, when the 14th was a Sunday. The earliest year before 1285 when 14 January was a Monday was in fact 1280, and that is the date I have employed here.

51. *Chauvency*, 18, 22. The same is found in the tournament at Montargis in *Sone*, lines 13237–72, where four stands were erected on the lists at Montargis, in front of which *commençailles* jousts were run by the new knights present, as in the days of William Marshal.

52. *Chauvency*, 31.

53. *Chauvency*, 14.

54. *Chauvency*, 21, 'fors et belles', 24 'moult bien fait', 29.

55. *Chauvency*, 42.

56. *Chauvency*, 57, 89, 91.

57. For the balancing of the sides, Vale, 'Chauvency, Le Hem and Edward I', 7–8.

58. *Chauvency*, 111.

59. *Chauvency*, 116.

60. *Oeuvres complètes de Rutebeuf*, ed. E. Faral and J. Bastin (2 vols, Paris, 1959–60), i, 459, 499, 501–2.

61. MP, v, 557; *Ann. Dunstable*, 218–19; for his French excursions, M. Prestwich, *Edward I* (London, 1988), 34–35.

62. Denholm-Young, 112–13.

63. *The Chronicle of Walter of Guisborough*, ed. H. Rothwell (Camden Society, 3rd ser., lxxxix, 1957), 210–12; *Willelmi Rishanger Chronica et Annales*, ed. H. T. Riley (Rolls Series, 1865), 79–80.

64. Denholm-Young, 115–16; *Ann. Dunstable*, 280, 283, 285. It is worth noting that the canons of Dunstable cannot be relied on to mention every tournament that occurred near their town; the tournament which we know met there at some time late in 1273 or early in 1274 was not mentioned in the annals, see Denholm-Young, 117n., and neither was the tournament at Dunstable in 1309.

65. *Ann. Dunstable*, 51.

66. *Chronicle of Walter of Guisborough*, 224–25.

67. *Statuta Armorum*, in, British Library, MS Harley 69, fo. 17r.

68. Denholm-Young, 117n.

69. Denholm-Young, 118–19.

70. J. Vale, *Edward III and Chivalry*, 61–62.

71. *Ordonnances des roys de France de la troisème race*, ed. M. de Lauriere, i (Paris, 1723), 329.

72. Ibid., 509.

73. See on this, R. W. Kaeuper, *War, Justice and Public Order: England and France in the Later Middle Ages* (Oxford, 1988), 208–11.

74. M. Vale, *The Princely Court: Medieval Courts and Culture in North West Europe, 1270–1380* (Oxford, 2001), 189; van den Neste, *Tournois, joutes, pas d'armes*, 123–24, 127.

Notes to Chapter 9: Knights, Technology and Equipment

1. D. Crouch, *The Image of Aristocracy in Britain, 1000–1300* (London, 1992), 155–58.

2. D. Crouch, 'The Earliest Original Charter of a Welsh King', *Bulletin of the Board of Celtic Studies*, xxvi (1089), 131.

3. *Memorials of St Anselm*, ed. R. W. Southern and F. S. Schmitt (Auctores Brittanici medii aevi i, British Academy, 1969), 97–102.

4. See discussion in, K. de Vries, *Medieval Military Technology* (Peterborough, Ontario, 1992), 66.

5. De Vries, *Medieval Military Technology*, 64, 67, surveys the Bayeux evidence, and also the extant examples of such helmets all but two of which have lost their nasals. See also generally on this, I. Pierce, 'Arms, Armour and Warfare in the Eleventh Century', *Anglo-Norman Studies*, ed. M. Chibnall (Woodbridge, 1987), 237–57.

6. Wace, *Le Roman de Rou*, ed. A. J. Holden (3 vols, Société des anciens textes français, 1970–73), i, pt 2, lines 555–6. A similar comment is to be found in

the contemporary *Roman de Thèbes*, ed. F. Mora-Lebrun (Paris, 1995), line 10534.

7. Reproductions of the seals referred to here can be found in C. H. Hunter-Blair, 'Armorials upon English Seals from the Twelfth to the Sixteenth Centuries', *Archaeologia*, 2nd ser., lxxxix (1943), 1–26; P. Bony, 'L'image du pouvoir seigneurial dans les sceaux: codification des signes de la puissance de la fin du xie siècle au début du xiiie siècle dans les pays d'oïl', in *Seigneurs et seigneuries au moyen âge* (Comité des travaux historiques et scientifiques, Actes du 117e congrès national des sociétés savantes, Paris, 1995), 367–401.

8. For the distinction between *coife* and *ventaille*, see *HWM*, i, lines 1245, 2957. The knights illustrated in the Bury St Edmunds Bible of *c.* 1135 clearly wear ventailles bunched around their chins. For evidence of separate mail coifs before 1150, I. Pierce, 'The Knight, his Arms and Armour, *c.* 1150–1250', in, *Anglo-Norman Studies*, ed. M. Chibnall (Woodbridge, 1993), 254–56.

9. *La Chanson de Roland*, ed. F. Whitehead (2nd edn, Oxford, 1946), lines 710, 1031.

10. F. Lachaud, 'Armour and Military Dress in Thirteenth- and Early Fourteenth-Century England', in *Armies, Chivalry and Warfare in Medieval Britain and France*, ed. M. Strickland (Stamford, 1998), 355.

11. *Roman de Thèbes*, lines 6752–56.

12. Literary sources began to mention horse trappers in the mid twelfth century as being expensively fashioned out of silk and as being the possessions of kings and counts. Like those of Simon de Senlis and William fitz Empress, they were cut fashionably ragged (*detrenché*) along the bottom, see *Raoul de Cambrai*, ed. W. Kibler and S. Kay (Paris, 1996), lines 324–30; Thomas of Kent, *Le Roman de Toute Chevalerie*, ed. B. Foster (2 vols, Anglo-Norman Text Society, 1976–77), i, lines 1629, 1864, 4066–70; *Roman de Thèbes*, lines 7193–94.

13. See generally, Crouch, *Image of Aristocracy*, 230–35.

14. As demonstrated in, A. Adam, 'Les usages héraldiques au milieu du xiie siècle d'après le *Roman de Troie* de Benoît de Sainte Maure et la littérature contemporaine', *Archivum Heraldicum*, 77 (1963), 18–29, see also Crouch, *Image of Aristocracy*, 229–30.

15. *HWM*, i, lines 1474–76.

16. Niger, 98.

17. Niger, 101.

18. Niger, 107, 114. In a description of c. 1190 of his arming, Duke Naimes likewise puts on genelliers of thick leather (*ganbais*), *La Chanson d'Aspremont*, i, lines 1900–7. *Genoilleres* are mentioned as customary knightly armour in an inventory of knightly equipment in a romance of the last quarter of the twelfth century, *Guillaume d'Angleterre*, ed. A. J. Holden (Geneva, 1988), line 2713.

19. Niger, 102. J. France, *Western Warfare in the Age of the Crusades, 1000–1300* (Ithaca, New York, 1999), 16–17, marshals evidence that dates the appearance of the visor plate (as a novelty) to around 1170.

20. See Pierce, 'The Knight, his Arms and Armour', 259–61, expanding on C. Blair, *European Armour* (London, 1958), 30. De Vries, *Medieval Military Technology*, 70–71, summarising recent literature, dates the appearance of the visor and the enclosing helm a generation later than here.

21. *HWM*, i, lines 3101–12. It may be that the poet is anachronistically crediting the Marshal in the 1180s with the equipment of the 1220s, but if that were so then the story would make no sense.

22. Laon, 223.

23. Jehan was armed with a *bacinet c.* 1235 x 40, in the romance *Jehan et Blonde*, lines 3989–4012.

24. Niger, 104–5.

25. *La Chanson d'Aspremont*, ed. L. Brandin (2 vols, Classiques français du moyen âge, 1923–24), i, lines 1904–6.

26. Lachaud, 'Armour and Military Dress', 355–56.

27. *Lancelot*, iv, 386: 'Et tuit cil de la Table Reonde estoient seingnie a rouletes de cordouan par desus les couvertures'.

28. In the second decade of the thirteenth century the *Prose Lancelot* gives an inventory of the complete knight's harness as a hauberk, helm, *chausses, genoillieres* and a surcoat (*cote a armer*) of samite, along with shield and a barded horse, *Lancelot*, iv, 184–5.

29. *Select Charters and Other Illustrations of English Constitutional History*, ed. W. Stubbs and revised H. W. C. Davis (9th edn, Oxford, 1913), 183. See for an assessment of this assize, M. Powicke, *Military Obligation in Medieval England* (Oxford, 1962), 54–56.

30. For the haubergeon, Lachaud, 'Armour and Military Dress', 362.

31. Lachaud, 'Armour and Military Dress', 353–54. Lachaud (ibid., 360) notes the difficulty of distinguishing between gambaisons, pourpoints and aketons. But she does note the purchase of woollen cloth for the making of a pourpoint for King John in 1208, and the *Chanson d'Aspremont* talks of the sort of knee armour which Niger tells us was made from leather as made of *ganbais*, which implies that gambaisons were leather quilted jerkins (see above).

32. *HWM*, i, lines 3255–59.

33. *HWM*, i, lines 8792–95, 8803–7.

34. Ralph of Coggeshall, *Chronicon Anglicanum*, ed. J. Stevenson (Rolls Series, 1875), 94–96.

35. *Jehan et Blonde*, ed. S. Lécuyer (Classiques français du moyen âge, 1984), lines 4023–26.

36. *Statuta Armorum*, British Library, MS Harley 69, fo. 17r.

37. British Library, MS Additional 46919, fo. 90v–91r, printed as appendix 1 in M. Evans, 'An Illustrated Fragment of Peraldus's Summa of Vice: Harleian MS 3244', *Journal of the Warburg and Courtauld Institutes*, no 45 (1982), 45–46.

38. For the slow rise of the English squire, P. R. Coss, *The Origins of the English Gentry* (Cambridge, 2003), ch. 9. For squires in English tournaments, N. Denholm-Young, *The Country Gentry in the Fourteenth Century* (Oxford, 1969), 141n.

39. Liechtenstein, 165.

40. A *garlandesche* of twisted silk was tied around Jehan's bascinet in a description of *c.* 1240, *Jehan et Blonde*, lines 3989–4012; for the crest, *Ham*, 309.

41. S. Lysons, 'Copy of a Roll of Purchases made for the tournament of Windsor Park in the sixth year of King Edward the First', *Archaeologia*, first series, xvii (1814), 305.

42. Barker, 181.

43. Barker, 181–2.

44. N. Vincent, 'The Earliest Nottinghamshire Will (1257)', *Transactions of the Thoroton Society*, 102 (1998), 51.

45. M. Prestwich, *Armies and Warfare in the Middle Ages* (New Haven, 1996), 21–22.

Notes to Chapter 10: Aristocratic Violence and Society

1. For the preudomme, see D. Crouch, 'Loyalty, Career and Self-Justification at the Plantagenet Court: The Thought-World of William Marshal and his Colleagues', in *Culture Politique des Plantagenêt (1154–1224)*, ed. M. Aurell (Poitiers, 2003), 231–35; idem, *The Birth of Nobility: Constructing Aristocracy in England and France, 900–1300* (London, 2005), 30ff.

2. *The Ecclesiastical History*, ed. M. Chibnall (6 vols, Oxford, 1969–80), vi, 348.

3. For Guibert de Nogent's charges against Thomas, *Self and Society in Medieval France*, trans. J. F. Benton (Toronto, 1984), 184–85.

4. *The Waltham Chronicle*, ed. and trans. L. Watkiss and M. Chibnall (Oxford, 1994), 78–80; *Chronicon abbatiae Rameseiensis*, ed. W. Dunn Macray (Rolls Series, 1886), 327–34.

5. A point well made by R. W. Kaeuper, *Chivalry and Violence in Medieval Europe* (Oxford, 1999), 161–63.

6. Bertran, 118–21.

7. Bertran, 148–50.

8. Bertran, 32–35.

9. Walter Map, *De Nugis Curialium*, ed. and trans. M. R. James (revised edn, Oxford, 1983), 146.

10. This section draws on work published elsewhere in D. Crouch, *The Birth of Nobility: Constructing Aristocracy in England and France, 900–1300* (London, 2005), ch. 12.

11. An interesting example of women as transmitters of social memory, a role considered broadly in E. M. C. van Houts, 'Introduction', in *Medieval Memories: Men, Women and the Past, 700–1300*, ed. E. M. C. van Houts (London, 2001), 1–16.

12. Jacques Bretel, *Tournoi de Chauvency*, ed. G. Hecq (Mons, 1898), 31–34.

13. Baldwin, 84.

14. d'Oisy, 240–4.

15. Baldwin, 86.

16. *Couci*, lines 954–61.

17. *The Exempla of Jacques de Vitry*, ed. and trans. T. F. Crane (New York, 1890), 63.

18. Jakemes, *Le Roman du Castelain de Couci et de la Dame de Fayel*, ed. M. Delbouille (Société des anciens textes français, 1936). James de Vitry by contrast praises a noblewoman who had the maid beaten and ducked in stream who conveyed advances from a would-be lover, *Exempla of Jacques de Vitry*, 106.

19. Joinville, *Vie de Saint Louis*, ed. J. Monfrin (Paris, 1995), 206.

20. *Le Roman de la Rose*, ed. D. Poirion and J. Dufournet (Manchecourt, 1999), lines 2115–24. The same advice is to be found in Raoul de Houdenc, *Le Roman des Eles*, ed. and trans. K. Busby (Utrecht Publications in General and Comparative Literature, 17, Amsterdam, 1983), lines 325–36.

Index